FROM PRAHA TO PRAGUE

FROM PRAHA
TO PRAGUE
Czechs in an Oklahoma Farm Town

PHILIP D. SMITH

University of Oklahoma Press | Norman

This book is published with the generous assistance of the Wallace C. Thompson Endowment Fund, University of Oklahoma Foundation.

Library of Congress Cataloging-in-Publication Data

Names: Smith, Philip D. (History professor), author.
Title: From Praha to Prague : Czechs in an Oklahoma farm town / Philip D. Smith.
Description: Norman : University of Oklahoma Press, 2017. | Includes bibliographical references and index.
Identifiers: LCCN 2017001127 | ISBN 978-0-8061-5746-7 (paperback)
Subjects: LCSH: Czech Americans—Oklahoma—Prague—History. | BISAC: HISTORY / United States / General. | HISTORY / Europe / General. | HISTORY / United States / State & Local / Southwest (AZ, NM, OK, TX). | SOCIAL SCIENCE / Minority Studies. | SOCIAL SCIENCE / Customs & Traditions.
Classification: LCC F704.P82 S65 2017 | DDC 305.8918/6076635—dc23
LC record available at https://lccn.loc.gov/2017001127

The paper in this book meets the guidelines for permanence and durability of the Committee on Production Guidelines for Book Longevity of the Council on Library Resources, Inc. ∞

Interior layout and composition: Alcorn Publication Design

For Phil and Jill
And for Cody

Contents

Illustrations

Figures

All photographs appear courtesy of the Prague Historical Society.

Map

Acknowledgments

THE DEBTS I HAVE ACCUMULATED IN WRITING *From Praha to Prague* go back to my days as a graduate student at Oklahoma State University and have continued during my tenure as a professor at Tulsa Community College.

I would like to thank those whose teaching, friendship, and encouragement have enabled me to complete this study. Without the help, advice, and encouragement of my mentors, colleagues, and friends, this work would never have reached completion. The suggestions and advice of my Oklahoma State teachers Dr. Joseph Byrnes, Dr. David D'Andrea, Dr. Richard Rohrs, and Dr. Michael Taylor strengthened underdeveloped ideas and enhanced the overall structure of the study. I truly appreciate the many hours each spent reading and editing this work.

I owe so much to Dr. Ron Petrin that it is nearly impossible to write without sounding maudlin. Dr. Petrin made me think and rethink several propositions in the paper and pointed out any faulty logic. For this, I thank him and extend my deepest respect. I will always cherish the hours we spent together talking and discussing immigration and ethnic questions.

Dr. Kenny Brown and Dr. James Kearney read the manuscript and provided valuable feedback. The final version is due to their insights. Thank you both!

John Phillips at the Edmon Low Library at Oklahoma State University helped me immensely with census materials and government documents. The library staff of the University of Tulsa granted me access to their government documents and copy privileges. I would also like to thank the staff at the Museum of Pioneer History in Chandler, Oklahoma, and the Prague Historical Museum for their assistance. I especially would like to thank Diana Kinzey and Norma Foreman of the Prague Historical Museum. Norma allowed me complete access to the holdings of the museum, and Diana spent the better part of four days helping me locate photographs, family histories, and cemetery records. Ms. Kinzey also spoke with me at length on the Kolache Festival in Prague and what it means to the current generation. The churches of Prague allowed me access to their membership and baptismal records. Their kindness and help were greatly appreciated.

A huge thank you goes to the Bohemian Hall of Prague. One of the great pleasures of a researcher is to be led to an ancient cabinet filled with dust-covered records, many over a hundred years old. I want to thank the members of the Bohemian Hall for affording me this experience. Wayne Opela and Ray (Sala) Reynolds met me every morning for a week at the Hall and helped me ten hours a day sort through the financial, monthly minutes, and membership records of the organization. It was an honor and a great pleasure to meet and befriend these descendents of the original Czech settlers. I also want to thank Valdean Sestak, the current treasurer of the Western Bohemian Brotherhood Association, for visiting with me and providing valuable insights into the current disposition of the Bohemian Hall.

Cody Tice, a former student, read the rough draft of the manuscript and provided valuable criticism on both style and substance. Our luncheons at Panera Bread were more than intellectual conversations about the manuscript; they always included lively banter about politics and, more important, baseball. Cody has passed away, and I deeply miss our conversations and his scholarly insights.

Gary Patton, professional photographer and lifelong friend, turned the ancient photographs in the Prague Historical Museum into clear prints for the book. Without his expertise, the illustrations would have been of poor quality. Gary also drew the map of Prague, Oklahoma, and took the photograph of Prague's Bohemian Hall and the author. Thank you, Gary, for your immense help.

Kent Calder and Steven Baker of the University of Oklahoma Press guided the manuscript to publication. Elaine Otto copyedited and polished the work to its final form. I appreciate everything they did for me.

Lastly, I would like to thank my wife, Pam. Her understanding and encouragement were indispensable. She has been steadfast in her commitment to this work, despite the added burdens it has placed on her. Without her, I would never have succeeded. Thank you, Pam, for your love and support.

FROM PRAHA TO PRAGUE

Introduction

IN 1902, THE FORT SMITH AND WESTERN (FS&W) Railroad Company, seeing an opportunity for large profits, made plans to build tracks from Fort Smith, Arkansas, across Indian Territory and into Oklahoma Territory. Its goal was to tap the exploding towns of central Oklahoma, especially the Guthrie–Oklahoma City area. The railroad identified the southeastern part of Lincoln County as a perfect spot for a refueling station. The FS&W needed a place on its line where its trains could take on coal and water. Initially, the railroad company championed the tiny village of Lambdin as the refueling site. However, when a local farmer rebuffed its monetary offer as too small, the FS&W looked elsewhere, specifically to the farmland of an immigrant Czech community.[1] Two Bohemian (Czech) immigrants, Anton Simek and Vencl Kozak, recent buyers of the land-run homesteads of Eva Barta and her son, Frank, agreed to sell part of their holdings. In a goodwill gesture, the railroad allowed Josephine Barta, Frank's wife, to name the new town. She decided on the name Praha to honor her birthplace of Praha, Bohemia. However, Frank (Squire) Vlasak, an influential merchant in the Czech community, persuaded her to Americanize the name to Prague. With the deal done, town lots went on sale May 20, 1902, and the brand-new settlement of Prague opened with the great benefit of being a railroad town.[2]

Frank Barta, an original homesteader in the 1891 land run, took immediate advantage of the opportunities offered by the embryonic village. In the summer of 1902, with great difficulty and just as much excitement, Barta hoisted and moved his entire farmhouse into the new town and reopened it as Hotel Barta. He also opened a general store and restaurant; however, it was his family's hotel that proved lasting.[3] It operated on a continuous basis until 1961.

Figure 1. Frank and Josephine Barta.

The area that became Prague, Oklahoma, began after the 1891 land run as an isolated agricultural colony of Czech immigrants. Once the newly plotted lots went on sale, an influx of non-Czechs, including German immigrants, African Americans, and U.S.-born whites rushed for the opportunities that a developing town afforded. The original land-run settlers, the Czech immigrants, quickly found themselves in the minority. How these sons and daughters of Bohemia and Moravia carved a niche for themselves while maintaining their ethnic identity, despite never numbering above 30 percent of the town's population, is the focus of this book.

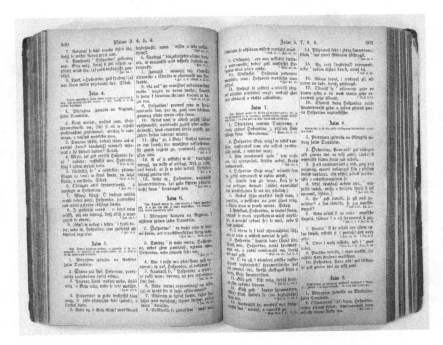

Figure 2. Catholic Bible of Frank Vlasak's mother.

Although Czech immigrants settled in Prague at a time of heightened nativist feeling throughout the United States, this Slavic group apparently suffered little rejection or resistance from the larger community. Furthermore, because of their history in Europe, the Czechs of Prague adjusted quickly to the dominant culture of the United States, which continued to be centered on Anglo-Saxon law and traditions. These newcomers chose to interact with the larger community rather than isolate themselves as a separate element within the town and resist any encroachment on their traditional way of life. Nevertheless, they battled to maintain their heritage and identity, albeit with mixed results. Although the outcomes were probably not exactly what the original settlers intended, today many Prague Czechs still attend St. Wenceslaus Catholic Church, while others meet regularly in the same Bohemian Hall as their ancestors and continue to cling to their ethnic identity and celebrate their heritage, even if only at an annual cultural festival.

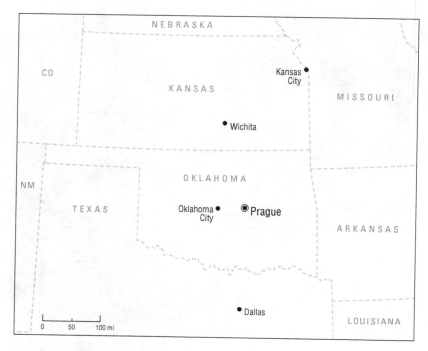

Prague, Oklahoma, in the southern plains. Cartography by Erin Greb. Copyright © 2016 by the University of Oklahoma Press.

The Czechs settling in the area of Prague, Oklahoma, claimed as their homeland the provinces of Bohemia and Moravia in Central Europe. In the late nineteenth and early twentieth century, these areas were part of the vast polyglot Austrian Empire ruled from Vienna by the Habsburg family. Austria would control these regions until the conclusion of World War I when the Slavic provinces, along with Czech Silesia and Slovakia, united and formed the independent nation of Czechoslovakia.

Although many, especially the initial arrivals, referred to themselves as Bohemian or Moravian, over the years the linguistic term "Czech" became commonplace when speaking or writing about these Slavs of Central Europe. In the early twentieth century, the non-Czech residents of Prague, Oklahoma, usually referred to their Czech-speaking neighbors, whether they originated from Bohemia or

Moravia, as "Bohemian." Thus the terms "Czech" and "Bohemian" in this case are synonymous.

Regardless of where Czechs settled in the United States, they grew accustomed to being a minority within a larger culture. Beginning in 1621 with the defeat of the Czechs at the Battle of White Mountain, the Austrian crown controlled the areas of Bohemia and Moravia, resulting in a strong Germanizing of Czech territory. The German language became the primary tongue of the government, military, and universities, as well as most of the aristocracy and professional class. As a result, for several centuries the Czech language served as nothing more than a peasant patois. Nevertheless, the historic language of Bohemia and Moravia persisted despite repeated attempts by the Habsburg rulers to extinguish it.[4] In addition, the Austrian lords inundated their conquered dominions with Germanic culture, which not only included western European ideas of governance and law but even delved into culinary tastes, including beer making. For example, Czechs claim that pilsner, considered by most a German beer, originated in the Bohemian town of Plzen and was a joint creation of the Czech inhabitants and a hired Bavarian brewer.[5]

The Habsburg domination resulted in two seemingly contradictory mind-sets. This paradox helped Czech immigrants simultaneously adjust to American culture and resist complete assimilation or "Americanization." The centuries-long foreign domination fostered in Czechs the ability to sustain their heritage and identity under harsh conditions, while their intimate contact with German culture caused a partial adoption of German ways as their own.[6] Thus Czechs became the most western-oriented of all Slavic groups, and though considered part of the "new immigration" of the late-nineteenth-century and early-twentieth-century United States, Czech immigrants differed significantly from their Slavic neighbors. Many arrived earlier than other Slavic groups, and many came as family units with every intention of staying and making the United States their home.[7]

This "Germanization" or "westernization" proved valuable to Czechs once they were in the United States. American culture, though definitely unfamiliar, did not intimidate Czechs to the extent it did the Slovaks and Poles. Czech immigrants entered North America with a distinct advantage over other Slavic groups. For example, many of the original forty-eight Czech families in the Prague, Oklahoma, area were only a few years removed from the farming villages of Central Europe, villages oriented around the community rather than individual households, which served the Czechs well in their new environment.[8] Czechs stuck together. This tendency enabled them to succeed when many U.S.-born farmers, who were more fiercely independent, failed.

Nevertheless, the story of the Prague Czechs centers on their ardent desire to maintain their ethnicity while simultaneously diving into the culture of their new homeland. This dual lifestyle in a town dominated by U.S.-born whites resulted in rapid acculturation and incorporation into the mainstream, but also in these small-town Czechs carving a permanent niche as a distinct group. Because of the frontier setting, they reacted pragmatically to their adopted environment and, despite their numerical inferiority, succeeded in establishing a stable presence. The Czechs of Prague gradually lost many of their European ways, but they preserved their ethnic identity. They stubbornly maintained an internal sense of distinctiveness, a sense of who they were.[9]

By 1930 most ethnic Czechs fit comfortably in their new environment. Their children attended public school, played baseball and football with as much fervor as anyone in the community, went to work for whoever paid the highest wage regardless of ethnicity, and married outside the group with little or no condemnation from other Czechs. Czechs' Prague experience resulted in a sense of identity akin to, but slightly different from, "symbolic ethnicity," in which ethnicity is more a question of "feeling ethnic," centered primarily on traditional foods and festivals, than of actually being a member of a distinct ethnic group.[10] The persistent and deep ethnic distinctiveness forged by the early Czechs of Prague laid the groundwork for a lasting and more far-reaching ethnic identity than the label "symbolic ethnicity" suggests. Instead, the Czechs of Prague, Oklahoma, trod a middle path on their journey toward assimilation into American society. This middle path, or birthright ethnicity, evolved out of the strong desire among the earliest Czechs to take a practical approach in maintaining their group's identity while embracing their new home.

Historians have focused only modest research on minority ethnic groups in American farm towns, preferring instead to concentrate on the larger groupings of immigrants in urban neighborhoods in large cities such as Boston, New York City, or Chicago, or on rural areas completely dominated by a specific ethnic group. This preference is understandable. These concentrations of immigrants provide an excellent view of how ethnic groups deemed the "other" by the dominant culture huddled together in an attempt to survive and ultimately succeed in a foreign setting. Nevertheless, an examination of a smaller grouping of immigrants living in a frontier setting provides a view of how these isolated and demographically inferior newcomers used various tactics to persist and prosper. First, a brief examination of overall Czech immigration is important in understanding exactly who the Prague Czechs were. Next, I look at the settlement of Lincoln County, Oklahoma, and the beginnings of Prague. The succeeding chapters focus first on factors encouraging the maintenance of ethnic identity and conclude with discussions of the evidence for assimilation into the wider economy and culture.

CHAPTER 1

Czech Immigration to the United States to 1930

THE YOUNG MOTHER, DRESSED IN A SIMPLE PEASANT SKIRT and blouse, ushered her children into the small, badly lit room to see their grandmother one last time. The children hugged and kissed the tearful lady, who valiantly forced a smile as she lovingly ran her fingers through their straw-colored locks and told her grandchildren how much she loved them. When the children finally pulled free, their grandmother rose from her wooden rocker and stretched out her arms to her daughter. The younger woman bounded across the plank floor and squeezed her mother fervently. Knowing it might be the last time they ever touched, they embraced for well over a minute. Although neither sobbed openly, both felt the warm trickle of tears down their cheeks. When at last they separated, the young mother promised to write often and then, with children in tow, marched toward the waiting wagon that would take them to the steamship and on to America to join their husband and father.[1]

This nineteenth-century vignette depicts the heartache many emigrants felt when leaving the village of their birth. The emotional state expressed by many emigrants included a mixture of enthusiasm, apprehension, and sorrow. The sorrow of leaving one's home, one's extended family, and one's lifelong friends must have been traumatic. For many emigrants, this resulted in not only personal discomfort but disillusionment over the move.[2] This disillusionment did not end once the emigrants set sail. Indeed, soon after their arrival, immigrants faced fresh obstacles: an unfamiliar language, a new culture, and an energetic, highly competitive economy where jobs went to those willing to work long hours in dirty and dangerous occupations. This early phase of immigration and its sudden and drastic changes caused many to become disheartened to the point of returning to their homeland.[3]

Although all immigrants faced this dilemma, it proved especially true for single, male immigrants arriving for purely economic reasons. Many emigrated to work, saved their money, and then returned home. These "birds of passage" lived a frugal existence in company dormitories or row houses close to the mill or refinery with their goal of returning home always foremost in their minds.[4]

Why did Czechs leave Bohemia and Moravia? Why did they uproot their families—often including grandparents—and come to a foreign land? What caused them to take such drastic action? Was it the lure of the New World and its promise of prosperity? Or did things become so bad in their own country that they lost hope for a better future. In many early accounts of the immigrant experience, scholars held that the traditional pull of the American economy and the vast opportunities it offered were the prime motives underlying immigration.[5] The idea of the United States as a beacon of hope and liberty and the opportunity to obtain prosperity attracted millions, causing them to leave everything behind and cross oceans to realize their dreams.[6]

Nonetheless, the political and economic situations in their homeland emerged as the primary reasons for Czechs coming to the United States and explained why they overwhelmingly came in family groups. Both push and pull factors are important, and neither should be discounted. However, before anyone would even consider leaving their village, they must conclude that things were not going to get better.[7] People normally do not simply up and leave the country of their birth. Their situation has to become desperate and discouraging; there has to be a push. What was the push? Why did hundreds and later thousands of families sell everything, board a ship, and set sail for a new land? Early on it appears that religious reasons caused many Bohemians and Moravians to cross the Atlantic and settle in the United States. However, in the nineteenth century, the impetus for emigration shifted to economic factors as the industrialization of Europe spread from west to east.

The first known Czech to settle permanently in America was Augustine Herman, who came to the New World sometime during the 1650s.[8] He settled in New Amsterdam, present-day New York, but eventually migrated to Maryland, where, after Herman had published a detailed map of the colony, Lord Baltimore awarded him 20,000 acres. Herman established his home on this tract of land and christened it Bohemia Manor. Though living in a British colony, Herman proudly acknowledged his heritage. He dubbed the two rivers running through his property the "Big Bohemia River" and the "Little Bohemia River." When the well-to-do farmer died in 1692, the inscription on his tombstone read, "Augustine Hermen, Bohemian."[9]

The vicious Thirty Years' War, then ravaging Bohemia, prompted other Czechs to follow Herman. Approximately 500 Czechs fled Bohemia searching for a more tolerant place to live. These small numbers of Protestants settled mainly in Pennsylvania alongside the more numerous German immigrants and quickly lost their cultural identity and native tongue.[10] Early immigrants from Bohemia seeking religious and political freedom continued to trickle into North America, usually settling near German communities until around 1850 when a new type of Czech immigrant began arriving—one leaving the homeland primarily because of economic factors.[11] Because Bohemia and Moravia contained rich natural resources, the Habsburg rulers of Austria-Hungary rapidly industrialized the areas, resulting in a deterioration of the way of life in many villages. By 1914, 70 percent of Habsburg industrial capacity was in the Czech lands with Bohemia alone containing about one-third of all the industrial workers in the empire. Agriculture changed from self-sufficiency to an emphasis on the market, which forever changed many European communities. Although unintended by the imperial government, this disruption of village life destabilized peasant culture and caused a rural-to-urban migration and ultimately an exodus.[12] The first to leave were usually craftsmen, artisans, and small independent farmers (cottagers) who felt threatened by the new, market-based economic order that emphasized large estates and the production of cash crops.[13] The industrializing forces specifically hurt the middle level of the Czech peasantry in southern Bohemia and eastern Moravia. It is chiefly these areas that supplied most of the mid-nineteenth-century immigrants to the United States.[14] Thus, despite Bohemia being the chief industrial center of Austria, the future appeared bleak, as thousands left to seek a better life. When asked by U.S. Immigration Commission agents sent to Bohemia in the early twentieth century as to why so many desired to leave their motherland, "In practically every instance . . . was . . . the answer 'to earn greater wages in America.'"[15]

Another motive that added to the economic woes emerged in the form of a European population explosion. Between 1800 and 1910, Austria-Hungary more than doubled its population.[16] Increased family size and the new economic order many times led to hunger and want, resulting in an almost fanatical effort to relieve the misery. In a study of the Nebraska town of Milligan, immigrants were asked why they left Bohemia. Of the 117 questioned, 92 gave "poverty and large families" as the primary reason for emigrating.[17]

In addition, in the 1840s, Central Europe experienced terrible droughts that decimated harvests and all but destroyed potato crops. As a result, many Czechs decided that it simply had to be better in the United States. Thus the loss of hope in the land of their birth catapulted Czechs across the ocean. Many were of the cottager class from small villages in Bohemia and Moravia. Once in the United States, they sought a similar lifestyle. Therefore, when they arrived, rather than migrating to the established German-Czech communities of Pennsylvania, many sought out inexpensive land in the West, thus becoming the only Slavic group to farm extensively.[18] These Czech families established themselves in Wisconsin, Nebraska, Iowa, Illinois, and Minnesota, and despite battling a harsher climate than they were accustomed to in Bohemia and Moravia, they became successful husbandmen growing wheat, rye, oats, and corn.[19] The cooperation and community-mindedness of these farming areas closely resembled the European villages the Czechs had recently left. In these north-central states, many Czechs broke away from the German American influence and flourished on their own. This pattern proved especially true in the rural states of Nebraska and Iowa.[20]

From 1850 to 1890, emigration from Bohemia and Moravia continued, and most of these newcomers to the United States bypassed the eastern destinations so dear to other Slavic groups and headed for the midwestern farming communities. As decades passed and the cheap western land filled up, Czechs were forced to look elsewhere for a new start. Some chose to settle in New York and Cleveland, but many continued west, settling in cities like Chicago, Omaha, and Racine.[21] St. Louis, in 1854, was home to the first sizable urban Czech community. However, Chicago soon surpassed St. Louis in the number of Bohemian immigrants and by the turn of the century became the veritable, if unofficial, capital of America's Czechs.

By 1890, over 170,000 foreign-born Czechs lived in the United States.[22] This number does not take into account second- and third-generation U.S.-born Czechs, many of whom lived in rural Czech colonies or in urban ethnic neighborhoods. The sparsely populated state of Nebraska alone contained over 50,000 people claiming Czech ancestry.[23] The farming villages and midwestern metropolitan centers were not the only places Czechs chose to live. New York contained over 47,000 residents claiming a Czech background, and Texas, the destination for many Moravians, held over 41,000 ethnic Czechs.[24] Nevertheless, Czechs increasingly chose to live in the northern states of Illinois, Nebraska, Wisconsin, Minnesota, Iowa, and the Dakotas.[25]

Czechs came with their families to stay.[26] Americans considered them as part of the "new" immigration—those whose country of birth was in southern or eastern Europe, even though Czechs had been coming to North America since the seventeenth century.

Czechs differed from other "new" immigrants such as the Poles, Slovaks, Croats, and Hungarians in many areas. To begin with, Czechs had not culturally associated much in the past with their northern Slavic neighbors, the Poles, or their close linguistic relatives, the Slovaks. Historically the Hungarians dominated the Slovaks, resulting in Slovakia becoming a land of uneducated peasants rather than a western-oriented industrial society. To add to this separation, most Slovaks settled almost exclusively in the cities of the Northeast, particularly Pennsylvania, rather than traveling to the Midwest as many Czechs did.[27] These Slovaks sweated long hours in the mines and mills, saving as much of their paychecks as possible with every intention of returning home.[28] As previously mentioned, many were known as "birds of passage," and they rarely attempted to assimilate into the larger community. Instead, they were content living in company ho ing close to the workplace, unlike the Czechs, who came to Nevertheless, those Slovaks who decided to remain in th

States established close-knit neighborhoods complete with churches, Slovak-speaking businesses, and community associations much like other immigrant groups.

However, due to centuries of interaction with the German-speaking peoples to their north and west, Czechs shared more in the areas of customs and mode of life with the non-Slavic Germans than they did with either the Poles or the Slovaks. Thomas Capek, a nineteenth-century Czech immigrant and writer of the Czech experience in America, summed it up well when he wrote that Czechs "felt pretty much at home among the Germans."[30] Although Czechs felt somewhat at ease with western culture, they did not sail across the Atlantic Ocean, as the Germans had done, in appreciable numbers until after 1880. Thus, despite having a lot in common with their German neighbors, most Czechs definitely were part of the new immigration regarding when they came to America.

In general, these Czechs migrated west to the north-central region of the United States and joined their relatives.[31] A more specific look at where Czechs in the United States lived in 1900 validates that many traveled to the ethnic communities of their forebears. The census further illustrates that north-central states like Illinois, Nebraska, Wisconsin, Ohio, Minnesota, and Iowa contained comparatively large numbers of Czech immigrants (105,940). New York was the only north Atlantic state with any appreciable numbers of Czechs (16,347), and because it was the primary port of arrival, it is difficult to ascertain how many immigrants chose the state as their permanent home or were merely passing through at the time of the census. Maryland was the top south Atlantic state with 2,813 Czechs. However, its total was lower than most North Atlantic states. The state of Texas, which included the port of Galveston, contained a sizable Czech population with over 9,000 foreign-born, with Oklahoma Territory the only other south-central area hosting more than 1,000 Czech residents. The Oklahoma Czechs came primarily due to the land runs and, in most cases, represented a second migration.[32]

Czech immigrants who settled in Oklahoma Territory were mainly farmers from Nebraska, Kansas, and Iowa looking for a fresh start. Alongside these Czech newcomers, making their way to Oklahoma

Territory, were American-born Czechs who had already spent many years in the United States, thus giving the new state a relatively significant number of Czech residents.[33]

Of course, newcomers born in Bohemia or Moravia were not the only ingredients in Czech communities; ethnic Czechs were also important. Born in the United States, these second- and third-generation Czechs remained a vital component of many enclaves. These sons, daughters, and grandchildren of Czech immigrants would have learned much about their parents' birthplace, including knowledge of the language, customs, and folklore. In 1910, the census recorded 531,193 Czech ethnics throughout the United States. Their numbers swelled to 622,796 ten years later.[34] Compared with other ethnic groups, such as the Poles, Italians, and Germans, this total number is minuscule. However, several north-central states contained relatively large numbers of Czechs. For example, the rural state of Nebraska held over 54,000 people claiming Czech heritage in 1920, and neighboring Wisconsin had over 46,000. Illinois counted the most with 140,000, and Ohio placed second with slightly under 60,000. Thus the Czech community's influence in certain states or regions within a state where they were heavily concentrated was greater than their overall numbers suggest.

This brings us to Oklahoma. Although the overall numbers are small, Czech influence in several towns such as Yukon, Kingfisher, and Prague proved important during their formative years. Probably the oldest Czech settlement in Oklahoma was a tiny community named Mishak, located in Boone Township, Oklahoma County. Established as a result of the land run of 1889, the town no longer exists because the government forced the inhabitants to sell their property when they expanded what became Tinker Air Force Base.[35]

In the early years of statehood, the area in and around Oklahoma City attracted several pockets of Czech immigrants. Besides the foreign-born, Oklahoma's capital was home to over 1,100 ethnic Czechs by 1920. Yukon, Mustang, and El Reno in Canadian County also contained a sizable number of Czech immigrants and American-born Czechs. Czechs in Yukon Township built a Czech Hall housing their fraternal association and hosted many dances, weddings, and funerals, which continue today. The Czechs in Yukon proudly designated their town the Czech "capital" of Oklahoma, and they hold a yearly fall festival commemorating their Bohemian and Moravian ancestors.

North of Oklahoma City, scattered Czech farming enclaves sprang up in the counties of Garfield, Grant, and Noble. Although never a majority, these Czechs made an appreciable impact in the villages of Bison, Waukomis, Medford, and Perry. Besides these concentrations, Czech immigrants also settled in smaller numbers in the Grant County towns of Fairview, Hickory, and Jarvis and in Logan and Sherman Townships of Kingfisher County.[36]

Early researchers concluded that Czech Oklahomans were farmers. For the great majority, this was true. Czechs tilled their fields and tended their livestock, coming into town only for supplies and entertainment and to worship. However, as the following chapters reveal, these immigrant newcomers did much more than farm, and their impact greatly exceeded their numbers.

CHAPTER 2

Settlement of Lincoln County and the Formation of Prague, Oklahoma, 1891–1902

AFTER YEARS OF STRUGGLE, DISAPPOINTMENT, and grinding poverty, Frantisek Vlasak and his wife finally decided to leave the land of their birth—the land of their parents, grandparents, and forebears. After many heart-wrenching discussions, they sold most of what they owned and bought one-way tickets to the United States and the promise of a better life. In 1866, the Vlasaks and their young children left the tiny village of Bykosi, Bohemia, then part of the Austro-Hungarian Empire, and arrived in New York City several weeks later. Here they set up a new home in the bustling financial capital. However, their time there proved short. The Vlasaks moved inland to Ohio and then to Nebraska, joining the many Czechs already living in that state. After several lean years in Nebraska, the family relocated to South Dakota.

In 1891, with cheap land in short supply, Frantisek's now-grown sons, Frantisek Jr. and Vincent, and Frantisek's daughter, Fannie Koutnik, along with her husband, Frank, migrated to Waterloo, Iowa, hoping to buy their own property. Shortly after arriving, the siblings learned of an upcoming land run on the Sac and Fox Indian Reservation in distant Oklahoma Territory.

Jumping at the opportunity, they decided to participate in the land run. The Vlasak brothers and their sister's family packed their few belongings and left for the booming town of Oklahoma City. Once there, they discovered that the land run was still six months away. So they waited. Although conversant in English, their native tongue drew them into contact with other ethnic Bohemians also awaiting the run. This group of Czechs resolved to claim land close to one another.

When the gun sounded for the start of the race, the Czechs gal-loped and drove their wagons as fast as possible in hopes of acquiring prime farmland. Unfortunately for Frank Koutnik, his horse died only four miles into the run. He claimed the area under the dead animal, which lay slightly south and several miles west of his desired destina-tion. The Vlasak brothers strove forward and found desirable plots in the southeast corner of what later became Lincoln County, Oklahoma. Other Czechs joined the Vlasaks in the area, and almost overnight a small community of Bohemian farmers sprang into being.[1]

As the above narrative demonstrates, no single person or group arranged in advance the Czech settlement in Lincoln County. There was not a planned migration from Bohemia to Oklahoma or from any other state containing a large population of ethnic Czechs. Instead, prior to the 1891 land run, several Czech families and individuals hap-pened upon one another while waiting in Oklahoma City. Although most had never met, their common tongue drew them together, and they agreed to settle in the same area of the Sac and Fox Reservation.[2] These families, with names such as Barta, Hrdy, Sestak, Bontty, and Provaznik, successfully staked out homesteads in the townships of North Creek and South Creek.[3]

Most of these particular Czech immigrants came to Oklahoma after first migrating to midwestern farming communities. Twenty-four Czechs who participated in the land run claimed Nebraska as their preceding residence, while fourteen said they had previously lived in Kansas. Three migrating families declared Iowa as their prior home, and two claimed Wisconsin. Minnesota, North Dakota, Ohio, and Colorado each contributed one immigrant family. Only one set-tler asserted he came directly from Bohemia to Oklahoma. Regardless, most participating in the 1891 land run were but a few years removed from the farming villages of Central Europe.[4] Furthermore, as the opening anecdote shows, some of the settlers had lived in several states before making their way to Oklahoma.

While this band of Czechs strove to claim land in Lincoln County, others also raced to the area. A smaller group of German immigrants settled in North Creek Township, north of the Czechs, whose home-steads lay primarily in South Creek Township. However, native-born

Americans comprised the bulk of those involved in the land run. Even with the Czechs' attempt to settle together, in many cases someone quicker to the spot interrupted their claims. For example, the 1891 land run claims of Czechs Frank Barta, Frantisek Mastena, Frantisek Souva, and Vincent Martinek surrounded the holding of J. W. Harshaw, a non-Czech. Furthermore, U.S.-born settlers dominated the northeast corner of South Creek Township, while most Czech homesteads lay primarily in the southern and western sections of the area.[5]

Most of the original Czech settlers came in small family units with each adult male securing a homestead. They paid $1.25 per acre in installments for the former lands of the Sac and Fox tribe and immediately began building and preparing the land for cultivation.[6] Shortly after the land run, the U.S. government established mail service on the southeast corner of the homestead of Frank and Josephine Barta, and the area soon became known as Barta Post Office.[7]

Within two years, there were about fifty Czech homesteads bunched together in the Barta Post Office area.[8] These ethnic farmers prospered and, though preferring to form an isolated Czech colony, experienced good relations with the non-Czech population, including the Germans located to the north. Little or no hostility existed in the new land, probably because the Czech farmers associated almost exclusively with their European kinsmen as did the Germans and white U.S.-born population.[9]

Soon after the land run, several small settlements sprang up. Two of the larger were Lambdin, located two miles east of the future town of Prague, and Arlington, which boasted at its peak two general stores, a post office, a blacksmith shop, a Methodist church, and three doctors.[10] By the turn of the twentieth century, other tiny settlements dotted the rolling hills of Lincoln County, including Keokuk Falls, a popular swimming and fishing hole for Czechs, Bellemont, the birthplace of the great Sac and Fox athlete Jim Thorpe, and Dent, the smallest and closest community to Prague.[11] The area quickly filled up. Although the original Czech settlers arrived from midwestern states, after 1900 and especially following the formation of Prague, Czechs from Texas trekked north looking for opportunities in the thriving farm town. These newer residents differed from the first settlers in that some were

Moravian rather than Bohemian with more Catholics than Protestants included among their number.[12]

The Czech settlement lay in the southeast corner of Lincoln County.[13] Rolling timbered hills dominated the landscape with numerous streams lacing the area. Most of the region's brooks were nothing more than narrow, shallow trickles, but a few flowed wide and deep. These, together with the hills, created a terrain that, for the most part, was uneven and rough, which caused farming to be difficult at first. Rainfall, which could be heavy in the spring, many times all but disappeared in the hot months of summer. Only a few miles west of the Czech homesteads a vast expanse of flat prairie grassland emerged, part of the Great Plains region.[14]

Upon arrival, Czechs began clearing the land and transforming it into productive agricultural fields. Not surprisingly, they modeled their farms on the European pattern. The Czechs and Germans prospered and quickly became the leading farmers in the area. Czech farms usually included large whitewashed houses and out-buildings kept in good condition, with meticulously maintained fields. In addition, their houses were generally larger than the homes of non-Czechs.[15]

The Czechs' hardiness and productivity could have been predicted. When the U.S. Immigration Commission examined Czech farmers, they concluded that wherever they settled, "Czechs [were] regarded by their neighbors in the same light as the German and Scandinavian farmers."[16] One advantage Czechs appeared to enjoy over U.S.-born farmers was their communal attitude. Czechs formed a tight community and helped each other. This group-mindedness often took the form of simple encouragement liberally sprinkled on a struggling neighbor. But on occasion it resulted in the more prosperous individuals helping the straining ones.[17] Unlike most native farmers, who tended to be extremely individualistic, the group-mindedness of the Czechs boosted their chances of prosperity in the early days of settlement.[18] This cultural difference showed up later in their ties with the village of Prague when many Czechs sought opportunities in the new town, some even moving there on a permanent basis.

Nevertheless, the Lincoln County farming community did not resemble those in the motherland. Peasant villages in Bohemia and

Moravia usually consisted of one long street with houses along each side. The men of the village arose early, ate breakfast with their families, then walked to work in the outlying fields. In Oklahoma, Czechs built isolated farmhouses.[19] Even after the formation of Prague, the majority of Czech farmers spent most of their time on their homesteads, traveling to town only to buy, sell, attend church, or participate in social activities. None lived in town and commuted to their fields daily, as was common in the Czech lands of Europe.

Although living on remote farms, the early Czech farmers of southeast Lincoln County established social and religious ties with one another. In 1892, five immigrants living in the Dent area—about one mile south of the future Prague—formed a chapter of the Bohemian Slavonian Benevolent Society headquartered in St. Louis. Before the end of 1892, twelve others joined the organization, boosting the membership to seventeen. Five years later, they left the St. Louis organization and established a charter lodge of the Western Czech Brotherhood Association with headquarters in Omaha.[20] These benevolent societies provided Protestant and secular (usually freethinking) immigrant farmers with a sense of community and fellowship. Once established, the societies erected a permanent building, usually called Bohemian Hall or Czech Hall. The halls afforded Czech newcomers a place where farmers could meet and discuss the tough job of producing a crop from virgin soil, a place where both men and their wives could socialize with others who spoke their language, shared a common past, and culture; a place where everyone could just relax and enjoy a few hours of respite. Although the new Lincoln County Czech benevolent organization included no female members the first year of operation, twelve women joined during the next two years. Thus, almost from the very beginning, and unlike many American organizations, the Czechs' fraternal association welcomed both men and women.

Not all Czechs in the area joined the society. The 1900 census manuscripts of South Creek Township, where the association held regular meetings, showed that eighty-three Czech adult males lived in the township, but only nineteen were listed in the Bohemian Hall's membership rolls.[21] In most cases, both husband and wife were members of the fraternal lodge. However, one Czech, Frank Sestak, provides an interesting case. His name does not appear on the membership rolls from 1897 to 1904, but the lodge listed his wife, Terezie, as joining in 1899. Perhaps the exclusion of Frank from the rolls resulted from a simple clerical mistake. In addition, his name does not appear in the Bohemian Hall's membership books through 1913.[22] Thus, without more evidence, Sestak cannot be considered a member of the benevolent association during this period. For whatever reason, the wife joined the organization, while the husband did not.

Not all Czech immigrants joined Bohemian Hall. Catholics rejected the secular freethought tenets of the organization and stayed away. Instead, they formed a parish that, besides fulfilling the Czech community's spiritual needs, also offered opportunities for social interaction. Eleven of the forty-eight original Bohemian settlers became members of the new church, including the Barta and Simek families, who originally owned the land that became the town of Prague.[23] Later, the parish church moved to the new town of Prague. Hearkening back to their collective history, Prague's Czechs christened the church St. Wenceslaus after the famous medieval Czech duke. Regardless of whether the Czech immigrant was Catholic, Protestant, or a freethinker, most in the farming community prospered.

The 1900 census for South Creek Township counted 341 families in the area, of which 42 claimed Czech ethnicity.[24] Of these 42 families, 37 heads of household listed their birthplace as Bohemia. In other words, the primary wage earner in most Czech families was an immigrant. Furthermore, in 1900, Czech families constituted a little over 12 percent of the total population of South Creek Township. Thus, from the very beginning, the non-Czech population in the township dwarfed the Czech immigrant community.

A closer look at the Czech community in the 1900 census two years before the creation of Prague reveals that of the 42 families living within the township, 28 definitely resided in another state before migrating to Oklahoma Territory. This can be ascertained by the census manuscripts for 1900 that list the birthplace of each child. Although it is impossible to tell exactly when the family arrived or left by looking at the state of their child's birth, we can determine that they were living in a specific state at the time of the birth or, at the very least, that the mother lived there during this period. By using this method, we can ascertain with some degree of confidence their previous state of residence and, of course, the fact that they did not come directly to Oklahoma Territory from Europe.

Census records prove that most pioneer Czechs came to Oklahoma Territory from the Midwest. By an overwhelming number, most appear to have come to Lincoln County from Nebraska, with Kansas placing second as the previous place of residence. Other states listed in the 1900 census where Czechs lived before moving to Oklahoma Territory included Texas, Iowa, South Dakota, Wisconsin, and Minnesota.[25] With the creation of the farm town of Prague, the numbers of Czech residents in the area rose on the 1910 census. Again, as in 1900, most previously lived in Nebraska with the main difference in the ethnic community being an increase in the number of second-generation Czechs.[26] However, an examination of the 1920 census manuscripts reveals that the situation changed. From 1910 to 1920, Prague witnessed an influx of Czechs from other states, especially newcomers from Texas claiming Moravia as either their birthplace or that of their parents. Still, Prague's Bohemian population more than doubled the numbers of Moravians. Nevertheless, a substantial number of Moravian Czechs arrived during the second decade.[27] This later migration to Lincoln County appears to undermine the claim of an earlier writer, who argued that "Czech settlement in Oklahoma occurred almost entirely in the territorial period" and "by the time of statehood in 1907 the movement was complete, and future increases in the number of Oklahomans of Czech extraction resulted from the excess of births over deaths rather than a continued migration of people."[28] At least in the Prague area, migration continued, albeit from other states, primarily Texas, from 1910 to 1920.

This influx of Moravians from Texas does not hold true for Yukon, the self-declared "capital" of Oklahoma's Czechs. In 1910, out of almost 200 Czechs living in the town, only 3 claimed to be Moravians from Texas. The number of Texan migrants increased to 5 on the 1920 census manuscripts and dipped to 2 on the 1930 tabulation. Why many Texan Moravians after 1910 decided to migrate to Prague and not to Yukon is impossible to state with any accuracy. That it happened is clear. The answer is probably something as simple as one or two Texas Moravian families relocating to Prague, liking the area, and writing home to their friends about the abundant opportunities in the new Czech village only a few days' journey north. That Texas Moravians migrated to Prague, Oklahoma, and not Yukon is certain. Why they did so is not.[29]

Despite the town's Czech beginning and Czech name, non-Czechs showed no hesitation in buying lots. Quickly they outnumbered the immigrant population in the new town. Nonetheless, Czechs flocked in large numbers to the bustling village where construction of wood and brick buildings seemed endless. A comparison of South Creek Township in 1900 and 1910 shows the heavy influx of Czechs to the area. The 1910 census recorded 448 families in Prague. One hundred forty-eight (31 percent) of them were Czech, including 108 heads of household born in either Bohemia or Moravia.[30] As noted earlier, the Czech component of South Creek Township in 1900 was 12 percent. The 1910 numbers show that the Czech portion of the population jumped to 31 percent, a hefty increase. The lure of this small farming town named after the beloved Bohemian capital obviously proved great for many ambitious Czechs seeking cheap land.

Besides Czechs and American-born whites, other immigrants migrated to the new settlement to take advantage of the perceived opportunities in the railroad town. In 1910, nine heads of household reported their birthplace as Germany with another eight American-born heads listing either one or both of their parents' country of birth as Germany. Another four families claimed a Canadian background (one French Canadian, the other three English Canadian), and two immigrant merchants were Russian Jews. The final five foreign-born heads of household in the town listed their birthplace as Ireland, Scotland, Switzerland, Belgium, and Poland.[31]

In addition to an increase in the white population, the 1910 census also showed an upsurge in the African American presence in the community. In 1900, thirteen black families lived in the area. This number more than doubled to twenty-eight on the 1910 enumeration. An interesting variation from 1900 to 1910 deals with the arrival of African Americans and the states from where they came. In 1900, six of the thirteen African American heads of household living in South Creek Township listed their birthplace as Tennessee. Three heads declared Alabama as their state of origin and two listed Arkansas, with one each from Mississippi and Georgia.[32] However, in 1910 thirteen heads listed their birthplace as Texas. Tennessee remained second with five of the same families recorded in 1900 still within the Prague area. An additional black family from Arkansas came to southeast Lincoln County, and the 1910 census again listed two African American families from Mississippi and Georgia. A further addition to Prague's black community was two families from Kentucky and one from Louisiana.[33]

The white, nonimmigrant population of South Creek Township in 1900 consisted of 269 families. One in four of the heads of these families declared the neighboring state of Missouri as their birthplace. Arkansas, Tennessee, and Illinois also contributed significant families to the newly opened farmland.[34] However, an inspection of the 1900 manuscript census shows extensive and repeated movement of families throughout the United States. The William Harris family is a good example. William was born in Texas. However, he listed his father's birthplace as Illinois and his mother's as North Carolina. Georgie Harris, William's wife, claimed Mississippi as her place of birth with her parents born in Alabama. It is impossible with only census records to discern where the couple met or married. However, by following the births of their children we can roughly trace their migration to Lincoln County, Oklahoma. For example, we know that from 1885 to 1887 the Harrises lived in Texas, because their two eldest children were born there. We can also state that sometime before or during 1889, the family moved to Indian Territory and delivered another child. Then, in 1892, they were living in Oklahoma Territory, but returned to Indian Territory, where they had a son in 1894. For whatever reason, the Harrises had moved back to Texas by 1896, but their stay proved relatively short because they listed the birth of still another child in Oklahoma Territory in 1898. Finally, the census taker counted the Harris family's residence as Oklahoma Territory on the 1900 census. Thus, just from the birthplaces of their children as listed on the census manuscript records, we can trace the movement of the Harris family from the state of Texas to Indian Territory, then to Oklahoma

Territory, back to Indian Territory, a short return to Texas, and finally back to Oklahoma Territory. These movements took place within a fifteen-year period.[35] Moreover, the Harris family experience was not an anomaly. Of the 269 white, nonimmigrant families living in the South Creek area in 1900, only 29 appear to have moved directly from their state of birth to Oklahoma Territory.[36]

A quick glance at the birthplaces of non-Czech heads of households in 1910 shows that Missouri again led the way, with Arkansas registering the second most. However, Kansas replaced Tennessee with the third largest numbers followed by Illinois.[37] Thus most people migrating to Oklahoma came from neighboring states.

As can be seen from the above demographic portrait, from the inception of the farming community of Prague, the Czech community found itself at a numerical disadvantage. Unlike some farming towns in the Midwest, such as Milligan or Wilber, Nebraska, or ethnic Czech neighborhoods in Chicago, Cleveland, or New York that contained a majority of people of Bohemian stock, the Czechs of Prague constituted a minority group from the very beginning.[38] As a result, their experiences differed significantly from inner-city areas where ethnic groups, despite living among a diverse population, often isolated themselves culturally. They also differed from agricultural settlements such as Milligan, Nebraska, where the population was overwhelmingly Czech, and one could go days without even hearing the English language spoken.[39] In fact, it is this singular environment which sets apart the Prague Czechs from many urban and rural ethnic communities where cultural and social isolation and, in some instances, economic seclusion proved easy to obtain. Furthermore, the diversity of this small Oklahoma farm town and the interactions of the Czech community with the larger population are both interesting and important.

From the creation of the town, their minority status forced these rural Czech settlers to confront and cooperate with the larger and, to them, foreign society. This differed from the Czechs of Chicago who, after a long day's work, retreated to a crowded neighborhood filled with the sounds and smells of their beloved Bohemia. And it was unlike the experience of the residents of Milligan, Nebraska, who successfully, if only temporarily, created a Czech oasis on the Great Plains where English need never be spoken unless a stranger happened to pass through. The town of Prague daily challenged the Czech newcomers with obstacles in language, social interactions, customs, and economic realities that their relatives in other parts of the country faced at irregular intervals or, at the least, could escape. This is not to say the pressure to acculturate, especially in the cities, was not great. However, the second generation, not the immigrants, usually fulfilled the task of acculturation in urban areas. Having been born and reared in the United States, they attended public schools and spoke English as well as the descendants of Franklin or Lincoln. These sons and daughters of immigrants crossed the cultural bridge and mingled freely with the dominant society. In contrast, the diverse population of the Oklahoma farming community forced most Prague Czechs, including immigrant adults, to live a dual lifestyle embracing the new American ways while toiling to maintain not only their European customs and memories but also their identity as Czechs.

Nevertheless, the Czechs of Prague proved hearty both in numbers and purpose in maintaining a thriving ethnic presence within the larger population of U.S.-born whites and the small but strong German community located a short distance north. Most settlers quickly accepted the fact that they were a minority and adjusted. They merged a determination to maintain their ethnicity with an equal resolve to participate in every facet of community life. This resulted in a duality that enabled them to succeed economically and adapt to the larger community quicker and without some of the tensions and conflicts other ethnic groups encountered while living in large cities or in isolated, ethnically homogenous settlements throughout the Plains region. The Prague Czechs plowed a haven of success and held onto their ethnic identity, their internal distinctiveness within the larger U.S.-born society, while fully participating in every social, cultural, economic, and political activity the small southeastern Oklahoma farming town had to offer. However, the religious situation of Czech immigrants differed drastically from other ethnic groups. Rather than a primary ingredient of their culture and ethnic identity, religion frequently served as a source of disagreement if not downright enmity.

CHAPTER **3**

Religion, Freethought, and the Czech Community

ON THAT FATEFUL SPRING DAY IN 1918, several men and women anxiously and reluctantly entered the field of devastation. Splintered white-washed lumber, twisted shingles, and shards of glass sparkling in the late-afternoon brightness littered most of the four acres. Barely visible in the tall grass rested planks of various lengths with jagged edges and sharp nails protruding as if purposely and chaotically placed to injure any inattentive trespasser. Heaps of wood embedded with chunks of glass rested next to serene tombstones of loved ones gone to be with the Lord. Alongside the irregular scenes of destruction lay a few seem-ingly unharmed boards already painted, complete with shiny spikes ready for the powerful blows of the carpenter to hammer them into place. Juxtaposed with the vast carnage, the intact lumber appeared out of place, like a joke played by someone with a sick sense of humor. Fortunately, no one had been inside the church when the tornado roared down from the sky. As if not content with crushing the roof, the twister had hoisted the sanctuary from the ground and then dropped it back onto the foundation, causing it to explode on impact and scat-ter debris between the graves of deceased parishioners. Little remained that a competent carpenter might salvage. St. Wenceslaus Church, the center of activity for Prague's Catholics, had been reduced to four acres of rubble.

Over the next few weeks, the parishioners removed the wood and glass from the parish cemetery and discussed what to do next. Of course, the church had to be rebuilt. But where should they build and how would they fund the new construction? Some wanted to re-create the original church at the cemetery. Others wished to see an even bigger church built within the environs of the growing town. After locating a piece of available land, Prague's Catholic parish opted to relocate closer to the central business district. The next chore, raising funds and actually erecting the edifice, took more than a year. Josef Lanik, a devout Catholic from the immigrant Czech community, volunteered to head the drive for donations of money and labor. Lanik and his helpers visited every Catholic household in the area, not begging but advising fellow Catholics of their duty to support the parish. The community responded, especially the prosperous Czech farmers living in the countryside. Raising more than $2,500 for materials, Prague's Catholics constructed a much larger church on Main Street. The finish carpenters worked long hours to complete the intricate woodwork of the chancel and nave, allowing St. Wenceslaus to hold its first service shortly before Christmas in 1919.[1]

On their arrival in the United States, most immigrants clung to the religion of their past. Confronted with new laws, unfamiliar customs, and a strange, usually urban, environment, the newcomers tenaciously embraced their church and their beliefs. Uprooted from a simpler way of life, these rural cottagers and village artisans arrived with a sense of excitement and hope but also with an overwhelming apprehension. The psychological trauma experienced by many must have been great as they gathered their belongings, underwent the mandatory physical examination, and experienced their first noisy street. A friend or relative meeting them as they disembarked from the ship may have relieved some of the anxiety, but not all. New York City bombarded the immigrants with all things new. Boys stood on the crowded sidewalks and hawked newspapers written in the perplexing language of the United States. Salesmen in peculiar clothing and rounded hats jostled the new arrivals as they hurried past. Wagons, pushcarts, hacks, and carriages squeezed together on narrow streets as their drivers bawled at one another for any perceived illegality or social misconduct. The immigrants took it all in. Although most newcomers experienced sensory shocks, immigrants from southern and eastern Europe arriving after 1880 underwent an enormous transition. Strapped with a vastly different culture, religion, and language than the majority of Americans, is it any wonder that so many newcomers smiled when they beheld the spires of the church?[2]

Priests sympathized with the immigrants. In eastern cities such as Boston and New York, the Irish already dominated clerical positions to the point that many U.S.-born Americans equated Catholicism with being Irish.[3] By the end of the nineteenth century, Italians demanded and received their own priests and parishes and soon competed with the Irish in the number of churches. Poles and Slovaks migrated west and formed ethnic churches in the neighborhoods of Pittsburgh, Chicago, and St. Louis. Wherever they settled, most southern and eastern European immigrants looked to the Catholic Church for reassurance and provisional assistance while they struggled to adjust to their new surroundings. Indeed, regardless of their belief system, religion offered the dislocated a system of coping and a means of support, comfort, and reconciliation during difficult periods.[4]

Once an ethnic group gathered enough members, religious leaders within the group appealed to the Catholic hierarchy for their own church with their own clergy. Much of the initial impetus toward church formation focused not only on a shared doctrinal ethos but also on a desire to preserve the old ways—the traditions of home. Churches were meeting places for various social groups and became refuges for newcomers confused about their place in American society. In many cases religion morphed into a form of ethnicity, reinforcing specific customs peculiar to the members' region or nation. Although the religious zeal was authentic, conflicts sometimes arose within the magnificent cathedrals constructed by the early settlers. The ethnic members and religious leaders began clashing, and divisions formed between factions of clergy over the ideals of religious devotion and ethnic identity.[5]

These ideals became an issue in the 1890s. Leaders in the Catholic Church worried that the institution might develop into a church of the foreign-born rather than an American church.[6] This placed clergy at odds with their parishioners, who took comfort in the cultural distinctiveness of their services and fellowship. Secular leaders within the immigrant group itself became more threatening and aggressive as they pushed for increased ethnic rather than religious focus.[7] In other words, lay persons within the immigrant community resisted replacing the cultural emphasis of their local congregation with a solely spiritual one. At this period in their lives, many immigrants refused to become only Catholic Americans. To them, ethnic identity still held great importance.

Regardless of tensions arising between laity and clergy, immigrant churches continued to aid individuals and families in adjusting to their new surroundings. Religious institutions provided psychological relief from the strains of factory work and dismal, crowded living conditions. Catholic churches supplied material relief through immigrant aid societies that focused on helping women and children. These programs provided struggling mothers with staples such as bread, salt, sugar, and sometimes meat. Similar to secular agencies like Jane Addams's Hull House in Chicago, the church also educated mothers in practical matters and offered a sympathetic ear, in many cases in the immigrant's native language. Additionally, ethnic churches created organizations and offered fellowship activities that allowed immigrant families a place to congregate, make friends, and feel accepted.[8] Overall, immigrant churches softened the cultural and economic blows of the dominant society. Over time, these churches introduced a more American form of worship, usually less formal, including the usage of English rather than Latin in part or all of the corporate service. As incongruous as it may appear, ethnic churches provided immigrants with a way of holding onto things past, at least psychologically, while innocuously advancing modernism and Americanism.[9]

Nonetheless, no institution exhibited more disharmony and schism than the immigrant church. This is clearly seen in the situation of the Czechs. They were the only immigrant group in which a majority abandoned the Church. Many Czechs cut all ties to organized religion, and many arrivals became known as liberals, rationalists, and freethinkers.[10]

Freethought (svobodomysleni) is the name of a movement that evolved from various sources. The exact origins of the term are uncertain. However, by the late seventeenth century, a few writers, including Benedict Spinoza (1632–77), began using the word in its present meaning. Some scholars consider the period from about 1875 to World War I as the highwater mark of freethought in American society. Freethought is the philosophy that man rules his own destiny, rejecting the ideas of miracles and divine intervention. Belief centers around the idea that nature and natural law guide humankind and that the uses of reason and science are the means by which one should judge everything. Freethinkers argue that truth should derive from the application of observation and experiment without the cumbersome influences of tradition and superstition. This rationalist philosophy asserts that "all beliefs should be subjected to critical examination by exactly the same standards."[11]

When examined, the differing ideas regarding the origin of freethought in the Czech community form a muddy pool—but one that highlights the complexities of not only rationalism itself but Czech acceptance. The writings of radical thinkers such as the iconoclastic agnostic Robert Ingersoll and English philosopher Herbert Spencer heavily influenced early Czech freethinkers. The origins of freethought lay in the European Enlightenment with philosophies such as French Positivism, German Materialism, and Darwinian theories. Another view posits that the Czech movement gradually developed out of Hussitism and the questioning of the Church as the final arbiter of everything. Czech intellectuals absorbed the ideas of freethought through their close proximity and long association with the German-speaking peoples. Again, the dichotomy of Czech-German history comes into play. Czechs despised Germany's power and its historic ascendancy over the Czech lands. On the other hand, Czechs borrowed heavily from their Germanic neighbors in areas ranging from philosophy to food. Freethought gained a foothold among Czech intellectuals through the writings of George F. W. Hegel (1770–1831), Ludwig Feuerbach (1804–72), Friedrich Nietzsche (1844–1900), and others. Rationalists like Johannes Ronge (1813–87) and Robert Blum (1807–48) and the ideas of the ill-fated 1848 uprisings gained further traction among Czech thinkers. However, the ideas of freethought gained acceptance with the masses primarily out of rebellion against the authoritarian Habsburg government and the Catholic Church. Many Czechs viewed both the political and religious sectors as children of the same mother: tyranny. Among many Czech liberals, anti-Catholicism, especially enmity toward clerics, elicited strong emotions. Militant Czech freethinkers carried this anticlericalism with them when they crossed the Atlantic.[12]

Freethought rationalists dominated the Czech-language press in the United States. By the end of 1910, more than three hundred

Czech-language serial publications were circulating from American presses.[13] Except for the major Catholic weekly, *Hlas,* most Czech-language newspapers leaned heavily toward freethought or at least attempted to remain neutral.[14] The ratio of progressive to conservative periodicals was close to 6:1.[15] One of the more strident liberal publications came out of Omaha. Edward Rosewater's *Pokrok Zapadu* (Progress of the West) consistently opposed organized religion. Rosewater and fellow Czech and Omaha publisher John Rosicky were the first to publish thought-provoking rationalist articles throughout the Plains region, reaching immigrant communities as far south as Texas.[16] Despite Rosewater's and Rosicky's journals, Chicago, containing the largest number of Czech immigrants, became the axis of liberal publication and activity. In 1883 the Windy City had fifty-two freethought societies but only three Catholic parishes. By 1920, membership in freethought associations across the United States was twice the size of membership in Catholic organizations.[17] If the number of newspapers and periodicals is any indicator, from roughly 1860 to the end of World War I Czech rationalists dominated and controlled Czech American society and culture.

Even so, not all freethinkers believed alike. Their views ranged from outspoken, atheistic Free Congregations (Svobodne Obce) and benevolent agnostics to those who believed in a supreme being but not in miracles or divine intervention (deists).[18] Despite profound differences, a spirit of theological questioning and physical separation from organized religion provided common threads binding all rationalists. Their trust in science and empirical evidence trumped the faith of their fathers and placed them philosophically within the progressive matrix.[19] Freethinkers believed in the progress of man in the here and now. They embraced the principle of the goodness of man and confidence in the future of society. These universal ideas echoed middle-class aspirations in the early twentieth century and served to attract converts, especially those not holding extreme views on matters religious.[20]

Czech freethinkers differed from their fellow European rationalists in one important matter: Czechs incorporated an anti-German attitude into their beliefs. Czech rationalism expanded beyond simply questioning Church authority and teachings; a fiery finish of nationalism covered the entire movement. In Europe, the nineteenth century witnessed the birth of modern Italy (1861) and Germany (1871), as ideas of nationhood and citizenship gained acceptance and flourished, first among intellectuals, then filtering down to the masses. Because of the budding nation-state movement, the medieval martyr Jan Hus took on added importance. Hus's defiance of authority and spirit of independence appealed to Czech liberals more than his theological arguments. Freethinkers held Hus in high esteem, although not as a martyred cleric but as an independent thinker and aspiring nationalist.[21] Rose Rosicky, an early historian of the Nebraska Czechs, in her 1929 work relates the patented rationalist answer when asked why liberals revere the memory of a defrocked Catholic priest: "If Hus were living today, he would be a liberal."[22]

The early freethought press in the United States promoted Hus not so much as an enemy of the Church but as an embodiment of Czech resistance to domination and as someone searching for the ultimate truth. Hus, who was executed at the Council of Constance in 1415, became a symbol of rationalist inquiry and Czech nationalist impulses. On July 6, 1873, the city of Saline City, Nebraska, held the earliest known American commemoration of the burning of Jan Hus. The featured speaker at the ceremony was Vaclav Snajdr, then editor of the Omaha-based *Pokrok Zapadu,* one of the leading freethought weeklies of the Great Plains.[23] Czech communities throughout the United States read about the festivities honoring Hus and began hosting their own event every sixth of July. These yearly commemorations took on a more defiant tone with the advent of the Great War. The five hundredth anniversary of Hus's death in 1915 was particularly emotional, and the anti-Habsburg press used it to rally support for the nascent independence movement among Czech émigrés and American Czechs forming in London, New York, and Chicago. With reports of Austrian atrocities filling the pages of American and Czech-language newspapers, the commemorative events doubled as fund-raisers for the Bohemian National Alliance, the primary Czech independence organization. However, once the Allies secured victory in Europe and created the new Slavic nation of Czechoslovakia, emphasis on Hus gradually faded in Czech American communities.[24] It appears that Hus was actually more important to the typical Czech American as a symbol of nationalist desires and independence from Austrian domination than as an icon of epistemology.

Freethinkers controlled the early fraternal associations.[25] Fraternal lodges such as the Slavic Benevolent Society and Western Bohemian Fraternal Association, along with the liberal press, effectively persuaded many Czechs to leave the Catholic Church.[26] Before 1914, about 55 percent of Czech immigrants in the United States were freethinkers, with the rest maintaining loyalty to the Catholic Church or switching to a Protestant sect.[27]

Some freethought intellectuals, especially journalists, viewed their mission as a sort of crusade against all organized religion.[28] Without apology, these writers denounced traditional churches and spread their message through the printed word. Reading their articles and editorials would leave one with the impression that the freethought movement among Czech Americans was passionate and uncompromising. However, zealous journalists constituted only a small fraction of Czech Americans, and they garner too much attention when the philosophical boundaries of Czech rationalism are examined. Nevertheless, it is clear that a division existed between liberal and Catholic Czechs.

In Prague, practically no Catholics joined the local Bohemian Hall (Zapadni Ceske Bratrska Jednota, ZCBJ) during the first thirty years; their membership at St. Wenceslaus sufficed. Although the 1918 tornado destroyed the membership rolls of Prague's Catholic church, a comparison of Catholic cemetery records with ZCBJ membership rolls through 1930 reveals only a couple of possible dual memberships. Jan and Anna Babek and Anna Wostrcil, members of the ZCBJ, are buried in the Catholic cemetery. Furthermore, it appears that in Prague, the division between Catholic and secular immigrant was not based on economic status. For example, among the early immigrant leaders of the new town, Joseph Lanik and Frank Barta remained Catholic, while Frank Vlasak and C. M. Sadlo abandoned their European religious roots.

Despite little duplication in membership between the church and ZCBJ, Catholics and Bohemian Hall members enjoyed amiable relations and frequently socialized.[29] In the Great Plains region, tolerant

Figure 3. Bohemian Hall, Prague, Oklahoma. Gary Patton Photography.

liberals, not militants, dominated Czech fraternal associations.[30] This appears to be the case in Prague. These rural Czechs, experiencing either anger or apathy toward the Catholic Church, drifted into a kind of lethargic irreligion. However, most liberals, at least in Oklahoma, harbored little animosity toward the Church. They simply felt indifferent about it.[31] Few were evangelical atheists or even agnostics. They merely quit the church and concentrated on economic and family matters, usually joining the Bohemian Hall for life insurance and fellowship opportunities, not because they entertained a deep grudge against St. Wenceslaus Church or the Catholic faith. Nevertheless, Prague's ZCBJ members concealed no yearnings to return to the Church. Most remained unchurched, and those who began attending chose a Protestant denomination rather than return to the pews of the Catholic parish. There is simply no evidence of hatred against their former faith.

Although claiming no pretense of being a religious organization, Czech freethought associations such as the local Bohemian Hall evolved into a kind of secular church where weddings and funerals were conducted, usually with a judge officiating.[32] No record of the type of music played at Czech funerals in Prague exists. However, funerals held at the Milligan, Nebraska, lodge included church songs such as "God Will Take Care of You," "Will There Be Any Stars in My Crown?" and "Beautiful Isle of Somewhere."[33] Remembering that most of the original settlers came from Nebraska, it would not be surprising if religious hymns rang out at Bohemian Hall memorial services in Prague as well.

Unlike midwestern Czechs, Bohemians and Moravians in Texas were not as influenced by freethought; Catholicism and Protestantism remained strong in the Lone Star state. Differing from the Prague Czechs and their ethnic kin to the north, the Texas Czechs were atypical of the Czech population as a whole. The Roman Catholic Church in Texas predominated among the Czech immigrants and their descendants, accounting for almost 75 percent of the ethnic population. The Moravian Brethren Church also dominated a few ethnic communities. One such was Snook, Texas, which held a large Brethren congregation and a much smaller Catholic church. In areas containing nonsectarian lodges, religious Texas Czechs did not join these freethought organizations.[34]

Czech freethought in the United States, then, was slowly transformed through the lodges from a strident denunciation of everything Catholic and religious into a calmer, secular, ethnically oriented movement. Again, between liberal and Catholic leaders, the split was real and at times quite hostile. Religious disunity plagued Czech communities in the United States more than any other ethnic group. This became evident during World War I when Czech Catholics refused to merge resources with the secular Bohemian National Alliance in Chicago until late in the conflict. However, in rural locales like Prague, the two camps put aside their antagonisms in the name of shared ethnicity. When Prague's Bohemian Hall sponsored a dance or play, it was a Czech dance or a Czech play rather than a freethought dance or freethought play, and as time went on, dances included American tunes as well as traditional Bohemian songs and steps. This further weakened hostile feelings between the two groups. In the end, Catholic and non-Catholic Czechs transformed ethnicity into their common "religion." As freethought, especially the radical anticlerical form, lost its appeal, fraternal organizations focused more and more on sustaining and passing down Czech distinctiveness to the young. Rationalist ideals withered until, by 1980, lodge members were largely Catholic.[35]

In the late nineteenth and early twentieth centuries, Czech National Cemeteries were permanent monuments to the freethought movement in Oklahoma.[36] There is no doubt that in the technical sense, this is true. Throughout Oklahoma and other states, the secular freethought associations created these burial grounds and interred their members. Catholics preferred their parish cemeteries, and many Protestants chose the city cemetery. However, later generations and non-Czechs viewed Czech cemeteries as monuments to Czechs rather than to freethinkers. Unless the passerby happens to be a student of freethought or Czech immigration, the cemetery symbolizes the historical presence of Bohemians and Moravians in the area. The ethnic identity of the buried trumps their philosophical leanings. Today Czech National Cemeteries, although started by rationalists, are monuments to all Czech Americans rather than to the purveyors of a secular freethinking ideology.

As of January 1, 1903, eight months after its founding, Prague had seven saloons but no churches.[37] The rough-and-tumble frontier town attracted many of the coarser elements from the twin territories searching for strong refreshments after a hard day's toil. Drunken fights and revelries abounded in the embryonic town. Despite the raucous turmoil, Prague's spiritual-minded residents coalesced into bands with like-minded beliefs and began building churches. Although not the first sacral structure in the new town, the Catholic parish dated to 1891 and the land run.[38] Eleven of the forty-eight original Bohemian settlers claimed membership, including the Barta and Simek families, whose homesteads later became the town of Prague.[39] The Czechs' presence within the church grew until, by the late 1940s, their numbers topped 75 percent of the membership.[40] Unlike urban areas where Irish, Italian, and Polish Catholics dominated, these small-town Czechs faced no competition for control of church functions and activities. Recognizing the need for Bohemian priests in these rural Great Plains settlements, the Catholic Church advertised in the newspapers of Bohemia and Moravia for priests to come to the United States.[41] St.

Wenceslaus maintained a Czech-speaking priest for more than thirty years.[42] In addition, by the early twentieth century, the Catholic Church had become the largest Christian denomination in the United States. With growing numbers, mainly fueled by immigration, Catholics transformed from a tiny minority religion, ridiculed and belittled by some Protestant sects, into a proud, confident group.[43] It was under these circumstances that Prague's Catholics established St. Wenceslaus Church.

Although primarily interested in the salvation of souls, the Church throughout America also aided the poor and needy. In Chicago, the Catholic Benevolent Union helped Czech immigrants adjust to industrial capitalism and living in an overcrowded city.[44] Catholic churches in farming regions promoted Catholic holidays and sponsored dances and bazaars, which turned into community affairs attended by Catholics and non-Catholics alike. In an attempt to cultivate Christian fellowship among their congregants, Prague's Catholics established their own fraternal association, the Catholic Worker (Katolicky Delnik).[45] The organization sponsored dances, dinners, and festivals centered around important Catholic holidays. Renegade Catholics of the Bohemian Hall attended St. Wenceslaus celebrations viewing the events as community happenings every bit as much as religious galas.[46] Only sixty miles west of Prague in Oklahoma City, there was immense religious friction between Czech Catholics and the smaller congregations of Czech Protestants.[47] The differing groups in the larger town separated themselves and refused to cooperate. In the small town of Prague, things were different. Residents lived in close proximity and saw the same people on the streets and in the stores anytime they shopped. Constant interactions bred more of a community spirit than could be seen in most urban centers. The residents, regardless of religious preference or ethnicity, simply had to find a way to get along.

Nationwide, Czech Protestants were vastly outnumbered by freethinkers and Catholics. After arriving in the United States, if a Czech left the Catholic Church, rarely did he relocate to a Protestant pew. Among immigrants, Presbyterian churches attracted the most ex-Catholics. Czech Presbyterians traced their national and religious heritage to Jan Hus and the Bohemian Brethren, the first Protestants in the

Czech lands. In fact, one of the largest Czech Presbyterian churches in New York named its building Jan Hus Bohemian Presbyterian Church.[48] In the farming communities of the Midwest, a majority of Czech Protestants in Nebraska claimed Presbyterianism as their faith.[49] However, the most aggressive sect was the Methodists. Focusing their conversion efforts primarily on the young, Methodist churches attracted second-generation Czechs and their offspring. Over time, more Czechs claimed Methodism as their faith than any other Protestant sect.[50]

Members of the Methodist-Episcopal Church erected the first church building in Prague. The pastor, appointed by the Annual Conference, ministered in Prague every other Sunday because he also served a church in nearby Okemah.[51] Soon after opening, the Methodists agreed to allow other denominations, specifically the Presbyterians and Baptists, to use their building until they constructed their own places of worship.[52] Much like the Catholic church, Bohemian Hall, and Sokol Hall (a Czech gymnastic organization discussed in chapter 4), the Methodist church became a center of community activity hosting concerts and plays in addition to revivals and special Christmas services.[53] The membership rolls of the church show no Czech names on the register during the first decade of its existence. However, in the 1920s, Czechs began joining the ranks of Methodism with several holding positions of leadership. Church records list William Vlasak, son of the Czech pioneer Frank Vlasak, as a steward in the church and serving on the Sunday school and finance committees. In 1928, the members elected Mrs. Billy Urban as the treasurer. During this same period, her husband served alongside Vlasak on the Sunday school committee.[54] Other Czech members listed over the years included Cervenys, Svobodas, Jezeks, Novotnys, Klabzubas, Koutniks, Stoklasas, Voborniks, Opelas, and Bonttys. Some of these, such as Jan Svoboda and William Vlasak, were members of the ZCBJ, while others were the wives and children of ZCBJ members. For example, Emma Spevacek, a member of the Methodist church, married Joseph J. Klabzuba, and both are buried in the Czech National Cemetery. The pastor of Prague's Methodist church performed the Klabzubas' wedding ceremony in 1902 at his church. Joe Stoklasa, one of Prague's grocers and a believer in the tenets of Wesleyanism, was a member of the Sokol Hall and is interred in the freethinking cemetery.[55] Finally, when the longtime Bohemian Hall stalwart Jan Svoboda died, Prague's Methodist church held his funeral and buried him in the Czech National Cemetery.[56] The above list embraces some of the most active Czech Methodists. Apparently many more attended, because in 1927 the Methodists invited Dr. Karl Sladek, a Czech Methodist from Oklahoma City, to be the guest speaker at special Czech-language services.[57]

No primary source information exists concerning the town's Presbyterian church. However, it is certain that the church conducted services in Prague from 1906 until 1920, when it was disbanded because of the small and declining membership.[58] Furthermore, from newspaper accounts we can glean that the C. V. Sojka family were active members, holding a dinner for the Presbyterian Social Circle in 1916.[59] In 1928, Mildred Eret, granddaughter of Bohemian Hall member George Eret, married Charles Butler, a non-Czech, in the Presbyterian church in Okemah.[60] It appears the Eret family remained staunch Presbyterians because, despite losing their church in 1920, they held their daughter's wedding in a church in a neighboring town. Jumping to the conclusion of the newlyweds' lives, Charles and Mildred Butler chose the Czech National Cemetery as their final resting place. Mildred's parents, Joseph and Lillian Eret, also chose the National Cemetery over the city cemetery, again showing how the once freethinking cemetery had transformed into more of an ethnic cemetery rather than the final resting place for nonbelievers.

Few Czechs joined either the local Baptist church or the Christian church during the early years of the community.[61] Similar to the experience of the Catholic church, the Prague Baptist church lost all of its records during a storm.[62] However, a few snippets of Czech interest in these churches emerge from the pages of the newspapers. For instance, Rose Klabzuba married Harmon Veatch in the parsonage of the Christian church, and James Urban, a Czech, married Eula Nash in that church's sanctuary.[63] Both Czechs were third generation and both married outside the group. Neither ceremony took place in the Bohemian Hall or the Catholic church. The only mention of an early Baptist Czech centers on Rose Bouda. Bouda, a Czech, married a non-Czech, Ollie McAdams, and both became members of First Baptist Church of

Prague.[64] Of course, what does all this mean? What is the relevance for the Czech community in Prague and for Czech communities throughout the United States? Although these anecdotes are only a small sample, they suggest that many Czechs, especially the later generations, returned to some sort of faith, with most opting for Protestant sects rather than the Catholic Church.

Upon arriving in the United States, many Czech immigrants left the Catholic Church. Most of these immigrant apostates never returned to the fold, but imbibed the secular ideas of freethought. A few joined Protestant congregations, chiefly Presbyterian and Methodist. Freethought intellectuals, particularly journalists, espoused a highly anticlerical form of rationalism. Through their weeklies and journals, they contested against their historic faith and developed an "us vs. them" attitude. However, the rank and file leaned more toward apathy in religious matters rather than confrontation. This appears true in small towns like Prague. Although the freethinkers established a Bohemian Hall for their members, they openly advertised for anyone—Catholics, Protestants, Czechs, and non-Czechs—to attend their social functions. Likewise, the Catholic church held dances and bazaars that were as much community events as sacred affairs. In Prague, Catholics, freethinkers, Protestants, and those who simply did not go to church mingled socially at any venue that offered refreshments and entertainment.

As time and generations passed, more and more Czechs joined Protestant churches. However, many continued their association with the local chapter of their fraternal association, including burial in the Czech National Cemetery. Slowly Prague's freethinking Bohemian Hall became more of an ethnic club than a bastion of religious unorthodoxy. The 1920s increasingly saw both Catholics and Protestants joining the freethought organization, and by 1980 Catholics formed a majority of the lodge's membership. Thus the situation of Prague differed from urban areas, which witnessed bitterness and animosity between freethinkers and Catholics.

Rather than unifying the Czech community, religion caused divisions. In Prague, these divisions did not erupt into outright hostility. The differing sides realized the need to work together in the frontier village. Religion, an important factor in ethnic identity with most immigrant groups, was not as pivotal with the newcomers from Bohemia and Moravia. Czech immigrants did not coalesce around a specific sacred belief system as did other immigrants. Other types of associations provided the frontier settlers with paths to express their ethnic heritage. Of utmost importance were their fraternal and gymnastic organizations.

CHAPTER **4**

Czech Fraternal Organizations in Prague

FIFTY-SEVEN-YEAR-OLD OSWALD BLUMEL did not notice his fatigue after such a long journey. He was too excited. After they had spent almost a year of planning and raising money for the 1920 trip, Prague's Sokol gymnasts had arrived in Prague—Prague, Bohemia. Their express purpose was to take part in a gymnastic exhibition featuring Czech Sokols from all over the United States and Czechoslovakia. However, a bigger reason for the trip was to visit relatives and experience the newly independent nation of Czechoslovakia.

Less than two years had elapsed since the massive bloodletting of the Great War had ended. After leaving Chicago, the small group of Czech athletes arrived in France on May 23, 1920, and spent a few days in Paris. Prague's athletes then made their way to Austria and the former capital of the Austro-Hungarian Empire, Vienna. Although most in the party had never seen Vienna, both young and old identified the city as the center of Czech persecution. During the war, newspaper articles and speeches had depicted the shameful wickedness of the Habsburg regime in unflattering terms. However, after visiting Vienna, even the most virulent Habsburg critic had to admit the city's beauty. The Austrians further disarmed the Czech group by showing them nothing but kindness. From Vienna, the small band of Oklahomans traveled into southeastern Germany, through the Bavarian Forest, and across the international border into Czechoslovakia. The people they met along the way tended to speak German. But as they continued toward the capital of the new nation, Czech became the dominant tongue.[1]

Prague was as beautiful as Blumel remembered, and memories of his childhood and youth came flooding back. Nevertheless, Blumel still believed he had made the right decision in leaving more than twenty-five years earlier. He managed his own hardware business in the

Oklahoma farm town and owned a comfortable house. His three children had all been born in the United States, and he and his immigrant wife, Emelia, made sure they learned the Czech culture through the Sokol and Bohemian Hall. The Blumels also agreed that the costly trip was well worthwhile.[2]

The gymnastic exhibition, though exciting, proved only a small part of the trip. The Oklahoma Czechs, like all traveling American groups, were treated like royalty by their hosts. They ate well, and the gymnastic schedule allowed them ample time to explore the city of their ancestors. Blumel visited his childhood home and met friends and relatives he had not seen in decades. The entire trip was exhilarating, especially for the older chaperones. When at last the day of departure dawned, it was with bittersweet emotions that the Czech expatriate hugged and shook hands a final time with the memories of his former life.[3]

Oswald Blumel, like many Czechs in Prague, continued to love the country of his past. Despite realizing their families were better off economically in the United States, they never wanted to forget their heritage. For this reason, Czechs throughout the United States held fast to their European ways and earnestly tried to pass their Bohemian uniqueness to their descendants. With time and new generations of children, however, their attempts to safeguard specific traditions, especially the Czech language, quietly fell by the wayside. Nevertheless, despite failure in the grand attempt to create a Czech enclave in the midst of a foreign society, the Czechs in Prague, Oklahoma, succeeded in inculcating a permanent Czech identity for many descendants. Furthermore, the matrix of this lasting group identity emerged during the early decades of settlement and arose from the group's persistent efforts to preserve their distinctiveness in a torrent of change.

Czechs, like many Americans during this period, were joiners. In 1915, the *Prague News* published a directory of local lodges. The list included the Masonic Lodge, Knights of Pythias, Independent Order of Odd Fellows, ZCBJ (Zapadni Cesko Bratrska Jednota or Western Czech Brotherhood Association), Modern Woodmen of America, and Woodmen of the World.[4] Although every lodge included Czechs, the lodge that attracted the most Czechs was the ZCBJ.

The Czech community's original fraternal association was the Bohemian Slavonian Benevolent Society (Cesko-Slovansky Podporujici Spolek) with its headquarters in St. Louis. The Missouri Czechs established it in 1854, long before the advent of the "new" immigration. The St. Louis society was America's oldest and largest Czech fraternal association, and members provided help, both financially and psychologically, for Czech families throughout the country.[5] A year after the 1891 land run, five Czechs living within the Dent area of Lincoln County formed Lodge 214 of the Bohemian Slavonian Benevolent Society to encourage fellowship and cooperation and to provide aid and life insurance for the immigrant farming community. The charter members, Frank Vlasak, Jan Sefcik, Jan Vobornik, Jiri Walla, and Vaclav Ladra, did not erect a permanent meeting place but met regularly in private homes. The lodge meetings and social gatherings provided a respite for the newcomers from the intense labor and emotional struggle of creating functioning farms and finding their niche in a strange land.[6]

However, in 1896, a schism developed within the national association between the eastern and western lodges. The eastern lodges had an older membership and therefore received an inordinate proportion of the benefits being paid out to their aged members.[7] In addition, the Bohemian Slavonian Benevolent Society did not admit women to their ranks; it was strictly a men's club. Chafing at the rising monthly dues charged by the national headquarters and the desire to allow women to join, several western lodges seceded from the parent organization and established their own association in 1897, with headquarters in Omaha, Nebraska.[8] This new group chose the name Zapadni Cesko-Bratrska Jednota (Western Bohemian Fraternal Association). The Czech farmers living in the southeastern corner of Lincoln County, Oklahoma, joined this secession, establishing Lodge 46 in the brand-new organization. When Prague incorporated five years later, the ZCBJ lodge moved from the rural community of Dent to the big new town. In 1901, while still meeting in Dent, the lodge had fifty-three members, including sixteen women. By the end of 1902, membership had grown to seventy-three, and the number of women had jumped to twenty-six—over a third of the total.[9] Unlike many early-twentieth-century associations, both ethnic and native, the ZCBJ lodge welcomed women on an equal basis as men, and many Czech women eagerly joined their husbands as members.[10] Prague's Bohemian Hall was a community lodge in which family participation was the norm. Not only could husband and wife join, but their children could attend most functions as well. Moreover, as Czechs married non-Czechs, the lodge welcomed their spouses.[11]

Once relocated to Prague, members continued meeting in homes and sometimes at the local schoolhouse. As the lodge grew, members agreed that they needed a permanent structure. John Barta, a Catholic and not affiliated with the ZCBJ, offered to give the lodge an acre of land.[12] In return for his munificence, Barta received free admission to all programs held at the Bohemian Hall for the rest of his life. Finally, in 1917, after myriad fund-raisers and labor donated by members, a two-story building south of the Catholic church was completed. In the dedication ceremony, lodge members christened the redbrick structure Bohemian Hall. It became a focal point in the lives of many Prague Czechs, sponsoring all sorts of events, including dances, plays, coming-out parties, and lectures.[13] Membership in the lodge included a life insurance policy for husband and wife as well as financial help when a member became ill or injured. The national organization in Omaha published a handbook for all its lodges, and in addition to death benefits, the handbook states that lodges were established

> To unite its members fraternally and to furnish them with an opportunity for mutual education and advancement, and to furnish opportunity for relief and aid in event of their sickness, disability or distress.
>
> To arrange educational lectures and debates, to support Czech-American national understandings, especially schools and Sokol organizations, to establish and maintain Czech libraries, and to cultivate the mother tongue and culture in general among its members.[14]

The ZCBJ came out of an intellectual movement known as freethought. As discussed in chapter 3, many Czech immigrants left the Catholic Church soon after arriving in the United States. These Catholic apostates provided the backbone of the early fraternal movement and used their Bohemian Halls the way most believers used their church.

Figure 4. Sokol Hall, Prague, Oklahoma, ca. 1907.

Prague's Catholics rarely joined the ZCBJ, preferring to participate in parish activities.[15] So it is interesting that John Barta provided the land for the erection of a permanent building for the nonreligious fraternal association, because the origins of the American Czech fraternal movement contained deep roots in freethought, with many freethinkers openly expressing anticlerical and anti-Catholic beliefs. Obviously, this anti-Catholicism did not extend to the farming community of Prague, or at least John Barta separated his religious beliefs from helping his ethnic relatives.

Another popular organization of Prague's Czechs was the Sokol Gymnastic Society (Telocvicna Jednota Sokol).[16] This athletic club, originally the brainchild of Miroslav Tyrs and based on similar German organizations, was formed in Prague, Bohemia, in 1862 as part of a cultural revolt against Austrian domination.[17] The purpose of the initial society was to train young Czechs (both male and female) physically, but also, and just as important, to inculcate them with Czech pride and nationalism. Many Czechs worried that the German language and culture of the Austrian Empire would eventually extinguish the native language, traditions, and historical pride of the Czech people. The Sokols were a reaction to this fear, and the athletic clubs proved a huge success, especially among teenagers. Within a few short years, practically every village in Bohemia and Moravia of moderate size or larger sported a gymnastic association. Apparently Sokols succeeded in their mission of instilling nationalistic feelings in Czechs, because during World War I, the Austrian government dissolved all Sokols, declaring them treasonous to the empire.[18]

The idea of Sokol clubs quickly crossed the Atlantic Ocean. The St. Louis Czechs established the first Sokol in the United States in 1865, and the gymnastic order came to Prague in 1906.[19] Although the various fraternal lodges stressed the maintenance of ethnic identity and culture, Sokols were especially assertive in their quest to instill Czech traditions among the young.[20] Like the Western Czech Brotherhood and other fraternal orders, American Sokols soon became freethought in their outlook. Physical training, language maintenance, and cultural retention were the primary goals. Sokols also attracted many religious and political liberals, some harboring radical beliefs and opinions.[21] Sokols were the conduits that spread nontraditional ideas to rural areas.[22] Some Sokol clubs, evincing a decidedly leftist political stance, even wore red as their principal uniform color to signify their socialist viewpoint. Other clubs commonly referred to these groups as "Red Sokols." However, the more mainstream clubs that strictly focused on athletics and Czech culture wore the traditional white tops and blue bottoms.[23] Prague's Sokol fell into the traditional category. When competing, Prague's gymnasts wore the white and navy blue of the original organization, not the political red of the radicals.[24] This is not to say there were no socialists in Prague. Socialism held a strong attraction for many Oklahoma farmers during the early twentieth century regardless of their ethnicity. Prague would have been quite the anomaly among Oklahoma farm towns if progressive ideas and socialist theory were not discussed while customers were waiting for a haircut at one of the barbershops or on a family's front porch where neighbors gathered in the cool of an early evening to share a drink and discuss the weather. When Frank Vlasak, a charter member of Prague's ZCBJ, died in 1929 of accidental asphyxiation, the

Figure 5. Members of the Sokol Hall on parallel bars.

Prague Record included in the obituary the fact that he had proclaimed himself a "progressive."[25] Vlasak, whose mother appears to have been a Catholic, was not a member of any church. His family held his funeral at the Bohemian Hall, and he was buried in the Czech National Cemetery instead of in the city or Catholic cemeteries.[26]

Prague's Czechs established a Sokol on the first day of April 1906 amid much fanfare not only from the immigrant community but also from the town at large. The thirty charter members purchased the Prague Produce Market and began teaching gymnastics on Sunday afternoons and courses in the Czech language and traditional dance during the week.[27] The Sokol gymnasts proved extremely popular in the first twenty years, traveling to Ft. Worth, Texas, for regional competitions, Chicago for national meets, and even sailing across the Atlantic Ocean to show off their skills to their European relatives.[28] The Sokol and ZCBJ organizations helped both young and old. They provided athletics and social intercourse for Czechs, whether living in town or on a farm. Prague's Sokol concentrated on gymnastic events.

However, occasionally the hall held other athletic events, such as in 1929 when it sponsored a wrestling match and invited the entire

Figure 6. Male members of the Sokol Hall.

town.[29] In addition, the fraternal associations buttressed the minority ethnic community psychologically and enabled their members to confront and adjust to the larger dominant society with success. In his study of Oklahoma's Czech farmers, Russell Lynch, an academic from Oklahoma A&M College, who did an in-depth study of the Czech farming community in 1942, concluded, "Czech children due to the ZCBJ and Sokol were better rounded [educationally] than those of the native American farm youth."[30]

An interesting aside to the discussion of Prague's Sokol concerns the Sunday gymnastic classes. Many American towns during this period strictly enforced Sabbatarian laws, commonly referred to as blue laws. These regulations forbade certain businesses such as saloons to operate and athletic events to be played on Sunday. The town's baseball team occasionally played on Sundays, and the Czech community's Sokol held regular workouts on the Lord's Day. Whether there were protests in Prague against these practices is not known. There

Figure 7. Sokol Hall girls waving flags.

may have been entire sermons preached against the practice. However, there is no mention in the Prague newspapers of complaints against either the Sokol or Prague's baseball team. Nor is there evidence of city officials taking any official steps to discourage the events, such as occurred in nearby Wellston. The *Prague News* reported that in 1907 authorities arrested the entire Wellston baseball team for playing on Sunday. As a result, city officials discontinued all baseball games, and the residents of Wellston lost their team in the Frisco League. The franchise moved to Davenport, also in Lincoln County, and continued playing with many of the same players.[31] Why Prague appeared lax on enforcing blue laws is difficult to ascertain. Perhaps the isolation of the farming community separated them from the pressure to conform to other towns. A more likely explanation lies in the fact that early in Prague's history, and during the apex of the strict enforcement of blue laws, the Protestant churches did not hold much power in the community compared with the Catholic church and Bohemian Hall. Neither of them pushed Sabbatarianism, and in the case of the Czech fraternal

Figure 8. Farewell celebration in Prague for World War I soldiers, 1917.

lodges, they cared not a whit about abiding by primitive Christian rules. Thus the principal actors in the community allowed Sunday activities such as playing baseball and exercising on the pommel horse and parallel bars, which other towns dominated by Presbyterians, Baptists, and Methodists proscribed.

Few Catholics joined the Bohemian Hall, preferring to participate in parish activities, including their own mini-version of the Bohemian Hall.[32] The Catholic Worker (Katolicky Delnik), founded in 1904 by members of St. Wenceslaus Church, included many farmers and townspeople, and during the first two decades, it was one of the most active organizations in Prague.[33] However, besides containing fewer members than the secular Bohemian Hall, this and most Catholic enterprises focused on charity work rather than social gatherings and primarily strove to help the poor and needy families in the community through the giving of food baskets, Christmas gifts to young children, and direct relief to those suffering hardships. Because it concentrated on religious instruction, the Catholic Church did not set aside the financial resources to sponsor as many events as the Bohemian Hall. Thus their social events paled in comparison with the almost weekly affairs, especially dances, held just south of their building.

Nevertheless, many in the Catholic congregation mingled socially with members of the Bohemian Hall. Catholics, especially the young, were not averse to attending dances or plays sponsored by the ZCBJ.[34] It also appears that the Bohemian Hall did not belittle or disparage the beliefs of their Catholic kinsmen. The Western Bohemian Fraternal Association, unlike the older BSBS society, propagated a policy of impartiality in the matter of religion.[35] The younger generation of free-thinkers evinced more moderate thinking than their forebears. They definitely were not as confrontational and anticlerical in their beliefs.[36] Czech Catholics of Prague and their counterparts in the Bohemian Hall did not form enemy camps, as suggested by other writers.[37] For pragmatic reasons, such as the wish of people regardless of their philosophical or religious convictions to enjoy a community dance, band concert, or dramatic play about old Bohemia, the opposing groups laid aside their differences and got along. In the farm town of Prague, the limited population almost demanded it.

By 1914, some of Prague's Czechs had lived in Oklahoma for more than twenty years. Many had been in the United States even longer. Nevertheless, when war erupted in Europe, the rural Czech community instantly showed concern when the Austro-Hungarian Empire, of which ancestral Bohemia and Moravia were provinces, joined Germany to fight the Allies led by Great Britain, France, and Russia. With anti-German sentiment growing in the United States primarily because of a cultural affinity with the West and the persistent submarine warfare perpetrated by the Kaiser's Germany, bewilderment cascaded upon many Czech Americans. So they looked to their native land for guidance.

From the onset of war, the Czechs of Bohemia and Moravia despised the conflict. They saw the war and conscription of their young men as further German oppression. The imperial government in Vienna feared a rebellion and tried to forestall problems by issuing an official decree that suspended "many constitutional guarantees, including freedom of speech, public gathering, press, travel, the privacy of one's home, and the secrecy of the mails." Furthermore, a military court rather than a civilian judge and jury tried anyone accused of violating the decree. Nevertheless, Bohemians and Moravians ignored the diktat, and thousands were arrested.[38] Anti-Austrian sentiment worsened, and a long-suppressed nationalistic clamor rang throughout the Czech provinces. The Sokols took the lead as the most active Czech organization, opposing the war and attempting to awaken a nationalistic consciousness. Prominent and respected individuals such as Thomas Masaryk and Edvard Benes added stimulus to the anti-Habsburg feelings sweeping the Czech lands. When the Austrian government moved to stamp out all dissent, many Czech intellectuals, including Masaryk and Benes, fled to Switzerland and then to England.[39]

The dissidents formed the Czech National Alliance in Great Britain and began speaking and writing against the Austro-Hungarian Empire, specifically against Austrian oppression. Through pamphlets such as *The Case of Bohemia*, the alliance argued that the Czech struggle against German domination and tyranny went back to the fifteenth century and the martyrdom of Jan Hus in 1415. In this "case" against the Austrians, the Czechs proclaimed their national history to be "one long struggle against the Universal German Monarchy under whatever garb it should appear." *The Case of Bohemia* concluded its argument by appealing to the Allies to create a free Bohemia that would serve in the future as "a safeguard against a new German advance and a barometer of German pressure."[40] Still another pamphlet originating in London detailed imprisonments and atrocities committed by the Austrian authorities and military against the Czechs. This short tract, *Austrian Terrorism in Bohemia*, alleged that since the beginning of the war, the Austrian government had sentenced almost a thousand Czechs to death and "the total of [Czech] soldiers executed already amount[ed] to several thousands."[41]

Soon anti-German fervor spread to the United States. Chicago, with the largest concentration of Czech immigrants, became the center of anti-German activity. The leaders of the Chicago Czechs formed their own group, the Bohemian National Alliance of America, involving the Sokol gymnastic societies and the principal Czech fraternal organizations in the United States. At first, few Catholic organizations joined the movement. This was, with little doubt, because many movement leaders espoused a freethought or liberal religious philosophy, which disturbed urban Catholics. However, despite their concern, Czech Catholics eventually grasped the cudgel of Bohemian independence and joined the effort in the latter portion of the war. They formed their own national alliance in 1917 and then merged with the Bohemian National Alliance and the Slovak League to form the Czechoslovak National Council of America in 1918.[42]

The Chicago alliance began making speeches and printing pamphlets attacking the Central Powers, particularly Austria, and calling for Czech independence. Charles Pergler became one of the alliance's most prolific orators. In 1916, in an address before the Committee on Foreign Affairs of the House of Representatives, he explained to American lawmakers why Bohemia should become an independent nation.[43] Later that year, Pergler gave a stirring speech in Chicago in which he said: "It follows, therefore, that this war is not only one to reduce France to impotence, to destroy the British Empire, to thwart legitimate Russian ambitions, to destroy the Serbian nationality and to absorb Belgium, but it is also a War on the part of Germany and Austria against the Bohemian People, who have been the western sentinel of Slavdom for Centuries."[44] Pergler ended his talk by hoping that the Allies emerged victorious and that a free and independent Bohemia was a fruit of their triumph. Increasingly, the Bohemian National Alliance included calls for independence in their speeches and printed tracts. Vojta Benes, an exile and member of the alliance, wrote, "The Bohemian nation has always held the right of self-determination to be the inalienable right of every people."[45] When the alliance reprinted a London speech by Thomas Masaryk in which he declared it was time for the Bohemian people to strike out for themselves, the Czech nationalist capitalized and shouted in bold print his plea to the allies: WE ASK FOR AN INDEPENDENT BOHEMIAN-SLOVAK STATE.[46]

Apparently the Chicago Czechs received some criticism, because in a published position paper, the Bohemian National Alliance declared that they felt comfortable speaking on behalf of all Czech Americans because the alliance was expressing only the general will of the community. Indeed, Dr. L. J. Fisher, president of the American Alliance, contributed numerous articles to the cause with many published in both Czech- and English-language newspapers across the United States, including Prague, Oklahoma.[47] In addition, all Czech-language periodicals in America carried a standing entreaty to Czech residents to become, as quickly as legally possible, naturalized citizens to rid themselves of "the odium which Austro-Hungarian citizenship in their minds carries."[48]

Chicago was not the only major American city to take up the cause of Bohemian independence. The Czechoslovak Arts Club in New York City joined the Chicago alliance by printing and distributing pamphlets. Like the Bohemian National Alliance, they too declared the right of self-determination for Bohemia.[49] However, one of their more interesting tracts contained nothing but quotes, including many attributed to President Woodrow Wilson. This pamphlet was powerful and surely evoked tremendous hope for Czechs not only in America but around the world. In one example:

> Self-determination is not a mere phrase. It is an imperative principle of action, which statesmen will henceforth ignore at their peril.
> WOODROW WILSON[50]

The contribution of American Czechs proved vital in persuading the American people, and thus their government, that a free and independent Czech-Slovak nation would become a valued ally and buffer to German aggression in the future. The Chicago Czechs led the propaganda battle with speeches and printed material. However, any effort of this magnitude takes money and a lot of it. The principal support, both financial and moral, for the Czechoslovak independence movement came from the workingman in the cities and the farmers of the Middle West and Southwest.[51] The immigrant and ethnic farmer and urban working-class family provided the bulk of the monetary support for the cause. Like Bohemian and Moravian communities across the United States, the Czechs of Prague, Oklahoma, supported Bohemian independence and did so from the outset of the war. Furthermore, they assisted the movement through volunteer work and donations and vocally championed the independence movement and Allied war effort even if it resulted in hard feelings and physical confrontations with the German immigrant community in Prague.

Economically, the war proved a godsend for American farmers. In January 1917, the *Prague Record* published a report by the Commerce Department showing a doubling in exports of agricultural products from 1913 to 1916.[52] Additionally, before the United States entered the war, the newspapers covered the European war extensively. Prague's weeklies regularly published photographs and short articles about the conflict and always from a pro-Ally viewpoint. The *Prague Record,* even more than the *Prague News,* was unashamedly anti-German in its outlook. This is, most likely, partially due to the relatively large number of Czechs in and around Prague who were vocal in their support of the Allies. Although much smaller, there was also a German American presence in Prague. Despite the *Prague News*'s previous Republican bias in coverage, once the war in Europe began, both the *News* and the *Record* supported the foreign policy of the Democratic president. Eschewing domestic politics, the newspapers openly promoted the cause of the Allies and President Wilson as he slowly leaned toward the Allied position. The *Prague Record* published articles originating from the Bohemian National Alliance. These commentaries advocated independence for Bohemia and complained of Austrian atrocities committed on Czechs. One particularly emotional diatribe, written by L. J. Fisher, declared that "in the first two years of the war, four thousand men and women have been hanged for 'high treason' to the emperor."[53] Whether or not the accusation was true is not important. The importance of the article lies in its impact on the Czech community, because many readers, no doubt, believed the report in its entirety.

During the war years, emotions ran high in Prague. Some in the Czech community were only recently removed from their country of birth, and most, even if born in the United States, still communicated with relatives in the old country. C. M. Sadlo, who came to the United States in 1898, had a sister living near Prague, Bohemia. Wes Pospisil, a young man of twenty-three when the war broke out in 1914 and who worked in Prague's harness shop, had been in the United States only since 1909.[54] The town's shoe repairman, Mike Mitacek, came to Prague in 1910, leaving his mother in Bohemia.[55] Many in the Czech community kept in contact with relatives and friends. In addition to personal letters, the rural Czech community stayed abreast of what was happening in Europe through the local weeklies and through their Czech-language newspapers, primarily published in Chicago or Omaha.

Germans had created a community north of Prague, and many of these immigrants also retained ties with Europe. John Mertes, who ran a hardware store in Prague, was born and raised in Germany. The merchant came to the United States in 1897 at the age of twenty-two. Although Elizabeth Whitmore had been born in Illinois, both of her parents listed Germany as their birthplace. The same was true for Kate Hudspeth, whose husband ran a livery business. Many in the German community were farmers living only a few miles from town. These families with such names as Heinzig, Tripke, Benning, and Wagner had been in the United States less than a decade.[56] What were their feelings about the European war? No doubt, some harbored ambivalent emotions, especially as it became clearer that the United States preferred Great Britain and the Allies to Germany. However, in a time of war, some Germans naturally supported the fatherland. Even if they kept quiet, they were suspected of pro-German sentiment. This support, whether actual or illusory, on several occasions resulted in confrontations and even violence.

The Prague Czechs loudly voiced their support for the Allies and Czech independence, and unfortunately, emotions sometimes boiled over. Fritz Heinzig, a German American, stated that "fist-fights and near riots, caused by bitterness of feeling among foreign-born residents, were common in Prague." Ray Tower, a native-born resident of the farm town, remembered "two cases of near lynching in the Prague community over the expression of sentiment favorable to the cause of the Central Powers." He added, "Looking at the community as a whole during World War I, there was a general feeling of both patriotism and sadness coupled with bitter hatred [by the Czechs] against the Germans and Austrians in Prague." Granted, these are the memories of older men recollected many years after the war. The passage of time often dims and distorts facts. Nevertheless, emotions sometimes ran rampant in the small town and manifested in several ugly incidents.

Hostility against German Americans in Oklahoma was not exclusive to Prague. Throughout the state of Oklahoma, physical violence against German immigrants or anyone with a German surname occurred frequently during the war.[57]

In 1915, the Czech community formed a Samostatnost (independence) club. At the initial meeting, the charter members elected Charles Cerny, one of the town's barbers, as president and Prague's tailor, C. M. Sadlo, as secretary. The club met the first Sunday of each month in the Sokol Hall with the express purpose of raising awareness and funds for the independence movement. Moreover, the meetings were open to the public and advertised weekly in the newspapers, encouraging anyone interested in Bohemian independence to attend.[58]

The Samostatnost club, in conjunction with the other Bohemian societies of Prague, sponsored Professor Sarah Hrbek, teacher of Slavonic languages and literature at the University of Nebraska, to come to Prague and speak at the Czech community's commemoration of the five hundredth anniversary of the death of the Czech martyr Jan Hus. Professor Hrbek agreed to come and delivered two speeches to large audiences. Her afternoon speech was in Czech, followed by an English version that evening.[59] The program, which included traditional Czech songs, was not billed as a political rally, and Hrbek's actual speech was not published. However, Hrbek was an active member of the Bohemian National Alliance, whose sole purpose was to promote Bohemian independence. Thus it is difficult to imagine the professor traveling the many miles from Lincoln, Nebraska, to Prague, Oklahoma, and *not* mentioning the war in Europe or the Czech struggle for independence.

Two years later, the Samostatnost club brought another speaker to Prague. On its front page, the *Prague Record* carried an article about the upcoming lecture: "Professor Ferdinand Pisecky . . . will lecture at the Sokol Hall at 7:30 o'clock Thursday evening of this week. The professor was at one time a prisoner of the present European war, but made his escape and came to America about six weeks ago."[60] These public speeches were more than informational lectures, more than simple emotional appeals to get American Czechs excited about a new, independent Bohemia. They were fund-raisers. The Bohemian

Figure 9. The Busy Bee Café, opened in 1912 by Frank and Josephine Kucera.

National Alliance sent out speakers, not only to arouse public opinion for the cause of Czecho-Slovak independence but also to gather much-needed money to support the cause. The alliance raised more than $675,000 with many contributions being $5 to $10, and most of the financial support came from urban workers and rural farming communities.[61] Knowing how passionately Prague's Czechs supported their country of birth, it seems safe to assume both farmers and townspeople helped the cause of Bohemian independence with their pocketbooks.

Prague and the surrounding farm community sent 111 men into the military during World War I.[62] Three of these young men perished in battle. The first was Edward Walla, a Czech American, killed in 1918 at the Battle of the Meuse-Argonne Forest. To honor the young soldier, Prague named their American Legion Post after him. The community buried their fallen hero in the Prague National Cemetery and erected a small Washingtonian-type memorial so that everyone would always remember.[63]

Early in 1918, American Czechs expressed dismay when President Wilson announced that his preliminary peace plan provided some autonomy for ethnic groups within the Austro-Hungarian Empire but not complete autonomy. Czechs and Slovaks staged mass protests across the United States clamoring for an independent state. Had they not taken the side of the Allies early in the war? Had their young men not readily and energetically volunteered for the Allied cause? Why had they given their hard-earned money to the Bohemian National Alliance if not to see the dreams of their homeland at last fulfilled?[64] Finally, in September, after Wilson met with exiled Czech leader Thomas Masaryk, the president announced his support for the dissolution of the Empire and the creation of an independent Czech-Slovak nation. When the victorious Allies granted the Czechs and Slovaks their own country at the peace conference, American Czechs rejoiced, and the Czech community of Prague, Oklahoma, enthusiastically joined the chorus. The Sokols and fraternal organizations provided the organizational apparatus for the ambitious Bohemian National Alliance. The Catholic Church joined the effort, putting aside theological differences with the freethinkers. The year 1918 marked a new beginning for the Prague Czechs. No longer did they need to refer to their birthplace as part of the Austro-Hungarian Empire. They now hailed from Bohemia and Moravia, provinces of Czechoslovakia and home of the Czechs.

Czech fraternal associations served an important function within the ethnic community. Although not as large as the freethought organizations, they performed charity work and religious instruction. However, the much larger Bohemian Hall and Sokol Gymnastic Organization provided the bulk of the Czech population with entertainment, athletic training and competition, and a link to the past. The fraternal lodges actively sought to maintain Old World customs and the Czech language. Faced with a demographic and geographic situation that demanded they make concessions to succeed economically, the fraternal orders futilely bailed against the rising waters of the dominant culture. That they succeeded as long as they did is a tribute to their persistence; the Bohemian Hall continued to conduct all monthly meetings in the Czech language until 1938.[65]

Nevertheless, despite the determined efforts of the lodges, individual Czechs in an effort to prosper and find contentment, quickly decided to participate in the larger Prague community. Many did not forsake their traditional ways and culture but instead decided to live in both worlds. At the town's inception in 1902, Czech immigrants energetically joined the community in every way. Sounding almost contradictory, Czech members of both the Bohemian Hall and Sokol Lodge became some of the most notable citizens in the new town. Frank Vlasak was a charter member of the Bohemian Hall and very influential in the Czech community. He also owned a thriving grocery business in Prague and served as vice president of Lincoln County Bank. Others such as Josef Cerny, Frank and Josef Klabzuba, George Eret, and Frank Kucera became involved in the local economy and society of Prague while spending many hours sitting in the Bohemian Hall smoking cigars, discussing politics and business, and no doubt reminiscing about their lives in Bohemia.[66]

Ultimately, the resolute efforts by the fraternal orders to maintain their European ways ended in failure. Upon the formation of the town, Prague's Czechs, including many in the first generation, vigorously engaged in community affairs. This led to rapid adjustment and acculturation by most. Nevertheless, the stubborn, steadfast refusal of the fraternal lodges to give up the past resulted not in the preservation of a unique and separate culture but in the inculcation of the young with a distinctive identity. Long after the graves of many original Czech settlers no longer attracted flowery tributes on Memorial Day, and Sokol Hall was but a faded sepia print in a centennial memory book, Prague's Czechs remained Czech. That they participated fully in the social sphere will be seen in the following chapter. It was social acceptance by the native-born Americans that led to an amazingly speedy adjustment by the small-town Czechs to the way of life of the majority within the community. Nevertheless, regardless of their "Americanization," including marrying outside their ethnic group, many children, grandchildren, and great-grandchildren of the early Czech pioneers never forgot who they were. Even if somewhere in their family history their surname changed from Sala to Reynolds or Sefcik to Pritchett, many held fast to their Czech roots.

CHAPTER 5

Economic Life in a Small Town

WITH A BIBLE IN ONE HAND and a hatchet in the other, the stout but still energetic woman marched down the middle of the dirt street with a brigade of women in her wake. The bonneted matriarch halted the excited throng close to the front door of the nearest saloon and immediately launched into her practiced and polished tirade against the evils of alcohol. By the time she finished her blistering verbal attack, the crowd buzzed with righteous indignation and anticipation with what they knew would happen next. Closing the Bible and brandishing her weapon, Carry Nation turned from the crowd and strode into the emptying saloon. With swinging ax and cries to God for deliverance, the temperance leader splintered several wooden cases of beer before leaving the drinking establishment and proclaiming victory to the applauding crowd.[1]

Despite the determined efforts of Carry Nation in 1904, Prague's saloons flourished during the pre-statehood era. During the period before November 1907, the saloon business boomed for most of the communities in southeast Lincoln County. The reason was quite simple. Lincoln County, as part of Oklahoma Territory, allowed open and legal alcohol consumption. However, adjacent Indian Territory located a little over three miles east of Prague was "dry." Alcohol could not be transported, bought, or sold there. Thus evenings and weekends saw a veritable parade of Indian Territory residents crossing into Oklahoma Territory to relax and imbibe.

The prolific alcohol consumption by some customers on occasion erupted into heated arguments over perceived slights, in many cases ending in fistfights or worse, resulting in a Wild West aura enveloping many towns in the area. Prior to the formation of Prague, the most infamous was Keokuk Falls, home of the "Seven Deadly Saloons." Located only a short ride from Indian Territory, the taverns of Keokuk

Falls became a favorite destination for hardworking ranchers and hired hands as well as members of the Sac and Fox tribe. However, the easily available booze attracted unsavory characters as well. In this small settlement, less than a mile from the future town of Prague, "all sorts of outlaws, horse-thieves, cattle-rustlers, road agents, and murderers hung out during the last decade of the [nineteenth] century." Regardless of the violence, the saloons earned enormous profits. Thus, to combat the bloodshed, Keokuk Falls hired officers equally as tough as the customers to keep the peace.[2]

Upon the formation of Prague in 1902, drinking proved a profitable business enterprise. Within weeks, the *Prague News* listed seven saloons operating in the environs with three of the establishments serving drinks under nothing but a simple canvas tent.[3] The success of these saloons encouraged others to join the business. From 1902 until statehood, anywhere from six to thirteen saloons operated within the town's limits.[4] Like many immigrants from eastern or southern Europe, Prague's Czechs enjoyed drinking alcoholic beverages. Most primarily drank beer, and Czechs prided themselves on the Bohemian origins of Budweiser and pilsner.[5] Owning a saloon or working as a barkeep ranked high as desirable occupations. Many viewed tending bar every inch as respectable as teaching school, working in a bank, or committing to the priesthood or ministry.[6] The Bohemian immigrants of Prague were no different. One of the most popular drinking establishments in the early years was the Kentucky Liquor House, owned and operated by Josef Klabzuba, a Czech.[7] Another saloon was owned by Josef Hrdy.[8] Furthermore, saloons brought in much revenue. An example of the profitability of the liquor business is found in a May 1907 *Prague News* article reporting the town's receipts from licenses and fees. According to the town's treasurer, in 1906 Prague took in a total of $4,193.88. Of this amount, $2,549.00 came from the issuance of saloon licenses.[9] Drinking was definitely big business.[10]

Another activity that emerged during this time was the smuggling of liquor into Indian Territory, where even the possession of alcohol was punishable by fine or imprisonment. However, the legal prohibition did not deter some ingenious drovers and ranchers. A common practice was to purchase the forbidden brew in Oklahoma Territory, hide the alcohol (usually whiskey) inside their boots in nearly unde-tectable flat containers, and then ride back into Indian Territory with the contraband completely out of sight.[11] Even subsequent to state-hood and the political decision that the new state of Oklahoma would be "dry," the smuggling continued. Before the passage of the fed-eral Volstead Act, newspapers contained colorful stories of arrests of unlucky or inept wrongdoers, such as the *Prague Record*'s recounting of the arrest of a young man found with twenty-four quarts of liquor hidden on his person. The account does not specify where the officer discovered the booze. One might suspect the culprit concealed the bot-tles under a long heavy coat. The only problem with this seemingly astute deduction is that the arrest occurred during an Oklahoma sum-mer.[12] Another interesting account revolves around a young woman who lived near Prague. Apparently she made a daily habit of walk-ing to a nearby stream carrying her baby in one arm and a bundle of the baby's clothes in the other, presumably to wash the clothes. The local Methodist minister noticed her forays to the creek, became suspi-cious, and decided to follow her. To his astonishment, when the young mother passed by a group of men, she pulled several whiskey bottles from out of her bundle and sold them.[13]

When the two territories combined to form the state of Oklahoma, Prague's saloons were forced out of business, but not without a last hurrah. In a lengthy article about the final Saturday night before the "dry" laws went into effect, the *Prague News* reported, "Prague has had some rough Saturdays but the last one was about the roughest yet. The drunks were a little drunker and the fights a little harder and oftener if possible." However, in the same edition, the paper also reported that "the nine saloon keepers of Prague promptly quit business Saturday night, thereby proving themselves to be law-abiding citizens." A few weeks later, the newspaper put an optimistic spin on the loss of a large part of Prague's early economy by opining that "the empty saloon buildings will soon all be full again."[14]

After being forced out of business by the new laws, Joseph Klabzuba opened a general store selling food, clothing, and household goods. This enterprise did not take, however, so he then eked out a living by selling cotton and pecans. After these unsuccessful business ventures,

Klabzuba finally found his calling when he became a salesman of oil and gas leases.

During the early years, Prague's Czechs owned or ran more than a fourth of the businesses in town. This involvement in the economic sector continued throughout the second and third decades of the community. In addition, most businesses retained a close relationship with the Czech farming community. Besides working his fields, a farmer might own a store in town or a member of his family might work in town while still living at home. Alternatively, a specific business might rely heavily on the trade of Czech farmers to stay in operation.[15]

Regardless, the communal peasant environment in which most first-generation Czechs lived in Europe helped them adjust to their new surroundings. However, the immigrants found nowhere an equivalent of the Bohemian village in the United States.[16] The Czechs of Prague did not come from a central European enclave where most lived in the village and walked every morning to their fields and pastures. Prague's farming Czechs lived on the peripheral areas of the town on their own farmland. After the formation of Prague, some farmers moved to town, while others remained on their farms with members of their family working at jobs within the village. Still a few, like Frank Vlasak, owned farmland but also ran a business in town. This is not equivalent to the European peasant experience in the strict sense. However, one experience that did transfer from Europe to North America was the communal mind-set. This cooperative spirit melded the outlying farmers with the Czech town dwellers, as both worked to ensure the success of the other. Meanwhile, organizations such as the fraternal orders and the church solidified these relationships.

For many newcomers, the Americanization process proved painful. The emptiness of the prairie farm led to loneliness, and the market-oriented agriculture promised an agonizing adaptation to American life.[17] In addition, anyone moving away from his or her home and extended family undergoes extreme apprehension. This would be compounded further if you moved to a faraway place where the language was incomprehensible and your early efforts to learn the foreign tongue turned to frustration at the myriad idioms and colloquialisms. However, unlike some ethnic groups such as the Slovaks,

Czechs arrived in the United States with every intention of making a new home. They came with their families, intent on carving a niche in the new land not only for themselves but for their descendants as well. No doubt, many suffered anxiety and some depression. Nevertheless, the support system provided by their family, friends, and fellow Czechs helped most get through the tough stretches. Despite spending most of their time working on their farms, they could look forward to coming into town for church functions or a Saturday night dance at the Bohemian Hall. Moreover, Czech farmers proved more successful than their American-born counterparts did in productivity and persistence on the land. They lived in larger houses with well-kept yards and painted outbuildings.[18] Some of this success must be attributed to their group-mindedness and cooperative spirit.[19]

The new territorial town boomed. Within a few weeks after town lots went on sale, Frank N. Newhouse moved from Kansas to Prague and began publishing the weekly *Prague News*. In late August 1902, the front page contained the following: "Prague is but six weeks old, but she already has two banks, two hotels, five or six restaurants, one drug store, two meat markets, one furniture store, two hardware stores, one printing office, two lumber yards, one blacksmith shop, one livery barn, six saloons, one bakery, one tin shop, six stocks of general merchandise, three doctors, one real estate firm, and two barber shops."[20] From the beginning, the Czech farming community got involved in the activities of the new village. Some of the original townspeople included Czech families such as the Voborniks, Cervenys, Kratkys, Zaloudiks, Bendys, and Bartas.[21] The very first issue of the *Prague News* ran advertisements for Frank Barta's General Store and Restaurant and the Czech-owned Dobry Lumber Company.[22] Barta and his wife operated the hotel for twenty-seven years. Their daughter then managed it until her death. The hotel consisted of seventeen rooms. The daily rate included meals, and on Sundays the Bartas opened their kitchen to the general public, and folks could eat all they wanted for twenty cents.

Frank Vlasak, one of the original land-run settlers, soon caught the business fever and opened up a grocery and dry goods store. A few years later, his son operated a garage repairing the gasoline-powered automobiles that were becoming ubiquitous on the dirt streets of Prague.[23]

The Czech community actively participated in the economic realm of the new town, and the passage of time did not seem to slow down their excitement. Czechs, whether original settlers or relative newcomers to the area, energetically joined the business community. During the next three decades, Czechs provided many products and services to the residents of Prague. Frank Svoboda opened a blacksmithing operation, C. M. Sadlo prospered as the town's tailor, and Mike Mitacek repaired and dyed worn-out shoes at Mitacek's Boot and Shoe Repair Shop.[24] Frank Lanik, a Czech farmer, opened a cotton gin on the outskirts of town, John Cerveny sold real estate, and Frank Kucera served hungry customers at his Busy Bee Café, offering them the "best 25¢ meal in town."[25] Other Czechs earned money by advertising special services in the newspapers. George Sadlo offered violin lessons, boasting that he had studied under Gerald Mraz of the Musical Art Institute of Oklahoma City, who himself had studied under Ottokar Sevcik of the Prague Conservatory of Music in Prague, Bohemia.[26] In addition, during the early 1920s George Sadlo and his wife, Emily, taught music for Prague's public schools.[27] Another Czech, George Eret, directed the first town band, and latecomer Jake Zabloudil cashiered at Prague's First State Bank during the Great War, dabbled in the oil business, and served a stint in the state legislature.[28]

The first permanent building constructed in Prague was a bank. Within a few years, the town boasted three financial institutions, and although none of the bank presidents were Czech, Frank Vlasak, one of the most respected of the Czech citizens, served as vice president of Lincoln County Bank.[29] Vlasak also built a two-story structure in downtown Prague that became home for several economic enterprises. As the first decade passed, the growing town attracted businesses of all kinds, many operated by members of the Czech community.

These Czech merchants and artisans were a part of the larger business community that included people with German, Irish, and Jewish backgrounds. The *Prague News* reveals advertisements for non-Czech businesses operated by people with names like Crow, Fowler, Bond, Ayers, Alexander, Taylor, and Berger.[30] By 1915 Prague contained

Figure 10. Horse-drawn wagons tied up along Broadway, Prague's main street, ca. 1909. Photograph donated to the Prague Historical Museum by First Rate Company, Oklahoma City.

thirteen mercantile establishments, and although the number dropped slightly during the 1920s, the town continued to attract enterprising entrepreneurs.

The Leader, one of the largest stores in town, belonged to Morris Blumenthal, a Jewish merchant. Blumenthal, quite the promoter, in 1937 invited Robert Wadlow, the world's tallest man at 8'7", to his store for a shoe promotion.[31] During the first three decades of Prague, two other Jewish families operated retail stores. Sol White operated a dry goods business until his retirement, and Sam Kolodny, a Russian Jew, managed the popular New York Bargain Store for nineteen years before relocating to Wetumka in 1926.[32] One of the oldest firms in Prague was Emmet O'Kane's One Price Store, formed in 1903. O'Kane, of Irish ancestry, proudly advertised himself in the *Prague News* as "the red-headed feller," and he ran weekly advertisements encouraging everyone to buy from his "friendly store."[33] And if you entered the Irishman's

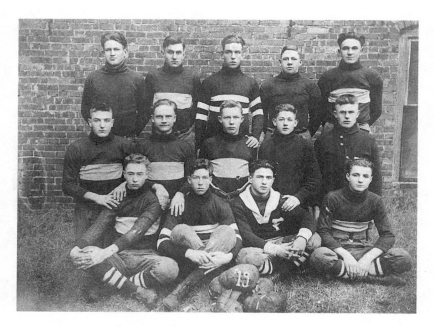

Figure 11. Prague High School football team, 1919.

establishment, you could also buy a hat from Nola Mertes, a member of the German community who operated a millinery parlor and hat shop inside O'Kane's mercantile.[34] Another ethnic Irishman, Vern McKim, ran a livery business, while two Irishmen managed one of the pharmacies in Prague during the second decade of the twentieth century.[35]

Neither the first local dentist nor the postmaster was Czech, and only one of the doctors during the early period of Prague claimed Bohemian stock. In 1904, that Bohemian doctor, John Z. Mraz, advertised himself as a physician and surgeon in the *Prague News* with his office located at Biggs Drug Store.[36] Mraz practiced medicine in Prague until he moved to Chicago in August 1905.[37] Another Czech ethnic, John Mastena, opened a chiropractic clinic in the fall of 1920, and later in the decade Frank Klabzuba returned to Prague after attending Creighton University in Omaha and opened a dental office.[38] Prague even had a town crier in its early days, William Woods, an ex-slave, who drove through the streets of Prague each day in a horse-drawn hack, ringing a bell and proclaiming the important news and upcoming events to pedestrians. When not employed shouting the news, "Uncle" William performed odd jobs for the local inhabitants.[39]

Woods was not the only African American living in Prague. Although the black population remained small throughout this period, the blacks who migrated to Prague did not receive the same economic opportunities as other residents, including the Czechs. Examining the decennial censuses from 1910 to 1930 reveals a similar result. While all African American families listed their occupation as "farmer" on the 1900 census, with the formation of Prague, the status of newer arrivals changed. While a few still claimed farming as their livelihood, black Americans in Prague overwhelmingly worked as laborers. The specific jobs listed on the various census manuscripts ranged from "odd jobs" to "cook" to "cotton picker" with a few blacks claiming employment as "cake punchers" at the cotton oil mill. On the 1920 census, Augustus Gray claimed that he was self-employed as a "scavenger." Many black women also worked. Their job descriptions varied from "cook" to "laundress" to "servant."[40]

Unlike members of the immigrant Czech population, no blacks served on the board of a bank; no blacks owned a building in downtown Prague; no blacks supervised a lumber company or operated a dry goods store. Instead, the white community, which controlled the overall economic apparatus, relegated to the black residents of Prague only the most menial and low-paying jobs. This is yet another reason for the acceptance of the Czech community by the native-born white population. Czechs were Caucasian. Czechs were white.

While the Czech immigrants of Prague enjoyed a higher economic status than blacks in the area, such was not the case in most northern cities. When the "new immigration" began around 1880, most northern cities contained only small numbers of African Americans. Thus when the massive wave of southern and eastern European newcomers crowded into the restricted confines of metropolitan areas like Chicago, Cleveland, and Detroit, they placed enormous pressure on the infrastructure and services of the cities. These low-paid factory workers usually sought apartments close to their work and ethnic relatives. Entrepreneurs responded by building "dumbbell tenements," which housed thousands of immigrants on a single city block. The areas with high immigrant concentration soon degraded into unsanitary, crime-infested slums with the Italians, Poles, Czechs, and other groups becoming the focus of ridicule and blame by many native-born Americans. Nativists attacked the newcomers for their popish faith, their strange languages, and unfamiliar customs. Occupying the bottom rung of the social and economic ladder, the immigrants became the whipping boy for any perceived societal problems. Many Americans did not accept immigrants and saw them as a threat to their way of life. This was not the case in Prague. There, the face on the bottom rung did not look Slavic; the face was much darker.

Thus the presence of an even more despised group in Prague resulted in an early acceptance of the immigrants who were scorned by many in the North. The native-born white residents of Prague overlooked the Catholicism and freethought tendencies of these central European émigrés, in part, because at least their skin was white. The existence of a small black community in Prague displaced ethnic persecution prevalent in northern cities. Having another minority group perceived as less worthy than your ethnic community could only appreciate your value to the village.[41]

Plentiful economic opportunities abounded in the early years of Prague. The territorial frontier town welcomed anyone willing to work and contribute to its success. Czechs found little discrimination or harassment about their "strange" customs. Czechs from other states also found their way to Lincoln County. While most of the original settlers came from the Midwest, many later arrivals migrated from Texas. These included a number of families proclaiming to be from the Czech province of Moravia rather than Bohemia. Although Moravians and Bohemians spoke the same language and both considered themselves Czech, there were a few differences primarily centered on religion. Most Bohemians either held to the Catholic faith or claimed freethought as their principal belief with a few drifting toward Presbyterianism. However, Protestant sects such as Methodism and later the Baptist church attracted many Moravians. According to the 1900 census manuscripts of South Creek Township, only three Czech families listed their last state of residence as Texas.[42] This shrank to two families on the 1910 census.[43]

The 1920 census shows that thirty-three families of Czech stock recorded their previous residence as Texas with twenty of them claiming to be Moravian. Unlike the two earlier national counts, the 1920 census differentiated between Moravians and Bohemians. Although Prague's Bohemian families dominated with seventy-six, Moravians showed a strong minority with twenty-eight families.[44] The native-born Anglo population of Prague referred to all Czechs as Bohemian. This remains true even today. All the same, regardless of which province Czechs claimed to originate, many did well in their new environment. In fact, by the 1920s, many were relatively prosperous.[45]

In the early days of Prague, Czech merchants, because of their shared language and group identity, attracted many customers from their ethnic relatives. The collective mind-set of the group suggests that Czechs stuck together for the benefit of the whole. Although impossible to prove, it appears logical to suggest that many Czechs carried on business with other Czechs. Despite the census records claiming that by 1920 most Czechs spoke English, some preferred to communicate in their native tongue. If a farm wife frequented a Czech-owned grocery or dry goods store, it was not uncommon for the clerk to address her in her native tongue. Sometimes Czechs offered their services in either Czech or English. For example, in 1920 Wes Klabzuba, an auctioneer, advertised in the newspaper that he "cried in either English or the Bohemian tongue."[46]

However, Prague's Czechs did not practice economic exclusivity; they eagerly interacted with non-Czechs. Czech farmers sold crops to Benjamin F. Whitmore and had their cotton ginned at his mill.[47] The *Prague Record* reported that Joseph Lanik (Czech) and Cliff Parks (non-Czech) traveled to Shawnee together on a business trip.[48] Although it is impossible to determine which specific stores individual shoppers favored, whether Czech or non-Czech, a glimpse at their hiring practices suggests there was little or no prejudice. Moreover, the economic interaction began soon after the construction of the town. For example, Frank Griffin tended bar at John Zabloudil's saloon and John Pierson and M. J. Tarpey cut hair at Czech immigrant Joe Eret's barbershop in 1905. Furthermore, Eret's establishment included a boot black. Normally, the man who shined the shoes of customers was African

American. So it is quite possible that Eret counted a black man as one of his employees.[49] The *Prague News,* proud of Eret's new barbershop, bragged about his operation:

> As evidence of his faith in the future of Prague, Joe Eret has invested more than two thousand dollars in a barber shop and its equipment and now presides over one of the finest shops to be found in Oklahoma. His shop has been furnished with all the latest designs of furniture, consisting of three chairs, four elegant mirrors, mug cases, wash basin, boot black's chair, etc., and in addition to this he has added a bath room with two fine porcelain tubs, hot and cold water supplies. A wind mill and tank furnishes the water and a hot water tank keeps on a supply of hot water all the time. . . . The people of Prague should show their appreciation of his enterprise by turning him a liberal patronage.[50]

A Czech and a non-Czech, Charles Vobornik and C. E. Kinsey, formed a partnership and operated the Broadway Meat Market for several years.[51] In addition, Czech newcomers erected buildings in Prague and accepted any businesses within the community as tenants regardless of ethnicity.[52] This inclusive trend continued into the second decade of the town. In 1915 Vern McKim, the Irish liveryman, took a job at William Vlasak's garage. Happy to have the Irishman working for him, Vlasak proudly advertised McKim's presence at his establishment and urged everyone to bring their malfunctioning motor vehicles for McKim to fix.[53] Another of Vlasak's employees was Carl Fiel, an ethnic German.[54] Julius Bontty, a Czech farmer, advertised "for help to bale 200 acres of prairie hay."[55] Bontty did not specify in the advertisement that he wished to hire only Czech hands. He probably wanted any strong young men to aid him in the tough, hot job of baling hay.

Auctioneer Wes Klabzuba shared calling duties with another Czech, A. J. Balaun, and two non-Czechs, William Alexander and H. E. Bevers. The four men advertised together weekly in the newspapers before World War I.[56] During the 1920s, Wes Klabzuba joined a non-Czech named Ogburn to form an auctioneer business. Later in the decade, Klabzuba formed yet another partnership with another non-Czech auctioneer named Barrett. Klabzuba and his partners advertised their services practically every week in the local paper.[57] Furthermore, non-Czech business establishments hired Czechs when they needed help or even to oversee their business. The Amsden Lumber Company employed P. J. Bartosh, a Czech, to run its operations, and a young Czech woman, Henrietta Sosenko, worked as a sales clerk at the New York Bargain Store for the Russian Jew Sam Kolodny. Kolodny also employed Eva Shumate, who was neither Jewish nor Czech.[58] Frank Vlasak's vice presidency of Lincoln County Bank shows that many native-born businesspeople in the Prague area concerned themselves more with earnings and permanence than with nativist emotions prevalent throughout much of America during this period.

With the discovery of oil in 1915 in nearby Paden, a minor oil boom came to Prague.[59] The tiny village of Paden sat nine miles east of Prague with the larger town benefiting through increased economic activity. People visited Prague to purchase luxuries in addition to staples, causing a brisk business and an increase in the number of mercantile firms and restaurants. The discovery of oil deposits on farmland near Prague continued into the 1920s. The explorers never found any oil in the immediate environs of the town. However, oil was discovered on Morris Blumenthal's Leader Ranch directly outside of Prague. The oil booms caused people to pay close attention to the price of oil. In August 1915 the *Prague News* rejoiced that "the price of oil stood at sixty cents a barrel, an increase of twenty cents in only ten days."[60]

Many Czechs earned money via the oil industry by leasing some of their acreage to oil companies. Joe Eret leased part of his pasture to the Illuminating Oil Company and Pennsylvania Oil Company, while Terezie Sestak leased eighty acres to the Prairie Oil and Gas Company. Other Czechs leasing acreage for oil exploration included Stanley Kolar, Frank Terfler, and Mary Leder. Frantisek Hnat, Jan Spaniel, and George Sestak sold the right of way through their holdings to the Sinclair Pipe Line Company to construct an oil pipeline.[61]

The discovery of oil in the Prague area occurred a couple of years after Henry Ford perfected the moving assembly line in automobile production. Car dealerships opened in the bustling town, and with the increase in automobile traffic came the call to improve the roads.[62] "Wish we had a good dirt road from Prague to Chandler. The shape of the road is in now is a fright," lamented the *Prague Record*.[63] The call did not go unheeded. The citizens of Prague mobilized, forming the Good Roads Boosters. The next two years witnessed caravans of cars traveling throughout the county "boosting" for everyone to urge their state representatives to build wider and smoother roads.[64]

One such trip ended disastrously when in August 1916 a group of Prague boosters set out in five cars to travel across the county. The group was ethnically diverse, including at least two Czechs, Van Sojka and Henry Prykrill, who agreed to drive. While crossing a bridge near Davenport, the expanse collapsed, plunging Prykrill's vehicle twenty-five feet into the shallow creek below. Miraculously, all the passengers, except the driver, received only minor cuts and abrasions. Prykrill was knocked unconscious for several minutes and awoke to find his nose was broken, his back injured, and his face bleeding.[65] Luckily, the incident only temporarily set back the Good Roads Boosters and their quest for easier travel. If anything, the accident strengthened their argument. Both the town and county roads did undergo improvements, including the paving of Prague's Main Street in 1926.[66]

Prague's merchants answered the call for more automobiles. The Jones brothers began selling Buicks in 1915, followed by F. S. Irvine and his Maxwells. Irvine sold his Maxwells for only $695, attracting many who did not wish to pay the $950 to $1,485 asked by the Joneses for their Buicks.[67] Not to be outdone, Preston G. Rawdon opened the Prague Garage in 1916.[68] Rawdon sold the even cheaper Fords to cash-strapped farmers and townspeople. One Czech who got into the auto industry was Charles Klabzuba, son of the aforementioned saloon-keeper. In 1927 Klabzuba resigned as a cashier of the First National Bank and started the Reliable Chevrolet Company, selling and repairing Henry Ford's primary competition.[69]

Despite the oil boom, cotton and the railroad formed the basis of Prague's economy until the late 1920s. In 1900 Lincoln County grew more cotton than any other county in Oklahoma Territory and by 1910 led the entire state in cotton acreage.[70] In October 1904 the *Prague News* proudly proclaimed that two hundred bales of cotton had sold in Prague on that day.[71] The advent of World War I spurred even more cotton activity. Although a major hailstorm damaged crops in 1916, the newspaper, only a few months later, wrote of the large war profits made by farmers not only around Prague but throughout the United States.[72] Despite the overall success of producing and selling cotton, several farmers sold their farms during the war. Most appeared to be non-Czechs selling their holdings, but the newspapers also included Czechs selling their acreage. Frank Vlasak sold his farmland during the winter of 1916 and focused on his economic ventures in town.[73] However, in 1928 boll weevils destroyed Prague's cotton farming region. Thereafter, farmers looked to other commodities, especially livestock and growing hay for feed.[74]

The first train passed through Prague on July 4, 1903. The townspeople, now numbering more than six hundred, celebrated the train's arrival with a parade, barbecue, and baseball game. Benjamin Franklin Whitmore, local mill owner and mayor, gave a grandiose speech about the rosy future of the growing town.[75] Excitement expanded exponentially. Some envisioned a town that could one day rival nearby Chandler or even Shawnee in size and prosperity. Throughout the railroad era of Prague, six trains normally stopped daily, three heading east and three heading west.[76] During the next thirty-six years, the Fort Smith and Western transported crops and passengers, helping Prague become the hub of economic activity for many farmers in southeastern Lincoln County.[77]

Of course, not all Czech immigrants and ethnics succeeded economically. In the United States' competitive market economy, Czech enterprises, like non-Czech ventures, failed and went out of business. Others closed for personal reasons, such as Vlasak's Cash Store, which closed upon the Prague pioneer's sudden death by asphyxiation at his home in 1929.[78] The introduction of automobiles and tractors ultimately ended Frank Sekera's dream of establishing a harness shop.[79] Nevertheless, many Czechs thrived in the bustling small-town economy to the point of being considered by some as excessively materialistic in their outlook.[80]

Several Czechs in Prague quickly succeeded in rising higher than most of their urban counterparts who struggled in sweaty jobs year after year. Urban immigrant businessmen lacked access to large amounts of capital, and thus their enterprises remained small, serving only a neighborhood clientele.[81] This may well be true concerning America's inner-city immigrant population as a whole. However, as early as the 1880s, observers of the Czech urban population in Chicago noticed that many succeeded quite well. In a long article published in the *Chicago Tribune* in 1886, a reporter who spent three days wandering around in the Bohemian district of the Windy City wrote, "It is a mistake to think that the Bohemians are only common laborers and wood-shovers. They are blacksmiths, watchmakers, and wood-turners . . . and they are all steady, sober, active men." The reporter went on to say that "many of them are excellent cabinet makers and upholsterers" and described the entire group as prosperous. Thus, despite the hardships of being newcomers, Czechs did succeed in America's cities.[82]

Likewise, in rural communities like Milligan and Wilber, Nebraska, and Snook, Texas, where Czechs numerically dominated to the point of ethnic exclusivity, the group thrived. Despite arriving comparatively poor and with few skills other than farming, some realized the opportunity for success and became retail storekeepers supplying their ethnic kin with the goods they needed. After only a few years, the town of Milligan included a doctor, dentist, hotel owner, and several schoolteachers of Czech ethnicity. As in Prague, the immigrant populations of Milligan and Wilber enjoyed spirits and recreation, prompting some Czechs to operate saloons and dance halls.[83]

The town of West, Texas, offers an interesting contrast to Prague, Oklahoma. Formed in northeastern McLennan County during the 1870s from several small farming communities, West became the dominant town after the arrival of the railroad. The town incorporated in 1892 with few Czech residents. However, Czechs began to arrive thereafter. Some arrived directly from Moravia, but most matriculated from their nearby, isolated farming villages to come to the larger and more prosperous town.

In the first year of West, Czechs founded both a Catholic parish and a Moravian Brethren church. By 1910, Czech businesses were ubiquitous throughout the railroad settlement. In that year, the immigrants established a fraternal association, a Sokol gymnastic society, and a Czech-language supplement to the weekly newspaper. Still the migration persisted, and by 1920 Czechs demographically dominated the town. Like the Prague Czechs of Oklahoma, most of the West Czechs originally lived on self-sufficient farms in a rather clannish ethnic community. However, once the railroad chose West as a station, rural Czechs left their homes to participate in the profitable activities of the economically thriving town.[84]

Regardless of where Czechs settled, they generally succeeded in rising above the poverty level, with many enjoying the fruits of the American economic system. Two reasons emerge for the success of so many Czechs wherever they lived, namely, their cooperative mindset and their western outlook. As documented in chapter 2, the U.S. Immigration Commission, created in 1907, also noticed the Czechs' peculiar success, especially compared with Slovaks and Poles. The commission explained it this way: "Czechs were thoroughly imbued with the progressive spirit of the West."[85] Again, German-speaking lands, such as the Holy Roman Empire and later the Austro-Hungarian Empire, both centered in Austria, dominated Bohemia for centuries, endowing the Czechs with a familiarity with western European ways and customs. This obviously helped them adjust and prosper in their new homeland.

Nevertheless, there remained differences in the Czech communities. This especially held true when comparing rural and urban. A popular immigrant synthesis stated, "In reality two immigrant Americas existed. One consisted largely of workers with menial jobs. The other, a smaller component, held essential positions, which pursued personal gain and leadership. Immigrants did not enter a common mass called America but adapted to two separate but related worlds, which might be termed broadly working class and middle class." Writing specifically about immigrants from Czechoslovakia, a Czech writer argued that, for the most part, the successful newcomers learned the English language and a profession and got "lost within the American inundation and very seldom associate with the rest of the Czechoslovaks of lesser importance. They pride themselves on their 'Americanism' and assiduously avoid social contact with the immigrants on the other side of the social fence."[86]

Generally speaking, this did not hold true in the farm town of Prague, especially with first-generation Czechs. There were, to be sure,

Czechs who left the city for better economic opportunities, such as Gerald Mraz. Mraz relocated to the much larger town of Oklahoma City to attract more students to his music school. Nonetheless, he apparently maintained contact with his friends in Prague and loved the small farming community because upon the death of his wife, he arranged her burial to be in Prague, and practically the entire town turned out for her funeral.

Another successful Prague Czech who left, probably due to personal problems, only to return later, was Jake Zabloudil. Born in Ord, Nebraska, in 1881 to immigrant parents, Zabloudil completed only the third grade and hunted and fished for a living. When his sister, Emma Zabloudil Urban, married and moved to Prague, Jake joined her and worked as a tailor making suits for the local businessmen. In Prague, he met Vivian Wilson, a non-Czech, whom he courted and married in 1906. An obviously ambitious young man, Zabloudil got a position at Prague's First State Bank, rising to president in 1916. He then ran and won election to the Oklahoma House of Representatives, serving one term. However, after the fulfillment of his term, his wife left him and filed for divorce. Zabloudil, discouraged and divorced, abruptly left town for Abilene, Texas, where he remained for several years, even marrying again. Zabloudil eventually returned to Oklahoma and farmed until his death in 1960 at the age of seventy-nine. In his middle and later years, he lived near and became friends with several American Indians. His love and admiration for the Sac and Fox tribe blossomed, with the tribe reciprocating by making Jake Zabloudil an honorary tribal member.[87]

Perusing the membership rolls of the Western Czech Brotherhood, Prague's primary Czech fraternal association, shows that their numbers included farmers, tailors, blacksmiths, and businesspersons. Some of them, such as Frank Vlasak and Joe Hrdy, who erected one of the early brick buildings in Prague and operated the COD Meat Market, gained much success and acceptance by the larger community and, relatively speaking, became quite wealthy. Others, such as the farmer Joseph Rubac or Frank Sekera, acquired less wealth but were content with growing cotton or operating a harness shop and raising their children in the usually peaceful farming village.[88]

An important distinction between the urban cities and the small town of Prague is the wealth ceiling. The opportunities to acquire extraordinary financial gain in a city such as Chicago or New York dwarfed the prospects of a rural community like Prague. Quite simply, the economic ceiling was not as high in Prague as in New York, Chicago, or even Omaha. This meant that the wealth divide was not as wide among the residents of Prague, whether they were Czech or not. With the exception of the Blumenthal family on whose land petroleum explorers found oil, most of the "wealthy" residents of Prague would have been considered middle class at best if they had been living in St. Louis. This resulted in a stronger feeling of community among the residents within the farm town. There was not an exclusive suburb for successful Czechs to escape their fellow compatriots. There were no private country clubs where the wealthy elite gathered to avoid the masses. Successful Czechs did not segregate themselves from their fellow immigrants.

Instead, both Czechs and non-Czechs, because of their isolated geographical situation, learned that if their community was to be successful, they had to get along. The diverse population incorporated into such a small town forced quick acculturation and amalgamation. If a Czech blacksmith, barber, tailor, or grocer wished to succeed, he simply had to attract at least some non-Czechs to his business. Likewise, with the American-born or non-Czech ethnic business enterprises, they needed Czech customers to survive economically. This is not to suggest that everything was harmonious or that Prague was an economic utopia. It was not. Businesses failed, people moved, the black population suffered hardship and lacked economic opportunities afforded others, and during World War I ethnic tensions rose between the Czechs and Germans of Prague. Nor is this to suggest that Czechs gave up being Czechs and forsook their European culture. As will be seen in the next chapter, they did everything they could to maintain their language, customs, and shared history. They battled to inculcate into their young their ethnic identity, the internal uniqueness of being Czech.

CHAPTER 6

Family Ties and Everyday Life of Prague's Czechs

A TIRED GEORGE SADLO WIPED AWAY THE SWEAT dripping from his brow. He glanced over his shoulder at the searing August sun and peered intently at Mose Case, squatting almost serenely behind the dusty slab. An athletic-looking man from the county seat of Chandler, a man Sadlo and Case barely knew, stood beside the flat slab waving a menacing stick of ash as if he intended to charge the tiny hill Sadlo stood upon and do him harm. Sadlo massaged the grass-stained orb resting in his right hand and in determined staccato gestures nodded at Case. From Sadlo's left came the encouraging chatter of Lester Hooter, while from his right John Reel and Fatty Oplinger expressed their confidence and support. Even the cheerful rasping of Wesley Pastusek's faraway voice filtered into Sadlo's ears. Lifting his left leg high into the air, Sadlo rocked backward before pushing toward the stranger from Chandler. Sadlo let loose the ball and stood stoically as it zipped past the helpless outsider. Mose Case caught the whizzing whiteness, stood, and held the ball high. The game was over. The Prague Sluggers had won yet another game. This week's victory came against the Chandler Nine by a score of 4–1. Prague's baseball club had not lost a single game that season.

The *Prague Record* covered the details of the August 17, 1916, baseball game between Prague and Chandler in a front-page article. George Sadlo, Prague's victorious pitcher, struck out sixteen Chandler batters on the hot day, giving up a mere six hits in the nine-inning game. Unfortunately for the team, they lost their first and only game of the summer the next week to Bristow's team by a score of 7–2. Prague's Sluggers won eleven of twelve games during the summer of 1916.[1] Both Czech players mentioned (George Sadlo and Wesley Pastusek) entered the U.S. Army in 1918 and served in Europe with the American Expeditionary Force under Gen. John J. Pershing.[2]

Like most Americans, rural and urban, in the first half of the twentieth century, the residents of Prague loved baseball. However, Prague's newspapers did not stop covering baseball just because the season ended. During the winter months of 1917, 1918, and 1919, most issues of the *Prague Record* carried short articles written by former Major League umpire Billy Evans. The column, Billy Evans Solves Baseball Problems, explained the complex rules of America's national pastime.[3] In 1919 the local newspapers ran articles on both the American and National Leagues of Major League Baseball, including photographs of each player on the World Series Championship team, the Cincinnati Reds.[4] In addition, during the 1920s the newspaper published pieces that included a biographical sketches, advice, and photos of stars such as Ty Cobb, Lou Gehrig, Tris Speaker, and George "Babe" Ruth.[5]

From 1910 through at least 1930, Prague fielded a town baseball team usually referred to in the newspapers as the Prague Sluggers.[6] During this period, most American towns and cities contained semi-professional or fully professional baseball teams. To put it simply, baseball was *the* sport in the United States during this time. Americans loved baseball. Whether one lived in an urban setting or in a small town, baseball held a prominent place in the hearts and minds of most residents. Despite never seeing a Major League game in person, Americans, especially males, followed the teams and players through the newspapers and beginning in the 1920s via radio. In addition, many small towns throughout the country formed teams and competed against other communities in their area. In 1920 the *Prague Record* reported that the area baseball teams were trying to revive the prewar league that again would be called the Frisco League.

Prospective participants included Prague, Chandler, Weleetka, Sparks, and Paden.[7] In general their players were not adolescents but young men in their late teens and early twenties who took the game seriously and played hard, hoping that a roving scout would see them on the diamond and sign them to a professional contract. Towns took great pride in their "nine" and flocked to the games. An illustration of the immense interest is found in the July 6, 1916, issue of the *Prague Record*. According to the paper, Prague's baseball game against Paden drew more than 450 fans. This may not appear a tremendous attendance until we consider that the total population of Prague at this time was barely more than 1,000.[8] Moreover, the town of Prague was no different in its interest in baseball from most communities across the United States. It should be noted, however, that these town teams were not professional. During the week, team members held full-time jobs. For example, in 1917 twenty-one-year-old George Sadlo identified himself as a musician. The hurler offered private violin lessons to the residents of Prague and later taught music at the public school. Wesley Pastusek, seventeen years old, and Lloyd "Fatty" Oplinger, twenty-three, worked during the week as sales clerks, Pastusek in a grocery store, Oplinger in a hardware store. Lester Hooter, Prague's twenty-one-year-old first baseman, worked for the railroad, while Ernest Blumenthal, twenty, worked alongside his father at the Leader general store.[9] The team practiced in the evenings and played on Saturday and Sunday afternoons. Normally players received a small portion of the gate receipts, but never enough to earn a living playing baseball. These young men were semiprofessional at best.

The people of Prague apparently evinced much interest in baseball and their home team. During summer months, the front page of the *Prague Record* usually contained an article about the previous Saturday's game. The Prague baseball team represented the entire town; it was not specifically a Czech team, and judging by the large attendance at games, it appears the town avidly followed the team. However, from 1916 until he left for the military, Prague's top pitcher was George Sadlo, a Czech and the son of the town's tailor. As mentioned, the 1916 Prague Sluggers won every game except one, a 7–2 defeat at the hands of the Bristow Browns. The town of Bristow lay thirty-eight miles from Prague. With the automobile still in its primitive stage and roads usually nothing more than grated rock or dirt in 1916 rural Oklahoma, thirty-eight miles was quite a trip, which again shows the love and importance that baseball held to these small agricultural communities.[10]

In April 1917 the *Prague Record* published the roster for the upcoming season. Most of the players sported Anglo names such as John Reel, Carl Wilson, Lester Hooter, Mose Case, and a second baseman named Smith. However, Lloyd "Fatty" Oplinger, from the German community, pitched and played shortstop, and Ernest Blumenthal, Jewish son of Morris Blumenthal, occupied left field. George Sadlo returned as the Sluggers' ace pitcher and was joined on the team by another Czech, Wesley Pastusek.[11]

Sadlo and Pastusek were second-generation Czechs. Their parents hailed from Bohemia and Moravia, respectively. Sadlo, born in Missouri, and Pastusek, born in Texas, probably had never been to Europe. Both attended school in the United States and could read and write in English.[12] They were American Czechs and made every effort to fit into American society.[13] What could be more American than baseball?

An early chronicler of Oklahoma's Czechs argued that "the Czechs of Oklahoma did not immediately embrace the larger society in which they lived" and because of this "they were not the most popular of settlers, partly because of their clannishness and partly because of behavior traits, which were all too common among them—quarrelsomeness, suspiciousness, and an inclination to carry small disagreements beyond the point of reason."[14] The above may very well hold true regarding the earliest settlers, the land-run pioneers of 1891, and the arrivals before the creation of Prague in 1902. The original Czechs in the area lived a somewhat isolated, exclusive ethnic lifestyle. However, once the farm village came into existence, the situation rapidly changed. Czechs participated eagerly in the economy of the new town, opening businesses, providing services, and buying and selling alongside the non-Czechs. There is little evidence of Czechs segregating themselves from the larger community, especially economically.

In *The Story of a Bohemian-American Village*, historian Robert Kutak wrote: "Immigrants in cities are often maladjusted because they lack control over their lives; they are moved and influenced by forces which lie beyond them. . . . This is not true in an isolated agricultural village where 90 per cent of the individuals are of the same nationality."[15] The above assessment compares an ethnic urban population with that of a rural community that was ethnically homogeneous. The analysis does not include farming communities like Prague where the newcomer population, though originally living in relative isolation, immediately became the minority with the creation of a town. The Czechs of Prague fall into this category. The early farming community was probably clannish. Czech farmers helped each other get through the tough times of cultivating the coarse prairie. In no source can one find that the Czech immigrants helped the native-born or ethnic German farmers in the area. The Czechs appear to have kept to themselves. However, when the Fort Smith and Western Railroad chose Frank and Josephine Barta's homestead as the site of a coaling station and Prague came into existence, circumstances changed. The Prague Czechs faced a decision: either actively participate in the new village or retreat to an even deeper isolation that would ultimately hurt not only them but also their children. Prague's Czechs proved pragmatic and realistic. Most chose to involve themselves in the inchoate community.

However, many did not envision participation as relinquishing their European culture. Like other immigrant groups, the Prague Czechs exhibited stubbornness in hanging onto their Old World culture, such as their language, cuisine, and music. They coupled their desire to retain the past with an acceptance of their present situation. To make life for themselves and their children as prosperous and conflict-free as possible, they chose to live a twofold lifestyle. Prague's Czechs made every effort to remain "Czech" while thriving in their new homeland. In a pessimistic study of American Czechs, one scholar posits that "when the first generation will have died there will not be much left of the Czech and Slovak culture patterns in the United States."[16] The evidence suggests that this is off the mark, especially in rural areas such as Milligan or Wilber, Nebraska, or Snook, Texas. Many rural areas maintained traditional customs well into the third generation.[17] Nor does it include the persistence of Czech identity, the refusal of many people of Czech ancestry to give up their identification as Czech, and their refusal to melt into the cauldron of Caucasian uncertainty. Many Prague Czechs, though rather quickly adjusting to a culture different from their own, did not lose their group identity or their sense of belonging to a group outside the native-born white mainstream. Again, this does not mean that Prague's Czechs refused to identify themselves as American or make concessions to the dominant culture. Many immigrants anglicized their children's first names—for example, Frantisek became Frank and Jiri changed to George—and beginning with the second generation, most Czechs proudly proclaimed themselves Americans. Nevertheless, most never forgot their origins or ethnic identity. As individual Czechs made the decision to participate in the activities of the farm town, their adjustment period shortened. Once Czechs took this irreversible step, some, especially the offspring of Czech women who married non-Czechs, began the journey away from the close-knit ethnic group to the ambiguity of an "American" identity. Sporting a non-Slavic surname, these American-born children, if they wished, could fade into the mainstream of society with little dif-ficulty. Regardless of accepting new associations and boundaries, some of Prague's Czechs resisted the slide into ethnic ambiguity and estab-lished a lasting presence centered on a birthright ethnicity that con-tinued long after they laid aside their cultural distinctiveness. Despite practicing a dual lifestyle in which they participated fully in the domi-nant culture while holding fast to their symbolic roots, Prague's Czechs remained firm in their ethnic identity.

Like all groups, whether Czech, German, native-born white, or African American, the fundamental unit was the family. Most Czech immigrants to the United States derived from the rural cottager class, and they brought with them the concept of the family as the center. In pastoral Europe, the family was of utmost importance in provid-ing workers to toil on the land. These were not urban professionals enmeshed in the capitalist dream of financial success through upward mobility. They worked many hours to get the most from the soil. Their ultimate goal was to own a fertile plot of land, build a comfort-able home, and raise their children. Their ideas of family solidarity remained intact even after arriving in the United States, and they were forced, out of economic necessity, into industrial jobs or, as in the case of the immigrant farmers living on the periphery of Prague, choos-ing to move into town and attempt to create a business. Furthermore, as historian Josef Barton asserted, "The locus of membership and alliance in the Czech community was the lineal unit of the family. . . . Czech immigrants, in short, allied themselves in families of three generations."[18]

The extended family was the norm and was of paramount impor-tance to the Czech community. However, regardless of the importance Czechs placed on unity and cohesiveness, this was the historical period known as the Victorian age. Like the typical native-born American father, a Czech father normally did not pursue close emotional relationships with his children.[19] This was left to the mothers. Mothers were the purveyors of affection. Czech fathers constructed a wall of authority and affection between themselves and their offspring. Fathers were the center of power, and respect was paramount. This contrived distance enabled fathers to maintain control over their children, and because of the more formal relationship, there were fewer chances of disrespectful behavior.

Once in the United States, the immigrant family came under intense stress. The family absorbed the shocks of the foreign culture, language, and economic system. It was to the family that the father, most likely the breadwinner, could retreat at the end of another workday in the new environment. Furthermore, if he and his wife had young children, as these children aged, in many cases they became culturally separate from their parents. This could place the entire family at risk.[20] Czech families grasped this tension and attempted to alleviate it through either the fraternal organizations or the Catholic Church, with the secular orders holding more sway in most Czech communities. Prague's Bohemian Hall was for the family, and the Sokol lodge specifically focused on the needs of the ethnic group's young.

Immigrant mothers may very well have had the easiest, as well as the most difficult, time of any in the ethnic group. Mothers remained in the home while their husbands went off to work, and therefore these women experienced less contact with the American culture, which allowed them more time to adjust slowly rather than being jolted by the new culture on a daily basis. In immigrant families, the mother transferred much of the family and ethnic traditions to the young. However, immigrant mothers also found it exceedingly difficult to deal with their children who grew up in American society and desired to conform in matters of fashion, music, and even food. This, of course, caused conflict.[21] When extrapolated to the village of Prague, this appears relevant, especially regarding the Czechs living on farms. These women came to town only to shop or attend a Czech or community event, and a fissure may very well have formed between them and their public school–educated children. However, the experience of mothers living within the environs of Prague differed. These women would have been aware of the goings-on around them and interacted more with non-Czechs than the rural mothers.

Nevertheless, the slower pace of the small town and the acceptance of Czechs by the majority–U.S.-born white population surely helped the immigrant women cope with the pressures of adjustment better than their urban kin. Regardless of the situation, everyday life centered on the family. Parents provided affection, security, and disciplined structure for the children and in return expected obedience and work.[22] It was through these ties of affection and obligation that immigrant families channeled ethnic identity to succeeding generations. In many cases in urban areas, these ties became strained due to the intense stimuli of the dominant society. However, in the comparative isolation of a rural farm or village, the family better controlled the habits of the young.[23] Parents were better able to oversee their children's personal habits, including recreational activities and social interactions. Furthermore, when the parents openly participated in the various aspects of community life, stress in the family lessened, resulting in less friction than if the children alone came in contact with the larger society.

Marriage was one important aspect of family life that immigrant parents attempted to control. It is not so much that they tried to choose specific mates for their children, although this no doubt occurred, but that they stressed the importance of choosing another Czech as their lifetime mate. Most ethnic groups in the United States married largely within their own group during the first and most of the second generation.[24] In the early years, Oklahoma Czechs insisted that their children marry within the ethnic group. Czech Oklahomans, in general, were conspicuously endogamous for perhaps two generations.[25] This is a broad, but true application regarding all of Oklahoma's Czechs. However, when extrapolated to Prague, it does not precisely describe the situation. The early and active participation of Czechs in the economy of the farming town resulted in social integration, dalliances of Czechs and non-Czechs, and ultimately exogamous marriages.

By using census manuscripts, newspaper announcements, and cemetery records, one can perceive the marriage patterns of the Prague Czechs. The census records show the birthplace of the individual, but also the birthplace of his or her parents. Thus it is relatively easy to determine who the immigrants are and who the second-generation ethnics are. The third generation proves tougher to unravel because both the birthplace of the individual and parents show up in census records as being somewhere in the United States. This can be especially taxing for third-generation females. With third-generation males, of course, most will sport obvious Czech surnames. When examining undetermined wives on census material in the later years of the study (1920 and 1930), it may be possible to revert to an earlier census manuscript, ascertain the birthplace of the grandparents of the individual in question, and thus determine the ethnicity of the wife. However, this can be possible only if the wife's maiden name is obtained. This is where the local newspapers and cemetery records can be of assistance. All marriage announcements in the Prague newspapers contained the wife's maiden name, and many cemetery tombstones displayed a woman's surname before marriage. Thus if the couple married in Prague or if their final resting place was in one of the Prague cemeteries, there is a good possibility of determining the wife's maiden name. By knowing the maiden name of the wife of a Czech immigrant or Czech ethnic, a supposition can be deduced regarding the existence of endogamous or exogamous marriage within the Czech community.

The 1900 census records show forty-two Czech households in South Creek Township, location of the future town of Prague. In all of these households save one, at least one of the married adults listed his or her birthplace as Bohemia.[26] In thirty-five households, both marriage partners were born in the Czech lands, while five families consisted of a second-generation Czech married to an immigrant.[27] The only possible exception to this endogamous portrait was Mary Banghain. Mary, a Bohemian immigrant, married George Banghain most likely in Nebraska when she was eighteen and he was around twenty-two.[28] George listed his birthplace as Nebraska and his parents' birthplace as Iowa. Their two daughters were born in Nebraska, with the younger being nine years old in 1900. Although it is impossible to state with complete certainty that Mary's husband was not a third-generation Czech, his last name suggests he was not. Thus, out of the forty-two households containing at least one Czech, only the Banghain family could be considered the result of an exogamous marriage.[29]

Does the above analysis support some scholars' idea that marriage patterns remained, for the most part, within the ethnic group during the first and second generations?[30] There is little doubt that the early Czech farming community in South Creek Township consisted overwhelmingly of immigrants marrying immigrants or immigrants marrying the children of immigrants. It shows the closeness of the early Czech community. Czech immigrants definitely looked for a mate within their group. Of the thirty-five immigrant-to-immigrant marriages, fourteen occurred in Bohemia before emigration. This reinforces the earlier position that many Czechs came to the United States in family units rather than as individuals. Furthermore, the twenty-one immigrant households that married after arriving in the United States consisted of many immigrants arriving at an early age, including ten who arrived before their sixteenth birthday and four aged sixteen to twenty. Most if not all of these likely arrived as a dependent member of an immigrant family and, despite claiming Bohemia as their birthplace, had already spent several years in America.

An obvious observation gleaned from the data is that rural Czech colonies in the Midwest clung strongly together. Most of the early Czech settlers in South Creek Township listed their birthplace as Nebraska, with the others claiming rural states like Iowa, Wisconsin, and Kansas. These immigrants lived in an environment where they came into social contact with other Czech immigrants. So although some arrived in the United States at an early age, their families quickly migrated west and joined close-knit immigrant colonies, which practically ensured the marriage of their children to others within the Czech community. Moreover, only eight married couples claimed to be married less than ten years. Considering that the first Czechs arrived in Oklahoma in 1891 with the opening of the Sac and Fox reservation to settlement, most couples married in the United States exchanged vows before migrating to the Sooner state. They met, fell in love, and formed a family before moving to Oklahoma.[31]

With the formation of Prague, things changed. During the next thirty years, interaction between the Czech community and the community at large in the economic, educational, and social spheres resulted in more exogamous marriages. Third-generation Czechs, those whose grandparents came from Bohemia, displayed little hesitation in choosing a non-Czech as a spouse.[32] Through the years, the *Prague Record* contained numerous marriage announcements covering the nuptials of third-generation Czechs with non-Czechs.[33] Even three granddaughters of the immigrant pioneer Frank Vlasak married outside the ethnic group. His oldest son's daughters, Marie and Gladys, married non-Czech men with the surnames Vanhooser and Crute, while his youngest son's daughter, Ednamae, married and divorced Herbert Kilgo of Asher, Oklahoma.[34] Considering that the third-generation descendants and the parents all grew up in the United States, it is not surprising that many married outside the ethnic group. This occurred in most ethnic groups. However, what about the second generation, those born in the United States of immigrant parents? Did Prague's second-generation Czechs remain endogamous, as earlier scholars argued?[35]

As already noted, the 1890s Czech farming community contained only six second-generation families, and all married within the group except for one whose head of household was unmarried at the time of the census. With the creation of Prague, more Czechs as well as non-Czechs streamed into the area until, by the 1920s, there were about one hundred Czech families living within the area, including thirty-six immigrant-to-immigrant pairings.[36] Again, by comparing cemetery records and newspaper marriage announcements with the census manuscripts, one can find a good depiction of second-generation Czech marriage practices. The 1920 census contained sixty-nine second-generation Czech families. Of these, forty-five married another Czech. Twenty-six of these forty-five married an immigrant, and nineteen partnered with a fellow second-generation Czech.

However, the remaining twenty-four second-generation Czechs married non-Czechs. Although these exogamous marriages constitute only about a third of the total second-generation unions, they are a significant number. Eighteen of the twenty-four exogamous marriages consisted of a female second-generation Czech marrying outside the group, including one Czech farmer's daughter, Agnes Sucha, who married a member of the German community, Max Brauer. Sucha, born in 1903, would have been a teenager during World War I.[37] Apparently the hostility between the Czech and German communities during this period did not affect her choice of a husband.

An examination of cemetery records reveals an additional five exogamous marriages involving immigrants with three of the five spouses being male Czechs.[38] Added to the twenty-four second-generation exogamic nuptials, the immigrant marriages bring the total of out-of-group partnerships to twenty-nine. Although endogamous marriages greatly exceeded exogamic marriages, the numbers are significant and suggest that Czech society was not closed. Marriages uniting Czechs and non-Czechs were commonplace beginning with the second generation. Thus it appears that the dual lifestyle many Czechs pursued, the pragmatic approach wherein Czechs participated fully in the community of Prague while attempting to maintain their traditions through the family and fraternal organizations, had already begun to break down by the second generation.

A final note on marriage patterns centers on how some Czech women who married outside the group continued to claim their ethnic roots. When a man married a non-Czech, his name remained the same. Despite marrying a German or Irish or Anglo bride, he kept his Czech last name. Thus, to his dying breath, his name proclaimed his Czechness; he was an Opela, Novak, or Jezek, no matter the nationality of his wife. Not so with Czech women. When they married, tradition demanded they change their surname to reflect their husband's. When Alice Babek, a second-generation Czech, married Cecil Olson, she became Mrs. Cecil Olson or simply Alice Olson to her friends and acquaintances. However, it is enlightening how several Czech women who married non-Czechs desired a return to their ethnic roots upon death. In the Czech National Cemetery, which required Czech heritage for burial, there are fourteen graves of Czech women of this period who married non-Czechs. Their husbands are not buried alongside them. The women's graves stand alone. Each woman's married name and Czech maiden name are etched on the tombstone with only one exception, Ednamae Vlasak, who divorced her husband, Herbert Kilgo. Why these women's husbands were not buried beside them is unclear.

Perhaps the wife died before the husband, and he turned the burial over to her family. Or perhaps the husband passed before the wife and she, in her dotage, decided in favor of a burial with her birth family and ethnic relatives rather than with her in-laws. Or maybe pride in their heritage prompted these women to ask for burial in the Czech cemetery. The true reason is unknown, and for each woman the motive probably differed. Nevertheless, these graves give testament that some Czech women, of which several were third generation, continued to view themselves as Czech. They held fast to their ethnicity despite going through much of their lives with a non-Czech last name.[39]

In addition, there are five graves of Czech women and their non-Czech spouses in the Czech National Cemetery.[40] These are worthy of note because in two instances, the non-Czech husband outlived his Czech wife, meaning he agreed to burial in the ethnic cemetery. In the other three cases, the wife outlived her spouse, implying she made the final decision on a burial site. However, two of the non-Czech husbands passing before their wives were in their seventies when they died, and the other, George Williams, was eighty-one or eighty-two. Thus it is likely that these couples discussed burial plans before their deaths and agreed on the Czech cemetery as their final resting place. Again this points out that these women, even though marrying outside the ethnic group, still identified themselves as Czech.[41]

Often the decision to marry in the United States marked the turning point in national identification and created the first tangible tie to the new land. Marrying someone outside your ethnic group is a visible and irrevocable step toward assimilation. Intermarriage affected the couple, their children, and the entire ethnic group. This impact appears especially true when women married outside the ethnic group. Their children would no longer keep the mother's ethnic surname but would take their father's. The descendants of these offspring are very susceptible to leaving the distant maternal heritage and becoming indifferent to their ethnic identity. Some even argue that pervasive intermarriage suggests the emergence of a new ethnic group, one defined by ancestry from anywhere on the European continent.[42] Although it is arguable whether or not more than one-third of second-generation marriages being exogamous falls under the adjective *pervasive*, nevertheless it is more than trivial. Furthermore, exogamy did nothing but increase with succeeding generations. Did these marriages outside the group result in the emergence of a new group or the disappearance of the old? Perhaps with some that indeed was the result, especially those descendents who were the product of several exogamic marriages incorporating three, four, or five ethnic groups. However, during this period, many clung tenaciously to their identity as Czech Americans regardless of their last name.

Besides the town name, Prague exuded a distinctive Bohemian flavor. The Czech population, both those residing within the town limits and those in the rural sections, did not isolate themselves from town activities. They were not an exclusive group, shunning contact with non-Czech members of the population. In this respect, Prague's Czechs appear different from urban ethnic communities where normally the children most readily accepted the dominant culture. In Prague, adults as well as their children participated in village events, working for and befriending non-Czechs. Similar to their experiences in a European village, the Prague Czechs participated in town activities and organizations. Additionally, friction between the Czech community and the other residents appears practically nonexistent—at least until the outbreak of World War I. [43] As mentioned earlier, nativist ideas and outright hostility toward immigrants pervaded much of the United States in the early twentieth century. Nevertheless, Prague's Czechs and the non-Czech inhabitants regarded each other with at least respect and usually friendship. However, many in the Czech community relied heavily on their fraternal societies or, if Catholic, the local parish church. These organizations helped the immigrants and their descendants cope with unfamiliar ways and customs, which enabled individual members to succeed not only in business but also on a personal level. The historical western orientation of these Slavs aided them well after their arrival in the United States. The Dillingham Commission, a joint congressional committee formed in 1907 to study immigration, found that the American Czech population was socially and educationally above other Slavic groups and almost the equal of German immigrants in education. These attributes assisted the Czechs well in coping with their new environment. [44]

Most of Prague's Czechs maintained a keen curiosity in the happenings in Europe, especially the Czech lands and in other Czech communities in the United States. At least three Czech-language newspapers enabled the rural community to glean information about their country of birth and others of their ethnic group in the United States that their local newspaper might not cover.[45] The primary Czech-language newspaper read in Prague was *Oklahomaske Noviny* (Oklahoma News). Published in Chicago beginning in 1905, the semiweekly kept the immigrant community apprised of Czechs throughout the United States as well as happenings in Bohemia. An Oklahoma farmer could have the paper mailed directly to him and could read about other Czech farmers in Iowa, Nebraska, and Wisconsin or keep abreast of events in Chicago, Cleveland, and other urban centers. For example, the October 19, 1905, issue offered a story about an anti-Habsburg demonstration in Brno, Moravia. The desire to throw off the yoke of imperial dominance did not begin with World War I. Another popular paper published in Chicago was the liberal-bent *Hlasatel* (Herald). Similar to *Oklahomske Noviny*, *Hlasatel* evinced a more politically progressive slant on the news and leaned toward rationalism on matters religious. Although there is no way of estimating the number of Lincoln County Czechs who read *Oklahomske Noviny* or *Hlasatel*, they were available and most likely read by many. The official newspaper of the Western Czech Brotherhood Association printed in Cedar Rapids, Iowa, was *Bratrsky Vestnik* (Fraternal Bulletin). Its primary purpose centered on informing members of upcoming events, meetings, and changes in leadership, dues, or benefits. This newspaper would have been readily available to all Bohemian Hall members.[46]

In 1902 Franklin N. Newhouse, a dedicated Republican, moved his printing presses from Baxter Springs, Kansas, to Oklahoma and began printing the *Prague News*, Prague's first newspaper, on July 24. The following year Frank Mullen started a rival paper, the *Prague Patriot*, which claimed independence in politics.[47] The papers carried stories from all over the nation as well as local news, and both actively sought to please their readers with articles about events in the Czech community. Czechs reciprocated by advertising their businesses and meetings in both newspapers. In 1909 Frank Nipper, a newcomer to

Prague, bought the *Patriot* and changed its name to the *Prague Record*. A few years later, in 1917, Nipper bought out Newhouse's *Prague News* and stopped publishing the rival sheet.[48] In 1919, deciding to move to Wyoming and begin anew, Nipper sold the *Record* to two men from Hennessy, Oklahoma, who in turn sold the entire operation in 1920 to Junia Heath Jones. She returned the newspaper to a Republican tilt and printed the happenings of the small town for many years.[49]

Prague's newspapers, like most small-town papers in the early twentieth century, covered all aspects of town life and the surrounding rural community. By reading the weekly newspaper, one could stay abreast of every happening in the town. Looking at a few stories covered by the *Prague Record* in a sixty-day period in 1916 reveals the wide-ranging scope of the newspaper: "Anton Pastusek building an addition to his house." Justice Balaun fined a man $16.50 for "hogging the road with his wagon and not allowing a Ford to pass." "Outside Paden [about eight miles east of Prague] last Thursday night, police had gun-fight with crowd of party men. One man shot in side after he fired his gun. He paid a fine." "Miss Henrietta Sosensko lost her gold wish-bone pin last Friday night. Finder please return to Miss Henrietta at the New York Bargain Store and receive reward." The papers even published accounts of seemingly ordinary activities such as "Some Wilzetta [a rural community about six miles northwest of Prague] people . . . out car riding Friday night," or "D. Bartek, John Barta, C. M. Sadlo, and several others went to the Canadian [River] Wednesday afternoon on a fishing party."[50] And "Lon Leder shot himself accidentally while hunting with John Cerveny and John Barta. Both barrels of a double-barrel shotgun hit him in the left leg. Dr. Mraz attended him."[51] The newspapers, especially the *Prague Record*, reported extensively on the everyday life of their readers. As seen, a resident could not build an addition to his house or even go fishing without the community finding out. When the wife of Dr. John Z. Mraz died, the *Record* covered her funeral, noting how beloved by the community the deceased was and that practically the entire town attended.[52] If one previously assumed that farmers and small-town residents rarely left home, they would be mistaken. Considering only the Czech community, the paper reported trips to various destinations throughout Oklahoma such as

Oklahoma City, Stroud, Guthrie, Bristow, and Tulsa. Furthermore, Prague's Czechs traveled out of state on visits and vacations to nearby states like Texas, Arkansas, and Kansas, but also to distant destinations such as Indiana, Illinois, Nebraska, Oregon, California, and New York.[53]

The papers reported on parties, families visiting other families, and even when a young single man paid a visit to the home of a young single lady. These social events and visits, whether friendly or romantic, show Czechs and non-Czechs personally and voluntarily involved with each other. The *Prague News* and *Prague Record* contain dozens of examples of Czechs and non-Czechs socializing, including a 1915 note where the Pospisil family (Czech) visited the Hensley home Sunday evening.[54] Apparently the Sojka family residence (Czech) was a popular destination because many non-Czech families such as the Emericks, Hammacks, Milligans, and Burnsides stopped there for visits.[55] When young Joe Bartosh (Czech) "called on Miss Fannie Nix, Tuesday evening," the whole town probably buzzed.[56] However, the relationship did not last, as the 1920 census shows the second-generation Bartosh married to Camellia, also a second-generation Czech.[57] Parties were always popular events, and Czechs enjoyed them as much as the next. When the Burnsides threw a party, the *Record* listed the guests attending, and they included several non-Czechs as well as Czechs such as the Vlasaks and Sojkas.[58] On Joe Heinzig's fourteenth birthday in 1926, his mother gave him a big party serving popcorn and birthday cake to the guests, which included Charlie, Louis, Fanny, and Agnes Opela and Marie and Anna Mae Simek. Young Heinzig's heritage was German. Obviously, the hard feelings of the prior decade between the German and Czech community were forgotten, as this German family allowed their son to invite his Czech friends to celebrate his birthday.[59]

Notwithstanding experiencing great success as farmers, artisans, and in business, the Czech community also suffered tragedy. One of the worst occurred during the summer of 1916: "Joe Rubac, a prominent Bohemian farmer . . . was run over by a west-bound passenger train Monday afternoon. . . . He died in a short time afterwards."[60] Apparently after disembarking, Joe Rubac realized he had left his suitcase on the train. He reentered the departing locomotive, retrieved his baggage, and then jumped from the moving train, falling underneath.

The weight of the passenger car crushed and severed one of his legs. The fifty-four-year-old Czech bled to death before some good Samaritans could carry him to a doctor. The Czech community and the entire town showered his widow, Anna, with their condolences and food. The Bohemian Hall of which Rubac was a member paid fifty dollars to Anna for burial expenses. The fraternal organization paid an additional fifty dollars to the widow as a death benefit.[61] Rubac's widow buried her husband in the Czech National Cemetery. To thank everyone for his or her kindness, Anna Rubac wrote a thank-you note, which the *Prague Record* printed.[62] However, this is not the end of the story. In the weeks to come, the *Record* reported various people visiting the widow, sometimes taking her to their house for a meal.[63] The community made sure Anna Rubac was not left alone while grieving.

Other than baseball, Prague fielded no other athletic teams during its first decade. The high school did not play their initial varsity football game until 1915, probably because of the amount of time and work most residents invested in building their homes, businesses, roads, and other infrastructure necessities. This is not to say that the early residents of Prague did not relax and enjoy themselves. As early as 1904, the town sported a racetrack, shooting gallery, and bowling alley.[64] In 1906 Prague added a roller skating rink for the young and old alike, and by the end of 1907 two billiard halls had opened.[65] However, beginning around 1915, the citizens of Prague ventured into other competitions. The *Prague News* reported the town organized a tennis team and challenged nearby towns to matches. Like the baseball club, the tennis team included adults, because the article listed Arthur P. Slover, a bank cashier and school board official, as one of the members.[66] George Sadlo, the baseball team's top pitcher, also played tennis. Other members of the tennis squad listed in the article included men with Anglo names like Fred Miles and Clifford Botts, and a Jewish man, Ernest Blumenthal. Thus, like the baseball club, the tennis team featured non-Czechs as well as Czechs. In March 1917 Prague held a townwide domino tournament that lasted several days and attracted many contestants, including Czechs. Sam Kolodny, the Jewish immigrant from Russia and owner of the New York Bargain Store, emerged as champion, defeating former mayor Benjamin Franklin Whitmore in the final game.[67]

Probably the most popular leisure activity in Prague was dancing, and the Czech community's Bohemian Hall emerged as the center of the dance craze. Saturday nights became the unofficial evening for taking a date for several hours of dancing and music usually featuring local Czech bands such as Bontty's Coronet Band or the Prykrill Orchestra.[68] The first town band formed in Prague in 1906. The twenty-three-member band chose George Eret, a Czech, as bandmaster and John Davis, a non-Czech, as business manager—still another example of interethnic cooperation.[69] From 1915 to 1930 practically every edition of Prague's newspapers contained an advertisement promoting a Saturday night dance at the Bohemian Hall. In addition, the weekly advertisements always stressed that everyone in town was invited. Despite being held at the Czechs' fraternal building, any couple paying the cost of admission (fifty cents before 1920 and seventy-five cents during the 1920s) could come and dance.[70] Although it was the most common venue for dances, the Bohemian Hall was not the only floor where one could waltz or practice the foxtrot. In 1917 Agnes Vobornik and Mary Pastusek held a "Big Social Dance" at the Sokol Hall. The *Record* reported that about seventy people attended the young women's party.[71] The American Legion also held occasional dances, as did the Catholic Church.[72]

Besides dancing, the townspeople enjoyed attending live plays. The Methodist Episcopal Church performed *The Thread of Destiny* at Prague's Folly Theater featuring youth from their church as the cast.[73] The high school drama department staged several plays with some of the performances also held during the evenings at the Folly Theater. In 1921 the high school presented *Valentine Vinegar's Vaudeville Agency* before a sold-out audience. Edward Shultz played the lead role, and the cast of teenaged actors included Eddie Klabzuba and Frank Kozak.[74] The Bohemian Hall sponsored plays as well. In April 1921, to raise money for Prague's American Legion organization, the Czech fraternal group performed a play two nights running.[75] A few years later, the Bohemian Hall advertised a play in the *Record* with the Czech title *Osel je Osel*, which roughly translates as "A fool is a fool." The advertisement bragged that the performance featured "Home Talent" and that the play would be followed by a dance. Although the advertisement did not specify the language of the play, the title was published in the Czech language. So the play was most likely performed in Czech.[76]

Residents of Prague almost certainly flocked to the Folly Theater in 1917 when it began showing motion pictures on a giant screen. The Savoy Theater, owned in 1921 by the Lanik brothers (Czechs), competed with the Folly for customers.[77] Besides reporting on the latest Hollywood movie coming to Prague, the paper carried news about neighborhood women holding rook and whist parties and who attended.[78] Traveling shows periodically stopped in Prague. Frank Still and his Wild West show performed before overflow crowds in July 1915, and the M. L. Clark and Sons Circus came to town in September of that year.[79] Burk's Big Show also arrived in Prague in 1915 and treated the residents to a parade and a rendition of the classic play *Uncle Tom's Cabin*.[80] The following fall, more than five thousand people gathered outside Prague on the Barta farm to watch Tex LaGrene demonstrate a flying machine, an airplane.[81] Vaudeville came to town in 1916 featuring dancing, singing, and comedy for three consecutive nights. The Franklin Show set up a giant tent and offered a different play each night with vaudeville performed between acts. Adults paid twenty cents, and the children got in for only a dime.[82] Prague held a Big Spring Festival in 1922, featuring eating contests, music, and a baseball game. Before the big event, the *Prague Record* advertised that the Terrible Turk, a professional wrestler, would be in town taking on "all comers."[83] The ensuing editions of the paper, however, did not report anyone defeating or even challenging the Terrible Turk. Perhaps when the young men in town finally got a glimpse of the Turk, he truly was terrible.

That Czechs attended these town events seems beyond doubt. An air show, which attracted more than five thousand, was held on Frank Barta's farmland. Czechs, like everyone in the community, enjoyed the shows and area happenings as much as their neighbors.

One community event Prague's Czechs loved was the annual Lincoln County Fair. Each fall, the newspapers listed the yearly ribbon winners, and Czechs always fared well. For several years Rudolph Pospisil was one of the best riders in the county, while Franny Walla, whose husband was an active member of the Bohemian Hall, won numerous first place awards with her canned blackberries and plum jelly. Lydia Sojka excelled in cake making, especially devil's food, while Rosie Vana took home prizes in tatting (lace work).[84]

However, the biggest town event during the year occurred every July 4. Festivities began early and lasted all day. The entertainment included music, singing, speeches, recitations, and contests such as foot races, an apple pie eating contest, a money-grabbing event, fat man's race, and various other attractions. Of course, food was plentiful, and the celebration normally concluded with a baseball game.[85]

Although the early Czech farming community appears to have been somewhat clannish, it is obvious that after the formation of Prague, most Czechs, both young and old, actively participated in community affairs. Beginning as early as the second generation, some Czechs married outside their ethnic group. However, despite choosing a non-Czech husband or wife, many continued their allegiance to the Czech community. In the social arena, as in economics, Prague's Czechs practiced a pragmatic approach in their relationships with the larger community. They took part in celebrations and befriended others outside their own ethnic group. This twin lifestyle quickly led to cultural dualism, an almost total immersion in the community, which resulted in rapid adjustment to the new American ways and acculturation into the mainstream culture. Nevertheless, some in the Czech community refused to undergo a full identity change; they refused to turn completely Yankee.

Still another aspect of the Czechs' decision to cooperate with the larger community concerns education. If these Czechs truly wished to maintain their European culture, they needed to teach their young the ways and language of their forebears. It was imperative. The following chapter reveals how they attempted to do just this while continuing to live in two worlds.

CHAPTER 7

Education and the Czech Community

BEN DAVIS, QUARTERBACK FOR PRAGUE HIGH SCHOOL'S football team, barked the signals to the offense in a clear voice that bordered on the musical to many spectators in the stands. Upon hearing the trigger word, the center snapped the football into the open, waiting hands of Davis, who wheeled to his left and deftly stuck the football into the midsection of Jim Sala, Prague's halfback and leading rusher, before the Seminole defense could tackle him for a loss. Sala tightly cradled the pigskin against his side with his left arm and followed the other halfback, Frank Kozak, as they charged into the maelstrom of the Seminole Chieftain line. Prague's linemen on the left side, Paul White and Charlie Klabzuba, threw their bodies at their husky counterparts, desperately trying to carve an opening in the Seminole defense, enabling Sala to speed through. Spotting a linebacker knifing through the gap, Kozak barreled into the opponent, knocking him to the ground. Jim Sala burst through the opening afforded him by the efforts of his teammates and sprinted several yards toward the goal line before the Seminole defenders finally dragged him to the turf.[1]

Jim Sala, with the help of his teammates, eventually scored a touchdown in a winning effort against Seminole High School. Sala, of Czech ancestry, joined two other Czechs on Prague High School's 1920 fourteen-man football squad. Frank Kozak, whose Bohemian-born father was the town's blacksmith, occupied the other halfback position, and Charlie Klabzuba, a third-generation Czech, played left tackle for the Prague eleven. Klabzuba's father and mother, born in Kansas of Bohemian immigrants, ran a general store in the downtown business district of Prague and owned one of the finer homes in town.[2] The three Czech players were born and reared in the Oklahoma farming community.[3]

Attendance at public school promoted patriotism, cultivated socialization, and, through peer pressure, enhanced cultural homogeneity.

Figure 12. Students of the Czech School, early 1900s.

Five days a week, several months each year, children from different socioeconomic and religiously diverse backgrounds sat at desks or tables and recited the alphabet, repeated the multiplication tables, and learned about their civic duties as American citizens. During recess, they played games like tag, hopscotch, jacks, marbles, and red rover. The boys chose a best buddy and soon the two become blood brothers, while the girls hung out in groups of four or five and talked about how disgusting boys were. By the time they became energetic teenagers verging on adulthood, they dressed alike, wore their hair alike, used the same idioms and slang words, and dreamed about the future. Sometimes the immediate future included marriage. It was not uncommon, especially in a small town, to marry a classmate. Rarely did a young man exclude as a possible lifetime partner a cute girl who laughed at his jokes simply because she or her parents claimed Bohemia as their birthplace. Nor did a young Czech normally find himself rebuffed by the slender redhead sitting next to him in geometry class because his last name was Opela or Jezek instead of Smith or Johnson.[4]

For ethnic groups, attending public school hastened acculturation or the "Americanization" of their young. Most immigrants realized that the confused look on their children's faces after the first day of school would soon disappear as they relaxed in their new surroundings, got acquainted with their classmates, and eventually became indistinguishable from them.

The first Czechs of Prague understood this all too well and during the early 1900s tried to establish a Czech school for their children. This school was not associated with the parish, but appears to be simply a brief attempt to form a secular ethnic academy. Unlike their energetic immersion into the economy of the farm town, many Czech parents in the early days of Prague wanted their offspring to attend classes taught in Czech. However, probably due to costs and losing students to the free public school, Prague's Czech school lasted only a short time.

Leaders in the ethnic group vainly trying to sustain Czech as the vernacular in the Bohemian community offered language classes at the Sokol Hall. Although popular in the beginning, the weekly instruction failed to stanch the inexorable flood emanating from the public schoolhouse. Czech students wanted to fit in, wanted acceptance from their peers. They wanted to be liked.

Immediately upon formation as a town in 1902, Prague established a public school district. The tiny wooden school building, which went through only the eighth grade, quickly suffered from overcrowded conditions.[5] After a quick meeting of ZCBJ officers, the Czech lodge offered Bohemian Hall as a temporary solution. The school board, chaired by ZCBJ member Frank Vlasak, accepted the invitation, and for more than two years the Bohemian Hall housed Prague's public school.[6] Two years later, the aspiring school district hired Dr. Adolph L. Lincheid, a German immigrant, as its superintendent.[7] With Lincheid's guidance, the town in 1909 established a sixteen-credit high school. However, the school remained housed in the cramped wooden structure. The first graduating class of nine seniors (seven girls, two boys) received their diplomas on May 6, 1913.[8] Prague built an eight-room brick schoolhouse in 1917. When it was declared unsafe in 1927, the city tore off the top floor and added a new wing.[9]

This short chronology appears somewhat to contradict or at least question the efforts of Prague's Czech community to establish their own school. The ZCBJ Lodge aided the public school with the use of their building for classes. Obviously not all Czechs worried about the school's impact on their children. Some, such as Frank Vlasak, promoted the public school system. Even the largest fraternal association in the new town supported it.

America's public schools eroded immigrant culture. Nearly all educators during this time promoted cultural homogeneity and the virtues of republicanism and capitalism to their students.[10] Public school teachers fostered universal literacy and through their efforts solidified English as the dominant language in the United States. They advanced and glorified the idea of the American Dream where, over time through thrift and hard work, economic success lay within anyone's reach. Another important outcome of public education, and for the most part unintended, was interethnic and immigrant-native socialization.[11] This invariably led to friendships, and if that friendship involved someone of the opposite sex, possibly romance. To fall in love with someone, you first must meet them and spend time together, and the schoolhouse placed pubescent teenagers in close proximity.

Leaders of ethnic communities quickly realized the impact of public schools on their young. Some groups formed private schools, which enabled them to preserve their religious and cultural heritage.[12] The Jewish and Catholic faiths successfully built and operated private schools stressing the doctrines of their beliefs along with a rigorous academic program. Unlike Jewish centers, which stressed Jewish culture, Catholic parochial schools focused on religious instruction. Thus, attending a private Catholic school did not necessarily mean avoiding cultural decline. Some historians argue that by holding onto the religion of their forebears, individual ethnic members retained something of their heritage and religion.[13] This thesis falters when transposed onto the experiences of the Prague Czechs.

When the piercing criticisms of Catholic policies, especially the selling of indulgences, by Czech priest Jan Hus resulted in his execution in 1415, Czechs revolted against the Church.[14] The terrible and bloody conflicts that followed took on a political cast as well as religious, pitting the downtrodden Czechs against not only the Church but also their German agents of war. From earliest times, national strife intertwined with religious strife.[15] Following the battlefield victories of the Czech Hussites under their legendary leader, Jan Zizka (1360–1424), Bohemia proclaimed autonomy from the Church. For more than a century, the Czechs preserved a wobbly religious independence despite rejoining the Austrian Empire in the sixteenth century. However, following the 1620 Battle of White Mountain, in which a combined force of Catholics that included troops representing the Holy Roman Empire, Catholic League, and Spain routed a much smaller Bohemian army, Emperor Ferdinand II restored Catholicism as the official religion of the Czech lands. The Catholic field commanders occupied the Bohemian capital of Prague and ordered all Protestants to reaffirm their faith or leave. Many left. Those who stayed never forgot.[16]

Upon arrival in the United States, many Czech immigrants abandoned the Catholic faith, which had been forced on their ancestors.[17] Many grasped the theological tenants of the freethinkers, some joined Protestant sects soon after arrival, others simply left the Church and concerned themselves with material issues. Unlike other ethnic groups like the Irish and Poles, Czechs found little refuge in the official religion of their native country. For many, the Catholic Church acted more as a wedge, splintering the community into two rival camps.[18] Because of the weakening of the Church, parochial schools struggled in Czech communities. Non-Catholic Czechs refused to allow their children to attend an educational institution run by priests and nuns. They much preferred public schools.[19] The situation in Prague, Oklahoma, differed little. Czech immigrants founded the Catholic church in Prague. However, they lacked the funds and students to open a thriving primary school. Instead, like their liberal relatives, they sent their children to the local public school and intensified their efforts of inculcating the Roman faith through church activities and Catholic clubs.[20]

The membership of the Czech community's secular associations, the ZCBJ Lodge and Sokol Hall, apparently understood the destructive impact of public education on their ethnic culture. They realized that after they were gone, their descendants might one day furrow their brows in incomprehension when hearing the melodic tones of their ancestor's tongue. Thus, in the early days of Prague, immigrants established a Czech school focused on passing their heritage and especially their beloved native language to their offspring. Unfortunately, the only remaining artifact of Prague's Czech school is an undated photograph with a list of students on the back. The children in the photo appear to range in age from five or six to the early teens. The oldest male student looks about nine or ten, while the eight girls in the back row all appear older.

Comparing the list of student names with cemetery records reveals that birth dates spanned from 1896 to 1902. Furthermore, only one student (Edward Bartosh) is buried in the St. Wenceslaus Catholic Cemetery. The Czech National Cemetery contains the remains of eight of the ten students found in the records.[21] Several of the young scholars identified later attended Prague High School. For example, Frank Kozak is pictured in the Czech school photograph. As noted in the opening anecdote, Kozak played halfback for Prague High School's 1920 football squad.[22] How long the school remained open is not recorded. However, the school shows an early attempt by members of the Czech community to inculcate their children with Czech culture.[23]

A later attempt to preserve the Czech language centered on the Sokol Lodge. The gymnastic society offered language instruction at the Sokol Hall in downtown Prague. Students conjugated Czech verbs, learned the different case endings, and corrected their pronunciation as if studying in a medieval Bohemian monastery overlooking the flowing blue water of the Vltava River rather than a rut-filled dirt street called Highway 62. The Sokol Hall's language classes continued at irregular intervals for many years.[24] As time progressed, parents stumbled in their efforts to convince their children of the importance of learning the language of a land they knew only through stories and faded photographs. However, the language did not entirely die out. Young people enjoyed using Czech words and phrases when telling an off-color joke or insulting someone. The new generation still exuded pride in their heritage. They liked who they were, yet they simply wanted to speak English.[25]

Czech mothers and fathers experienced a wide range of feelings when sending their children to public school. They understood that instruction would be in English. They understood that their sons and daughters would study alongside the offspring of native-born Americans. They realized, surely, that their children would change as a result. Some, no doubt, believed they could lessen the influence of the American school with increased participation in Sokol and Bohemian Hall activities. Others probably recognized the cultural fate of their progeny and sadly accepted it because of their decision to emigrate. Regardless, most Czechs comprehended the importance of an education for their young. As time progressed, more and more began sending their children to public school.

Melva Losch Brown, a 1970s resident of Prague, wrote that the Czech pioneers were well educated.[26] She based her conclusion on interviews with descendants of the original settlers, not on actual data such as certificates, diplomas, or college degrees. The Czech immigrants to Prague, with few exceptions, were farmers.[27] Most originated from small villages in Bohemia and Moravia where toiling in the fields was the future of most young people rather than a college education. This does not mean that Czechs did not value education; they did. Congress's Dillingham Commission found that Czech immigrants compared closely with German immigrants in literacy and fared much better in their ability to read and write than other Slavic groups such as the Poles and Slovaks.[28] However, planting crops, building fences and barns, and establishing a home emerged as their first priority, not schooling for the young and especially not advanced schooling. This mind-set continued even after the creation of Prague and included the U.S.-born and German immigrants. For several years, most students' education in the Barta Post Office area of Lincoln County and the early days of Prague ended with the eighth-grade graduation ceremony.

Although probably not "well educated" as surmised by Brown, the early settlers overwhelmingly arrived literate. The 1900 census for South Creek Township listed only four Czech adults (two men and two women) considered uneducated, with two of the four able to read but not write.[29] Thus only two Czech pioneers could neither read nor write. However, the ability to speak English reveals a somewhat different picture. Almost two dozen Czech adults in 1900 revealed to the census taker that they could not converse in English. This equates to almost a fourth of the total adult Czechs listed in the census. The number unable to speak English rises slightly when children (excluding infants and toddlers two years or younger) are included in the total. Although most children spoke English, the census manuscripts list ten youngsters unable to speak English. However, these ten dependents came from only three families. Furthermore, nine of the ten belonged to two families, the Pechaceks and Placas, containing no naturalized members.

Josef and Matilda Pechacek and their six children emigrated from Bohemia in 1897. They either arrived in New York and took a train to Texas or, what is more likely, landed in Texas, because Matilda gave birth to a seventh child, Vincent, in the Lone Star state in the same year. The family soon migrated to Oklahoma Territory and purchased a farm in the Czech community of South Creek Township.[30] The Pechaceks either arrived in the United States with some money or did quite well on their new farm; by 1900 they owned the property free and clear. Neither Josef nor Matilda could speak English. Their five oldest children, ages fifteen, thirteen, eleven, ten, and seven, attended school for three months during the preceding year. However, all claimed no ability with the new language.[31] How they received instruction without an understanding of English is unclear unless the Pechacek children attended the Czech school. As previously noted, records of the Czech School vanished over time with the only remaining relic being a single undated photograph with an incomplete list of students' names on the back. No Pechacek children are on the list.[32] Of the ten children listed on the 1900 census who could not speak English, five belonged to the Pechacek family. They had been in the United States less than four years.

The Placas, including five sons and a daughter, were born in Bohemia. In 1899, Frances and his wife, Francis, arrived in the United States with their five youngest children. They came to join their oldest son, Josef, who had emigrated two years earlier. Reunited, the Placas quickly made their way to Oklahoma Territory where they rented a farm. The four oldest sons, ages twenty-two, eighteen, sixteen, and fourteen, helped their father and mother work the farm. Only the two youngest children attended school and this for just two months. Of the eight family members, three claimed on the 1900 census an ability to speak English: Frances, Josef, and ten-year-old Jaroslav (Jerry). New to the United States, the Placas became immersed in creating a home and obtaining economic viability. Similar to the early settlers, the Placas worked the land as a unit, with the educational needs of the children considered secondary to the crops. They spoke their native language on the farm and probably encountered the strange-sounding tongue of the majority only on trips to town for groceries and supplies. So adding four Placa children to the list of non-English-speaking children brings the 1900 census total to nine.[33]

The tenth and final Czech youngster listed as not able to speak English was Annie (Anna) Kaiser. Her situation appears completely different from the Pechaceks and Placas. Annie, aged fifteen, was the second oldest of six children born to Jan and Anna Kaiser. Except for her infant sister, Francis, all of Annie's siblings spoke English and had attended school at least three months during the previous year. Annie did neither. Additionally, Annie could not read or write. Her father immigrated to the United States in 1868 at age fifteen or sixteen. Her mother was also born in Bohemia, but the census taker failed to record her arrival date. Annie and all her siblings except the youngest (born in Oklahoma) claimed Wisconsin as their birthplace. Since her brothers and sisters attended school and could read, write, and converse in English, it is safe to assume that Annie Kaiser was mentally challenged. Furthermore, Annie is buried in the Czech National Cemetery alongside her mother and father, and it appears she never married. Thus Annie's situation differed considerably from the Pechacek and Placa youths who were recent arrivals from Europe.

Unfortunately, the 1900 census does not reveal how many children could converse in both English and Czech. The suspicion is that the number would be great. Several families such as the Kolars, Bartoshes, Terflers, Spevaceks, Mertas, Kroutils, Smikas, and Novotnys contained at least one parent unable to speak English, usually the mother. However, in every instance, the children proclaimed an ability to converse in the new tongue. How did these youngsters communicate with their parents? They obviously spoke both Czech and English. What this suggests is that many Czech families continued to speak their native language at home even after most or all members acquired the facility to speak English.

Ten years later, with the town of Prague now in existence, eight adult Czechs declared they could not communicate in the English language. By 1920, the number of non-English speakers in the Czech community fell to three, each of whom was part of the 1910 total. Apparently none of the three ever learned English. They were a married couple aged seventy-two and sixty-eight and a sixty-seven-year-old woman whose husband could speak English.[34]

The 1900 census also tracked school attendance denoting the total number of months youngsters had spent in school during the previous year. Czech girls spent about six months per year in the classroom and Czech boys about half that time. In addition, under the rubric "Trade/ Profession," the census lists most girls' occupation as "At School," while beginning around the age of ten or eleven, Czech boys found themselves quantified as "Farm Laborer." This undoubtedly shows that the first priority for most farmers at this time was not an education for their young but economic survival. This survival depended on the sons helping the fathers in the fields as early in their lives as possible. As illustrated in the 1900 census records, boys attended school when they could, but if work needed to be done on the farm, then their sisters trekked to class without them.

Moreover, this data alludes to the patriarchal undertones of Czech family structure with two distinct possibilities. Czech fathers believed their daughters should not toil in the hot cotton fields alongside their brothers. The school attendance records of girls compared with boys lend credence to this assumption. On many mornings, the girls washed their hands and faces, brushed their hair, slipped on their homemade frocks, and sauntered off to school. At the same time, their brothers, some as young as ten, donned overalls and a floppy hat, slipped a patterned handkerchief into their back pocket, and took their place in the cotton field at their father's side.

However, a second possibility is that in some families, the daughters also provided field labor during planting and harvest. Once the cotton matured, farmers rushed to pick the yield as quickly as possible for fear of a sudden thunderstorm that could flood the fields and ruin the crop. Census data attests that this second scenario is probably true for some Czech families. In a minority of families, the months attending school by gender mirrored the other. For example, despite being recorded as a student, thirteen-year-old Mary Pechacek attended only three months of classes in 1900—the same number of months as her older brother, Joseph, cataloged on the census as a farm laborer. Likewise, in the case of Fannie and Albert Novotny, eighteen-year-old Fannie spent a single month in the classroom as did her younger brother, Albert, whom the 1900 census denoted as a farm laborer. In these families and others, girls carried the title of student, even if they spent relatively little time at the schoolhouse. Perhaps the fathers and American society or at least the census recorder preferred to think of female adolescents as students even if actual conditions confirmed a different conclusion.

Finally, a glimpse of either economic success or the importance of education to individual families can be garnered by examining 1900 census information. For instance, the school-aged children of Josef and Mary Leder, Frank and Fannie Provaznik, and Frank and Terezie Sestak all attended about six months of school in 1900. This included both boys and girls. Thus the economic circumstances of these families were such that they needed less help from their sons or else these particular parents valued education to the extent that they somehow circumvented the much needed and readily available labor supply in order for their children to attend school. The economic situation and ideas about the importance of an education differed from family to family. Some believed in and wanted their children to attend school regularly. However, some of these same parents decided the best chance for the family's economic success depended on their children laboring on the farm rather than sitting in a classroom reading Shakespeare or Hawthorne. Other families probably saw little value in an education beyond basic reading and math skills.

The experiences of school-aged children of non-Czech native-born farmers mirrored the latter Czech scenario. Quite simply, the offspring of some families attended class on a regular basis, while the children in other families went to school less often. However, a sharp difference observable in native-born families is that in almost every case, both sons and daughters attended the same amount of school during the year. If the daughters made it to school, their brothers went with them. This is a marked variance from some other Czech families, in which the brothers occasionally stayed home and worked on the farm while their sisters studied.[35]

Later census manuscripts did not enumerate the number of months children attended school. They simply listed whether or not an individual attended. Thus a detailed comparison between the necessity to stay home and work the farm versus sending the children off to school is difficult. However, some differences protrude from the data. In 1900, two seventeen-year-olds in the Czech farming community attended school. In both 1910 and 1920, only one young person of Czech heritage in Prague aged seventeen or younger did not attend school. The 1910 census taker recorded fourteen-year-old Agnes Martinek as not currently attending classes, and in 1920 the census listed Mary Piter, aged sixteen, as not attending.[36] Why these girls left school is uncertain. Conceivably, a serious illness to either of them or a close loved one forced one or both to forgo their education, at least temporarily. Perhaps the census taker simply made an error. In the case of Agnes Martinek, her seventy-eight-year-old Catholic father, Vincent Martinek, arrived in the United States in 1863 but still declared his language as Bohemian rather than English. Vincent owned his home free and clear and lived, according to the census, on his "own income."[37] Thus he may have placed little faith in the American educational system and may have even envisioned it as a hindrance to his family's religious or ethnic way of life. There is no way of telling for sure. Of course, the primary reason why so few older teens, regardless of ethnicity, attended school in 1900 compared with later years is that the early public schools in the area went only through the eighth grade. Once Prague built a public four-year high school, most town residents took advantage of the opportunity and sent their young to class.

This was not the case among Czech farm families living in the rural environs of South Creek Township in 1920. As mentioned, among Czech youths under age eighteen who resided in the environs of the town, only Mary Piter had not attended any school during the previous twelve months. However, looking at Czech families dwelling on farms in the outlying rural areas of the township shows almost a dozen teenagers under eighteen years of age not in school.[38] Why the discrepancy? Again, each family faced different obstacles, including economic, social, and sometimes physical illness or injury as they endeavored to establish a new home in America. Parents needed teenaged children to help on the farm. Cotton production was labor-intensive, and to a farming family, children truly were a blessing, not an added hardship.

A handwritten list found in the 1904 school notebook of Ellen Whitmore, daughter of the town's first mayor, provides the earliest record of Prague's students. Whitmore, a member of the first eighth-grade graduating class of six students, listed thirty-eight pupils attending the Prague public school, including three Czechs: Mary Sestak, Joe Leder, and Agnes Martinek.[39] The Sestak and Leder families belonged to the Bohemian Hall, while the Martineks attended St. Wenceslaus Catholic Church. The number of Czech students attending public school in 1904 was small. This is doubtless due to the existence of the Czech school. Why these three families opted for their children to attend public school rather than the ethnic school is unclear. Perhaps distance was a factor. Maybe the public school required only a short walk from their homes. Cost may have been an issue. Parents paid no out-of-pocket expenses to send their child to a public primary or secondary school. However, private schools received no taxpayer funds. Thus the expense of the private Czech school may have discouraged some families.[40] Regardless of the reason, the Sestaks, Leders, and Martineks chose the public school over the ethnic school. As the years passed, more and more Czech families chose to send their children to public school.[41]

Czech children rarely posed discipline problems at school, possibly due to their well-ordered home life.[42] Moreover, some did quite well academically. The *Prague Record* lauded Raymond Kolar and Lillian Pastusek as Prague's top seventh-grade students in English.[43] Frank and Eddie Klabzuba graduated from Prague High School and attended Creighton University in Nebraska.[44] Eddie Klabzuba later entered Creighton's dental school and earned his license in 1926. Henryetta Bartosh scored well enough on entrance exams for admittance to nursing school, and Oliva Cerny and May Mee Cerveny studied business in Oklahoma City.[45] George Sadlo, a member of Prague's very first graduating class in 1913, earned a teaching certificate and became a band director. In 1928, his Cleveland High School band won the Oklahoma

Class B State Championship. George and his wife, Emily, later returned to the town of their birth and taught music at Prague until their retirement.[46] In addition to Sadlo, two other Czech students graduated and entered the teaching profession during this period. Marie Vlasak and Clara Cerny taught at Prague's grade school during the 1920s.[47]

Czechs also competed alongside their non-Czech classmates in the sports arena, and a few acquired a reputation as outstanding athletes. The high school started a football program in 1915.[48] In the early years, Frank Kozak, Jim Sala, and Charlie Klabzuba were mainstays of the squad. During their four years on the team, Kozak and the younger Sala manned the backfield as halfbacks for the Red Devils. During the late 1920s, Wesley Kahanek anchored Prague High School's track team with his specialty being the pole vault.[49]

Nature bestowed many talents upon George Sadlo. Besides musical ability, Sadlo excelled at track and other sports. In 1913, Sadlo won the Lincoln County High School pole vault championship.[50] After graduation, he pitched for Prague's town baseball team and traveled to other communities as part of the tennis squad. If Prague fielded an athletic team, Sadlo participated.[51] Unfortunately for Sadlo, an older man from nearby Bellemont completely outshined him. While Sadlo was winning blue ribbons at county track meets, this man was winning gold medals at the Olympics. As Sadlo struck out batter after batter for the Prague Sluggers, this man scored touchdowns for the National Football League's Canton Bulldogs and hit home runs for the New York Giants. Regardless of Sadlo's talent in many sports, the fleet-footed Sac and Fox Indian born only a few miles outside Prague garnered all the attention. George Sadlo demonstrated exceptional athletic ability, and his exploits deserve praise. With little doubt, during the second decade of Prague's existence, Sadlo enjoyed the reputation as the town's best all-around athlete. However, no matter how good he was, he was no Jim Thorpe!

Rural schools dotted the landscape outside of Prague. These small, often one-room buildings attracted the children of farmers living too far from Prague to trek to the larger school. Most German farmers lived north of Prague, and their offspring usually attended either Center Point or Arlington schools. A few Czech farmers, such as Josef Cerny, Ernest Sala, Stanley Sucha, Frank and Lewis Bouda, and Antonia

Dostalik, owned land in the Arlington area and sent their children to school with the German youngsters. Other rural schools near Prague included Red Eagle, Prairie View, and Fairview. Frequently, these small country schools faced financial hardships. They held carnivals and pie sales to raise money for needed supplies and equipment or repairs to the schoolhouse. Another common practice involved teachers, usually single young women, boarding with local farmers. In Arlington, George "Grampa" Sala and his wife opened their home to many dedicated but penniless educators.[52] These schools remained small. In 1947 consolidation began. Prague swallowed several farm schools the very first year, including Fairview, Center Point, Red Eagle, and Bellemont. In 1900 Lincoln County contained 184 schools with most being small. By 2000 the count had dropped to 9.[53]

In education, Catholic and secular liberal Czechs refused to cooperate. Some attempted to operate a Czech school. However, with only one student positively identified as Catholic, it appears that most Catholic Czechs eschewed the ethnic school. When Prague opened a free public school, some leaders in the Czech community, such as Frank Vlasak, heartily endorsed it from the outset. As time went on, more and more Czechs began sending their children to the town's school. Nevertheless, they continued in their attempts to preserve their culture, especially their language, through classes held at the Sokol Hall. In addition, Prague's Czechs rejected a passive approach to their children's education. They encouraged the public school to recognize the special needs of their young, primarily the celebration and preservation of Czech culture. The decentralized structure of these small-town schools left them open to ethnic pressures, and in many cases ethnic groups successfully lobbied for favors they might not obtain in a larger, highly bureaucratized system.[54] For example, the public school in Milligan, Nebraska, where Czechs dominated numerically, offered the Czech language as a course in high school.[55] In Prague, Czechs focused on the arts, specifically music and dance. George and Emily Sadlo taught music to all grades, with George offering violin lessons on the side. The talented George Eret, Prague's first bandmaster, gave lessons to Prague students on various stringed instruments.[56] Prague Public School instructed its students in the Czech *beseda* (circle) dance and formed a *beseda* dance team that traveled in 1932 to teachers' meetings in Tulsa and Oklahoma City to perform their routine in traditional Bohemian dress. The *beseda* dancers included several students from outside the Czech population, such as Albert Brown, Clarence Fennel, Olene Roberts, Kathryn Forth, and Robert Slover.[57] Obviously non-Czech students enjoyed Czech dances, too.

Once Czech families decided to send their children to public school, they attempted to exert some control over the situation through active participation, and this proved especially successful in the arts. Their rural environment and minority demographic circumstances plus the refusal of the secular, Protestant, and Catholic segments to cooperate and form a unified private or parochial school left the public school as the best option for education.

CHAPTER **8**

Politics and Community Life in Prague

Charles Vobornik probably slept little the night of the election. Although backed by the Bohemian Political Association, Vobornik faced a tough competitor for town treasurer in fellow businessman Jacob Mertes. Mertes, a German immigrant, operated a thriving hardware store on the west side of Broadway Avenue not far from Vobornik's meat market at Broadway and Main.[1] The two Czechs already holding office in Prague, Frank Vlasak and Anton Pastusek, supported Vobornik, but as with any office seeker, the candidate felt uneasy. Similar to most residents of Prague, he liked Mertes but still hoped to receive more votes than the affable hardware dealer. Fortunately, neither Vobornik nor Mertes had long to wait. By the following day, it was clear that Vobornik would be Prague's next treasurer. In a landslide victory, the Czech immigrant defeated the German immigrant by 106 votes. Of the eight town officials for the upcoming year, 1907, three would be Czech.[2]

Earlier chapters demonstrate the rapid acculturation and accompanying marital assimilation of Prague's Czechs with the larger society. The frontier beginning, rural characteristics, and demographic situation of the farming town of Prague hastened the conversion of many Czechs, including the first generation, from "outsider" to respected resident. Indeed, with the inception of Prague, the minority-Czech population participated in every facet of the community. Paramount in this transition was the apparent absence of prejudice and discrimination from the very beginning against Czech newcomers by native-born Americans. This chapter reveals a public involvement in the affairs of the town by ethnic Czechs. Czechs were joiners who liked being engaged. This was true regarding their fraternal associations, and their participation overlapped into the community's civic lodges and local politics. Finally, these small-town ethnics assimilated into the larger society much faster than their relatives living in urban areas such as Chicago and Cleveland or those who made their homes in homogeneous rural settlements across the Midwest. From the town's inception in 1902, many Czechs made the decision to accept their new environment and actively take part in it. Furthermore, participation in civic institutions began earlier than the second and third generations; some of the early town leaders such as Frank Vlasak, A. G. Balaun, and Anton Pastusek were immigrants.[3]

With a membership of almost fifty, Prague's Bohemian Political Association promoted the election of good candidates, which normally was translated as good Czech candidates. Chaired by the ubiquitous Frank Vlasak, the organization, formed soon after the creation of Prague, declared no allegiance to a specific political party but instead searched for and backed anyone they believed to be good for the town.[4] Considering the party allegiance of most Czechs in Prague, the evidence is sketchy at best. With the Bohemian Political Association declaring partisan neutrality, one cannot simply state that all or even most Czechs belonged to a specific political party. Perhaps a look at other Czech communities will provide hints as to political affiliation.

A study of Milligan, Nebraska, noted that early-twentieth-century Czechs overwhelmingly voted for Democratic candidates, chiefly because of their loyalty and affection for fellow midwesterner William Jennings Bryan.[5] Due to the historical propensity for newcomers to attach themselves to the party of Thomas Jefferson, it appears likely that a majority of Czechs leaned Democratic, especially those living in urban areas and those arriving after 1880. However, the leading Czech (and freethought) weekly of the Great Plains region, *Pokrok Zapadu* (Progress of the West), consistently backed the Republican Party and must have influenced many citizens unsure about politics.[6] In addition, because the first migration of Czechs arrived in the United States earlier than other Slavs, many before or shortly after the Civil War, the Republican Party's antislavery stance appealed to them. It is most likely that urban Czechs favored the Democrats, while rural Czechs supported the Republicans—at least prior to 1900.[7] Czechs liked the Progressive policies and style of Republicans Robert La Follette and Theodore Roosevelt, but because of World War I and Woodrow Wilson's support for the creation of Czechoslovakia, many switched allegiance to the Democratic Party. Like religion, Czechs were politically divided.[8]

Besides the two major American political parties, socialism also attracted Czechs. Devout freethinkers especially tended to advocate the overthrow of the capitalist system. However, even among freethinkers, socialist ideas remained in the minority.[9] Thus Czechs, like most Americans, supported whichever party they believed best represented their views. Urban residents favored the Democratic Party, while rural folks split their allegiance and bounced back and forth, depending on the candidate and circumstances. Nevertheless, Prague boasted two successful Czech candidates during this period, A. J. Balaun and Jake Zabloudil, both Republicans. Balaun, a member of the local ZCBJ, served for many years as justice of the peace in Prague, holding court for minor offenses and proclaiming the marriage vows for numerous young couples. Zabloudil, originally from Nebraska, worked at the State Bank of Prague until winning election as a Republican to the state legislature in 1915.[10]

Populism, a grassroots movement focusing on the dreary plight of farmers, attracted many Oklahoma farmers and those living in rural towns. This movement, along with the later urban political philosophy Progressivism, exerted a powerful voice in territorial and in state and local politics during the 1890s and the first two decades of the twentieth century. In 1904, the *Prague News* reported that representatives for the People's Party (or Populist Party) were in town holding meetings and campaigning hard for their candidates.[11] Although amazingly silent on the affiliation of most city officers, the newspaper did list A. F. Wood, the town's police judge in 1904 and 1905, as a Progressive.[12]

When comparing the political participation of urban and rural Czech communities, one author wrote that "the rural communities were somewhat retarded, however, when compared with the development of Czech communities in the large cities of America in which its denizens achieved responsible positions in public, professional, and commercial life and in the trades."[13] This thesis does not consider the situation in Prague, which offers another scenario. The Bohemian Political Association came into being soon after the establishment of Prague, and within four years, three of the eight town officers were

Czech.[14] Keep in mind that from the town's birth, Czechs never enjoyed a majority; they constituted about 30 percent of the total population during this period. Thus to have control of almost half of the town's elected positions suggests that non-Czech residents showed no hesitation in voting for someone with a Slavic name. These local political victories also hint that Czechs voted as a bloc. If a Czech ran for office, most in the Czech community probably cast their ballots for him. Prague's Czech population historically stuck together. Regardless of the correct scenario, from the very beginning Czechs actively involved themselves in affairs of the town. They served on the city council and held positions from town treasurer to mayor.[15] However, Czech candidates were not always successful. The popular Frank Vlasak lost his town council seat in 1917 to the local photographer, William Shumate.[16] Nine years later, Jim Farley, a barber, bested his Czech opponent, Joseph J. Klabzuba, in another city council race by twenty-eight votes.[17] So, despite being a powerful voice in the town's political matters, the Bohemian Political Association was not a monolith; it was nowhere close to being a small-town reproduction of a big-city machine.

In addition to politics, Czechs energetically participated in civic lodges. Along with the Bohemian and Sokol Halls, the town of Prague hosted local chapters of the Masons, Knights of Pythias, Woodmen of the World, Odd Fellows, Lions Club, and American Legion.[18] Many Czechs joined these nonethnic organizations, especially the Masons and Knights of Pythias. Over the years, the Prague weeklies splattered Bohemian surnames such as Bontty, Balaun, Svoboda, Jezek, Cerny, Leder, Vlasak, and Sojka when listing the officers of these lodges.[19] In April 1927, Prague business leaders established a Chamber of Commerce to encourage and assist economic concerns. The group held their early meetings at Sokol Hall with Charles Klabzuba, proprietor of the Reliable Chevrolet dealership, serving as secretary-treasurer.[20] Other Czech businessmen in the Chamber of Commerce included John Stoklasa, co-owner with his brother of the Boston Store, one of Prague's busiest general stores. Stoklasa served on the Business and Trade Committee, while another retailer, Joseph J. Klabzuba, worked with the Roads and Highway Improvement Committee, lobbying both county and state governments for better transportation infrastructure.[21] Prague's Chamber of Commerce also listed Frank Svoboda, Steve Kanak, Charles Babek, and Joe Stoklasa as members during the 1920s.[22]

The Ku Klux Klan, a not-so-civic lodge, held meetings somewhere around Prague in the early 1920s. The reemergence of the Reconstruction era terrorist group swept into Oklahoma after World War I. Fueled by fears of communism and radicalism, many white rural residents panicked at the influx of Catholic and Jewish immigrants from what they saw as the backward parts of Europe. In addition, whites became alarmed at the perceived black defiance to the social order as witnessed in the Tulsa Race Riot of 1921. The earliest mention of the white supremacy group's activities in the area occurred on June 8, 1922, in the *Prague Record*. In a short article, the paper described how two Klansmen in full regalia visited a local Methodist church at the end of the service and handed the preacher a note and $38.50. The following week Prague's paper included a rumor "that an order of the Ku Klux Klan was organized last week."[23] Every edition of the *Record* during July and August 1922 contained at least one article covering the activities or beliefs of the organization. The Klan again visited a church in September. Several Klansmen dressed in fluid white robes and slitted hoods interrupted the Rev. William McElvany of the Methodist church during a revival meeting. The group marched down the narrow aisle of the small auditorium and ceremoniously offered the minister an undisclosed amount of money, which he accepted. The Klansmen then promptly left. This story in no way should be viewed as disparaging of the Methodist cleric. A minister accepting a donation from hooded armed men does not equate with agreeing with them. We do not know McElvany's racial beliefs. In addition, if the evangelist refused the proffered money, he risked open confrontation or the chance that the unknown men might drag him from his bed one night and whip him in front of his neighbors and family. Few whites brazenly defied the Klan. Reverend McElvany appears no different.[24]

Did Czechs join the Ku Klux Klan? One would hardly think so. The Klan despised immigrants, specifically those from southern and eastern Europe. For a Czech immigrant or even second-generation ethnic to enlist in a group that detested their very origin seems foolish. The proposition is absurd at its very core. Apparently, interest in the secret organization quickly withered because Prague's newspaper reported no more episodes of Klan activity after the fall of 1922. Whether for lack of support or the community's strict observance of Oklahoma's Jim Crow laws, activities of the hooded band either dissipated or went unmentioned. Finally, absolutely no Klan violence against anyone in the Czech community surfaced in the pages of Prague's newspaper. No immigrants suffered lynching, beatings, or any other degradation at the hands of the most prominent homegrown terrorist organization in the United States.

Turning to something less violent, Czechs loved music. Historically, "Czech" and "musician" were almost synonyms. Czechs prided themselves on their prowess with musical instruments, and the old Bohemian saying, "*co cech, to muzikant*" (if a Czech, then a musician) contained much truth. Of course, during the first decades of the twentieth century, television had not yet been invented, and radio did not air until the 1920s and even then only in metropolitan areas for a few hours each day. Residents of small towns relied on silent motion pictures (until 1927 and the advent of "talkies") and traveling troupes offering plays, burlesque, and vaudeville. Most entertainment in rural communities originated locally. School plays, concerts, and sports attracted large audiences. Traveling Methodist, Baptist, and Presbyterian evangelists erected huge tents and held emotion-packed services nightly for two or three weeks to overflowing crowds before moving to the next town.[25] Rural as well as town folk attended the worship meetings, enjoying the foot-tapping music as much as the fire-and-brimstone sermons. Revivals, although not overtly meant to be, took on an air of entertainment featuring local musicians and singing groups. Czechs attended these open-air services. Czech groups like the Makovsky Band played and sang sacred songs prior to the itinerant preacher expounding upon the genetic legacy of original sin or denouncing rebellious transgressions like gambling, alcohol abuse, and lust.[26] These religious meetings were as much social gatherings as attempts to produce another Great Awakening.

Besides sacred music, Czechs enjoyed playing and singing secular tunes. An early researcher visited several Czech homes in Oklahoma City in 1933 and 1934 and found musical instruments in practically every home and the residents willing to show off their talent on the violin, piano, or horn.[27] Prague's Czechs probably differed little from their western neighbors. Shortly after incorporation, Prague formed a town band. George Eret, a Czech, accepted the position as band-leader, and for the next thirty years members of the Czech community actively and no doubt energetically played at town events like Independence Day, Decoration Day, and the Washington and Lincoln birthday celebrations.[28]

In 1929, residents organized a Municipal Band and again chose a Czech as its leader. Julius Bontty met with band members every Tuesday and Thursday evening at the Sokol Hall for practice. The twenty-member ensemble included both Czechs and non-Czechs and, like the earlier town band, entertained Prague's residents at most community events.[29]

Music was a luxury in the small frontier town; however, public safety concerned everyone. An out-of-control fire could quickly devastate the brick and wood buildings that lined Main Street. In the early days of Prague, anyone physically able helped to put out fires. During scorching, dry summer months, fires could quickly spread out of control, so anyone in close proximity to the blaze lent their brawn. Real horsepower provided the impetus for the fire trucks, while the pumps and hoses relied on human muscle. When a fire broke out, anybody in the vicinity rushed to the scene and assisted in the hot and smudgy effort. By the 1920s, however, the town of Prague owned a motorized fire truck with a gasoline-powered pump. Similar to practically every community organization or activity, Czechs eagerly became involved. At least two Czechs served on the fire department with Charles Babek holding the position of assistant fire chief during the 1920s.[30]

There were no Andrew Carnegies or John Rockefellers or Cornelius Vanderbilts in Oklahoma, so the small farming town did not contain the wealth of a big city. Primary industries revolved around the production of cotton. The only manufacturing ventures attempted proved a short-lived effort by a blind Czech immigrant, Frank Mastena, who produced and sold brooms, and the Oklahoma Cigar Manufacturing Company, managed by another Czech, J. Hajek. The cigar factory employed between ten and fifteen people.[31] Possibly

the most successful business enterprise, one neither owned nor operated by Czechs, was the Union Cotton Oil Company. It attracted inves-
tors from as far away as Chicago. George Jepsen managed and owned
a share of the operation with additional financial backing provided
by Bertha Ambrister, a wealthy widow, and several out-of-town inves-
tors, including one from Chicago. However, when the price of cotton dropped after World War I and a boll weevil epidemic in the late
1920s bankrupted many farmers, the profits from the cotton oil mill
dropped precipitously.[32]

From Prague's founding, Czechs participated in every facet of its
development. From establishing businesses to serving on the school
board to holding public office, Czechs were an integral part of the community. Furthermore, with time and new generations, their degree of
contribution suffered no decline. In its 1920s promotional booklet *City
of Opportunities*, Prague published photographs of homes of its leading
citizens and short biographies of successful merchants and the principal educational and civic officials. Sandwiched between photographs
of impressive rock, brick, or painted frame dwellings owned by families with names like Long, Wilson, Whitmore, and Duncan are pictures
of spacious and well-kept Czech residences owned by the Klabzubas,
Bonttys, Kanaks, and Kolars. Also pictured was the Barta Hotel. The
last few pages of the booklet contained snapshots and biographies of
almost fifty religious, business, and civic leaders, including ten Czechs.[33]

Czechs showed no hesitation in joining community affairs.
Members of the immigrant community occupied civic and political
positions in the town ranging from municipal bandleader to assistant
fire chief to state representative. However, to gain a better understanding of Prague's Czechs, the situation of Czech populations in other
regions of the United States needs exploration. An examination of civic
participation of immigrants living in urban areas and rural communities like Milligan, Nebraska, whose population consisted overwhelmingly of Czechs, should provide a reliable assessment of what was
going on in Prague.

In urban areas, immigrants arriving shortly before or after the turn
of the twentieth century lived in the least expensive housing, usually
close to their place of employment. Often immigrants from the same

geographic region or village clustered together in ethnic neighborhoods and formed tight-knit communities that might constitute a city block or only a high-rise tenement. However, rarely did a single ethnic group reside exclusively in a single neighborhood. They usually shared their neighborhood with at least one other ethnic group but normally did not socialize with them. For example, "On New York's Lower East Side, Jews and Italians shared the neighborhood, but each group held domain over particular blocks. Thus, different groups could live in close geographical proximity and yet be socially isolated."[34] Czechs living in New York, Cleveland, Chicago, or other urban centers realized the same fate. Most worked long hours doing factory work or some other menial job and spent much of their downtime in the local saloon, Bohemian Hall, or if still loyal to their faith, in a church pew. In only a few exceptions did they pursue political careers or gain notoriety as city leaders.

Furthermore, even if they pursued a greater role in their city, anti-immigrant feelings of the native-born majority or negative reactions of an already entrenched group like the Irish rebuffed their efforts. Urban Czechs, like most "new immigrants," suffered from a lack of acceptance by the majority population. Most of these immigrants retreated to the security of their homes, lodges, or local saloon after a hard day in the factory. Many, long after their arrival, remained psychologically isolated to the point of loneliness.[35] They were in the United States but not truly a part of it. It fell to their children and grandchildren to incorporate fully the values, culture, and economic mindset of the new land.

A relatively homogeneous rural village like Milligan, Nebraska, offers yet another look at a Czech community. Established in early 1888, the village of Milligan, much like Prague, benefited economically from the construction of a railroad. However, from the beginning, Czech settlers numerically dominated the small town almost to the point of it being entirely Czech. In 1900, of 83 families living in the proximity of Milligan, 69 were Czech. By 1930, the community consisted of more than 200 households with a total population of 681. Of these, 313 of the residents were Czech immigrants, and another 290 were the immigrants' sons and daughters. Robert Kutak found only

53 people living in Milligan in 1930 who claimed no Czech blood, with another 16 stating that one of their parents was Bohemian. During this period, all village officials were Czech.[36] What did this mean for the isolated farming village? How did it differ from the situation in Prague?

Milligan Czechs controlled every facet of their environment. From the economic structure, to the social scene, to who ran the town, their voices and decisions dominated. Unlike the Czechs of Prague, who, from the very outset, found themselves at a numerical disadvantage, these Czechs living in Nebraska were in almost total control of their community. This proved especially true regarding language. If an individual chose never to learn English, he or she could shop, run a business, or attend church without fear of ridicule or feeling like an outsider. Although many younger people in Milligan knew English, Czech remained the primary spoken language in the home as late as 1930.[37] Even so, the community was not an unadulterated ethnic oasis in the midst of the Great Plains. American culture crept inexorably into the hearts of the young. On a regular basis, Czech boys congregated at a local field and played the American game of baseball, conversing and teasing each other in both English and their parents' tongue.[38] Attending a town dance revealed the girls in homemade patterned dresses but wearing their hair in the popular bobbed style of Hollywood starlets. Few young men wore jackets while dancing, preferring long-sleeved shirts rolled up to around the elbow. The local band interspersed fast-paced American music with traditional Czech tunes, and if anyone needed refreshments, there were hot dogs and soda.[39] This Saturday night dance probably mirrored thousands more across the United States during the 1920s regardless of race or ethnicity.

Nonetheless, the penetration of American ways into this isolated community advanced more slowly than in demographically diversified areas and primarily took hold with the young. During this time, the typical Milligan family still enjoyed roast pork, sauerkraut, and potato dumplings followed by a slice of *kolach* and coffee as their favorite meal.[40] Due to their isolation and dominance, the Milligan Czechs were rather clannish, not prone to intermarriage, and proud of their Central Hall, which alternated as a saloon and meeting place for several lodges. Prominently displayed on opposite walls of the Main Street structure hung portraits of the martyr Jan Hus and Thomas Masaryk, the Czech nationalist and first president of Czechoslovakia.[41] Unlike their counterparts in Oklahoma, the Milligan Czechs did not immediately feel pressure to adjust to everything new. Because of their majority status, they could survive economically and socially without a whirlwind tutorial in American customs and language.

Another Czech cultural island was Snook, Texas. Named Snook in 1895 after the surname of the Anglo-American postmaster, the farming village consisted almost exclusively of Moravian Czechs. Like the Milligan Czechs, these Texas Moravians felt no anxiety to conform to the dominant culture of America. In fact, the Snook Czechs seemed to believe themselves not only different but superior to their Anglo neighbors. A common phrase in the community was "We're Czechs; they're Americans." Mothers and fathers inculcated this expression into their young, which clearly implied that it was a privilege to be Czech and that they were better than the Americans with whom they associated.[42] These Texas Czechs simply believed they worked harder and did things better than their Anglo neighbors. Their Moravian origin also held great pride for the immigrants. For whatever reason, many Anglo-Americans referred to anyone from the Czech lands as Bohemians, even if they were from Moravia and not Bohemia. Most Texas Moravians resented this misnomer, preferring Moravian or simply Czech. In Snook, the newcomers held almost all the political offices, owned the largest stores in the town, and established a thriving Czech school teaching all subjects in their native language. They called it Moravia School. Like the Czechs of Milligan, Nebraska, these Texas Moravians assimilated more slowly than their ethnic counterparts in urban areas or farming towns like Prague, Oklahoma, who were inundated from the beginning with the dominant Anglo culture and language. Robert Skrabanak, who grew up in Snook, Texas, found that upon revisiting his hometown decades after he had left, the Czech cultural heritage still remained. He even heard a few conversations in Czech among townspeople.[43]

In the realm of civic participation and demography, the experience of Prague's Czechs differed from urban and ethnically homogeneous rural communities like Milligan and Snook. The farm town ethnic group faced much less discrimination than its city counterparts when aspiring to hold public office or participate in community affairs. From the beginning, the dominant, native-born Anglo residents accepted their Slavic neighbors. The community voted Czechs to leadership roles in the town government and saw no disgrace in playing instruments under the guidance of a Czech conductor. Some, perhaps with a quick wink of the eye, even performed the secret handshake of the Masons with their Czech fraternal brothers. Equally important to this lack of prejudice by the majority population was the decision by many Czechs to participate in community affairs. This decision was an individual's choice, not a group pronouncement, after a close or lopsided vote in the Bohemian Hall. A few Czechs probably hesitated or outright rejected joining the social life of Prague. They retreated to their homes, and little is known about their lives for that very reason. Some of them perhaps left the small town in search of a less-threatening environment similar to that in Milligan or Snook. Most of them probably just refrained from participating in any activity they did not understand or anticipated might make them look like a greenhorn.[44]

This early acceptance of the American culture and economic system implies a pragmatic decision to survive in their new surroundings. To succeed in a farming town that contained very little industry, one needed to adjust to the ways of the majority. This would be especially true for a member of an immigrant group. The fact that Czechs constituted a noteworthy portion of the town from its very creation helped. Indeed, the very name of the new settlement signified their presence. The existence of a small black community within the town, a less desirable racial group than the European immigrants, meant that Czechs did not occupy the lowest rung of the social ladder, which surely diminished any prejudice that might have been aimed at them. However, the rapidity and apparent entrance into Prague's general community of many within the ethnic group, including immigrants, suggests more than a hardheaded assessment of the circumstances. It suggests a fundamental change, a structural assimilation into their new environment. Individual ethnics, including several pioneer immigrants, voluntarily transformed their lifestyles to fit in. The Prague Czechs joined the new milieu, and they did so more quickly than most of their ethnic kin living in urban or homogeneous rural settings.

This does not mean they gave up their identity as Czechs and tromped into the haziness of American whiteness. They did not awaken one morning and see the visage of a Yankee staring back at them in the mirror. Despite attending public school and playing on the varsity football squad or performing in the municipal band or even serving the public as a respected member of the town council, these Czech immigrants did not exile themselves from their heritage. They held firm to their birthright and desperately tried to pass it to their progeny. They were Czech Americans in the truest sense—Czech in their ethnicity but American in their loyalty and outlook. The immigrant pioneers no doubt exhibited much more "Czechness" than their offspring. After all, Bohemia or Moravia was their birthplace and their cherished home. It was the second generation, those born in the United States, who maneuvered more easily in American culture. The young played the same sports as their non-Czech friends, listened to the same music, and equally enjoyed watching Clara Bow, John Barrymore, and Mary Pickford on the silver screen. A number of them even fell in love and married someone outside the group. By the third generation, most of Prague's Czechs were probably indistinguishable in their speech, mannerisms, and dress from their friends named Baker or O'Malley. However, like their fathers, mothers, and grandparents before them, they too joined the Bohemian Hall or participated in Sokol events and valiantly tried to repeat the tricky sounds of the Czech language when their elders spoke to them. By 1930, many of the original Czech settlers were gone. A few had moved away, but most had died. Their decision not to isolate themselves into an ethnic enclave but to participate fully in the larger community resulted in a legacy of rapid acculturation and assimilation to the brink of absorption—but not quite. Although outwardly they appeared as American as anyone born and raised in the United States, inwardly the Prague Czechs remained Czech. They retained their internal distinctiveness; they maintained their ethnic identity.

Even before the establishment of Prague, Frank Vlasak enjoyed a position of respect among Czech farmers. Known as "Squire," Vlasak operated a store in Dent, a small town north of Prague, and aided his fellow immigrants through personal loans. From 1891 to 1902, Vlasak reinvested his earnings in acreage and, by the formation of Prague, was one of the larger landholders in the community.[45] Vlasak quickly realized that a better economic future lay in the new town, and he relocated to Prague, opening a feed store. Despite his immigrant status, Vlasak's prescient decision not to shy away from involvement in the farm town resulted in success. The Czech entrepreneur bought some prime downtown property and built a two-story structure, the Vlasak Building on Broadway Avenue, selling groceries, dry goods, and general merchandise. Vlasak operated his retail business on the first floor and rented out the second floor rooms to temporary and long-term tenants.[46] He remained in business until his accidental death in the fall of 1929 at the age of seventy. Apparently the widower lit a faulty heater in his home and died of asphyxiation.[47] He went to sleep and never woke up. With Frank Vlasak's death and the death of Josephine Barta a year later, the two people most responsible for the appellation of the new town being Prague were gone.

Prague, Oklahoma, from its beginning was a demographically diverse farming community on the southeastern edge of the Great Plains region. Named after the capital of faraway Bohemia, the town affords a different perspective on assimilation and ethnicity than that found in populous urban areas and relatively homogeneous rural ethnic enclaves.

In an earlier study of the Czechs in Oklahoma, Karel Bicha summed up the ethnic group's experience when he wrote, "Their lives were simple. They farmed. These two words provide both a memoir and an epitaph for the first generation of Czech Oklahomans and a large majority of their descendants."[48] As a general statement referring to all Czechs in Oklahoma, this may well hold much truth. However, for the Czechs of Prague, I believe we can agree that they did much more than just farm.

Epilogue

THE DISAPPEARING SUN GLISTENED off the perspiring dancers as they bopped and swayed to the music of the band. The crowd of several thousand filling the main thoroughfare of the town gyrated to the rollicking tunes. A young blond woman, dressed in a blue skirt and a white, frilly peasant's blouse, danced with her boyfriend on the edge of the street while checking her hair to make sure her crown was still there. Only two hours earlier, judges had declared her the 2016 queen of the Kolache Festival, the annual birthday celebration and Czech commemoration of Prague, Oklahoma. The band, Czech & Then Some from Ennis, Texas, performed traditional Czech melodies and modern pop classics.

The yearly festival was the idea of Fr. George V. Johnson, the priest at St. Wenceslaus Church. Local organizations, including the Bohemian Hall, planned the first gala in 1951. The initial event served as a dress rehearsal for an even bigger celebration the following year, the fiftieth anniversary of the founding of Prague. The festivities began at 9:00 A.M. with a flag raising followed by the singing of both the American and Czech national anthems. A parade complete with bands, floats, and dignitaries strutted down Jim Thorpe Boulevard, Prague's main thoroughfare, while hundreds of onlookers cheered them on.

Celebrants then moved to the Prague City Park, where dozens of vendors sold quilts, wooden birdhouses, paintings from aspiring artists, and other homemade crafts. Concessionaires offered hotdogs, cheeseburgers, fries, and soda pop. But if visitors wanted a more authentic experience, they could buy *kolache*, the sweet pastry that gave the festival its name, or *knedliky* (dumplings), or even *brambory salat* (potato salad). Of course, they needed to wash it down with a *lemonada* (soft drink). Guests then proceeded with their food and drink to the nearby grandstand and watched a group of authentically clad dancers perform

Figure 13. Kolache Festival, May 2016.

the *beseda*, the traditional Czech circle dance. The Kolache Festival, held the first Saturday of May, attracts up to fifteen thousand visitors.[1]

The highlight is always the coronation of the queen. In actuality, there are three levels of royalty: a princess, junior queen, and queen. The princess is aged eight to ten, the junior queen is under sixteen, and the queen must be at least sixteen. Originally, all contestants had to be full-blooded Czech. Now a girl is eligible as long as one of her ancestors came from Bohemia or Moravia. The competition for all three awards is fierce. The contestants must wear traditional Czech dress, speak some Czech to the judges, exhibit a skill, and undergo questioning in front of the audience. The head judge crowns the girls at 6:00 PM on Saturday night right before the festival finale, the all-town street dance.[2]

Although the Kolache Festival is a city event, many Bohemian Hall members volunteer. Today's Bohemian Hall has more than three hundred members. The ethnic association still offers life insurance to its members and continues to rent the 1918 building for weddings, family get-togethers, Christmas parties, and Halloween spook nights. In order to attract higher numbers, the Czech members voted several years ago to open their membership rolls to anyone with an interest in the organization. Thus many current supporters have no Czech background. Saying this, all the officers trace their ancestry to the Czech beginnings of Prague. With Bohemian names like Sestak, Jezek, Kozel, and Fredrich, the officers of the Western Czech Brotherhood continue to honor the memory of their forebears and proudly assert their ethnic identity.[3]

However, the Bohemian Hall, like many historical organizations, suffers from a lack of funds and committed supporters. Few participants take an active role in the maintenance and beautification of the elderly structure. In the 1950s, the Bohemian Hall members installed a drop-down ceiling in the grand room, probably to save on heating costs. Recently this false ceiling collapsed. Few members volunteered to help clean up the mess, despite numerous calls for assistance. The ceiling is not the only problem with the Czech meeting place. As with any older building, the edifice needs constant care and preservation repairs. Amazingly, the collapsed ceiling may be a blessing in disguise. The original high ceiling is beautiful. Although the century-old hardwood floor needs some love and care, the finished creation would make the Grand Hall an attractive choice for weddings, parties, and dances. Nevertheless, the estimate is around $100,000 to restore the once magnificent Bohemian Hall.

Jarrod Sestak is leading a group of young Czechs to save the Bohemian Hall and continue the legacy of the Western Czech Brotherhood. Sestak and several young men and women have joined the effort to preserve and beautify the ethnic home of their ancestors. From fund-raising to clean-up detail, these young people have set aside time from their schoolwork and sports to pitch in at Bohemian Hall. It is to be hoped that the members, including this youthful cohort, will be able to find funding to complete the enormous task of renovating the structure of the original Prague Czechs.

Although many Czech descendants remained in the environs of Prague their entire lives, others sought their future outside the county of their birth. Jeff Ladra, a fourth-generation Czech descended from immigrant farmers Vaclav and Marie Ladra, now lives in San Francisco. His family's trek to the golden state apparently began during the 1930s when Vaclav's son, George, relocated to Maricopa, Arizona. Hundreds of Oklahoma families left the Sooner State during the Depression in search of employment. When the Ladras moved to California is unclear. However, George's son, Gavin (known as Dee J), died in California in 2014. Jeff Ladra, George's son, serves as CEO of Pladra, a San Francisco clothing company specializing in premium outdoor shirts.[4]

Edward Sefcik, the grandson of Czech farmers Jan and Rosa Sefcik, found his calling in the U.S. military. Sefcik attended Kansas State University prior to World War II on an ROTC scholarship. He graduated Phi Beta Kappa and earned a commission as an officer in the army. When America entered the war in 1942, Sefcik served as an infantry captain and suffered permanent injuries. After the war, he became active in the Veterans of Foreign Wars, American Legion, and the Disabled Officers Association. He died in 1976 at the age of fifty-seven in Kansas.[5]

Another Czech descendant who made the military his career was Jack Barta. Jack, the grandson of Josephine Barta, who gave Prague its name, was born in Wynona, Oklahoma, in 1922. His father, John, left Prague and first settled in Henryetta, Oklahoma, before moving to the small town in Osage County, northwest of Tulsa. Jack Barta graduated from the University of Tulsa in 1949 and later earned a master's degree during his career in the military. He married Jane Love of Tulsa, and together they raised three daughters. Jack Barta retired from the Air Force in 1975 with the rank of colonel and spent the rest of his life in Edmond, Oklahoma, actively working in his Bible church and traveling with his family throughout the United States. The retired colonel, whose grandparents were so instrumental to the formation of Prague, passed away on February 11, 2015.[6]

Oklahoma's first modern artist was a Prague Czech. Olinka Hrdy, the celebrated Oklahoma muralist, was the daughter of Josef Hrdy, who owned and operated one of the early saloons during Prague's "Wild West" days. However, Olinka's parents divorced in 1910. The girl lived with her mother, Emma Benes Hrdy, and her three siblings on land leased from the Seminole tribe. Her mother worked as a housekeeper, and work consumed most of the young girl's childhood. Nevertheless, Olinka loved to draw, and her artistic talent impressed her high school teachers. After graduating at the age of sixteen, she entered the University of Oklahoma in Norman to improve her skills as an artist. Needing money for tuition, she began painting pictures and murals for whoever would buy them. The university almost expelled her for painting nude figures on her dorm room wall. Keep in mind, it was 1920!

Hrdy continued painting murals after graduation. Unfortunately for us, only three of her murals still exist. The Oklahoma City University School of Law contains two of them, and the Will Rogers Middle School in Long Beach, California, has the third. She completed her California mural in 1939 as part of the Federal Art Project, one of President Franklin D. Roosevelt's New Deal programs. Olinka Hrdy, the gifted daughter of a saloon owner and a hardworking mother, died in 1987, but her life's work continues to amaze.[7]

One of the stalwarts of the Western Czech Brotherhood was Cyril (C. M.) Sadlo. He owned a prosperous tailor shop in Prague and participated in the ethnic association until his death in 1951. He and his wife, Emma, raised one of the amazing residents of early Prague: their son, George. George Sadlo was the star pitcher of the town's semi-professional baseball club, a member of Prague's tennis team, and a violinist. Historically Czechs have loved music, and the tailor's son proved no exception. He taught the intricacies of the violin to the children of Prague while only a teenager himself, and in 1917 he enlisted in the army and served his country during World War I. After the war, Sadlo married a second-generation Swedish immigrant, Ruth Gummerson, who shared her husband's love of music. The couple began a career in music education, taking the high school bands of Cleveland and Ponca City, Oklahoma, to new heights. Seeking new challenges, George and Ruth accepted jobs in Illinois, where George became the music supervisor of the Dundee public schools.

Along the way, the couple had a daughter, Kathryn Ruth. It was almost inevitable that their only child would also fall in love with music. Saving every penny they could, they sent their daughter to the University of Oklahoma, where she earned both bachelor's and master's degrees in music. Kathryn Sadlo then moved to Chicago and studied at Northwestern University and the prestigious American Conservatory of Music. The third-generation Czech from Prague, Oklahoma, became a concert singer and appeared with symphony orchestras around the country, including the American Opera Company. While preparing to relocate to New York City, with a concert tour of Italy scheduled, she met Walter W. Wilson. The two fell madly in love, and Kathryn decided to stay in Chicago. She canceled her European tour and said yes to Wilson's proposal. However, she refused to give up music, and she opened a dance studio in the Chicago area and performed in numerous musicals during the next fifty years. For whatever reason, she and her husband never had children, so the Sadlos' contribution to American music died with her in 2008. Nevertheless, the son and granddaughter of the immigrant tailor of Prague, Oklahoma, left an indelible mark on the future generations who learned at their feet.[8]

After more than a hundred years, the Prague Czechs continue to proclaim their ethnic identity. Although completely Americanized, the descendants of the original immigrant settlers still join the Bohemian Hall and reap the benefits of its insurance programs. Many prefer burial in the Czech National Cemetery rather than in the public cemetery, regardless of their religious beliefs. In fact, the history of Bohemian Hall being a bastion of freethought is all but lost.[9] Except for some of their last names, Prague Czechs today are indistinguishable from any other resident of the small farming community in central Oklahoma. They are American through and through, from their language to their hairstyles to their tastes in music. Nevertheless, they continue to hold dear to something the original Czech immigrants of Prague would completely understand—they proudly identify themselves as not only American but Czech American.

Notes

Introduction

1. William Ray Tower, "A General History of the Town of Prague, Oklahoma, 1902–1948" (MA thesis, Oklahoma Agricultural and Mechanical College, Stillwater, 1948), 9–10. See also Lincoln County Historical Society, *Lincoln County: Oklahoma History* (Saline, MI: McNaughton & Gunn, 1988), 186. Lee Watts was the farmer who turned down the railroad's offer.

2. Russell Willford Lynch, "Czech Farmers in Oklahoma: A Comparative Study of the Stability of a Czech Farm Group in Lincoln County, Oklahoma, and the Factors Relating to Its Stability," *Bulletin of Oklahoma Agricultural and Mechanical College* 39, no. 13 (June 1942): 44. For additional details, see Melva Losch Brown, *Czech-Town, U.S.A., Prague (Kolache-Ville), Oklahoma* (Norman: Hooper Printing, 1978), 32.

3. *Prague News*, 24 July 1902 and 17 December 1915.

4. See Robert A. Kann, *A History of the Habsburg Empire, 1526–1918* (Berkeley: University of California Press, 1974), 533–34.

5. There are conflicting stories of the origin of pilsner. The most accepted is that the inhabitants of Pilsen (Plzen) in 1838 hired Josef Groll, a Bavarian brewer, to instruct them in the German lagering method of brewing. He included Saaz hops in the recipe, resulting in the famous pilsner draft.

6. See Kann, *A History of the Habsburg Empire*, 533–34. German-speaking lands bordered Bohemia to the north, west, and south.

7. Czechs speak an Indo-European language related to Polish, Slovak, Russian, Ukrainian, Bulgarian, and several other southern and eastern European languages. The family of languages is known as Slavic.

8. Lynch, "Czech Farmers in Oklahoma," 89.

9. This internal sense of distinctiveness is one of the defining characteristics of ethnicity. See Stephan Thernstrom et al., eds., *Harvard Encyclopedia of Ethnic Groups* (Cambridge, MA: Belknap Press of Harvard University Press, 1980), vi.

10. Herbert J. Gans, "Symbolic Ethnicity: The Future of Ethnic Groups and Cultures in America," *Ethnic and Racial Studies* 2, no. 1 (January 1979): 9.

Chapter 1

1. Paraphrased and expanded from a story found in Emily Balch, *Our Slavic Fellow Citizens* (New York: Charities Publication Committee, 1910), 58–59.

2. Victor R. Greene, "Ethnic Confrontations with State Universities, 1860–1920," in *American Education and the European Immigrant: 1840–1940*, ed. Bernard J. Weiss (Urbana: University of Illinois Press, 1982), 153; Weiss, introduction to *American Education*, xviii.

3. Paul H. Elovitz, "Patterns and Costs of Immigration," in *Immigrant Experiences: Personal Narrative and Psychological Analysis*, ed. Paul H. Elovitz and Charlotte Kahn (Madison, NJ: Fairleigh Dickinson University Press, 1997), 14; Nobuko Yoshizawa Meaders, "The Transcultural Self," in ibid., 49.

4. The Slovaks are an example of this phenomenon. From 1908 to 1910, of the 71,172 Slovaks who entered the United States, 41,726 (59%) returned home. For an in-depth discussion, see Joseph Stasko, *Slovaks in the United States of America* (Cambridge, ON: Dobrá Kniha, 1974), 48.

5. For a brief discussion of early writing about immigrants, see John Bodnar, *The Transplanted: A History of Immigrants in Urban America* (Bloomington: Indiana University Press, 1985), 2.

6. U.S. Immigration Commission, *Reports of the Immigration Commission*, 42 vols. (Washington, DC: Government Printing Office, 1911), 12:385.

7. Bernard Bailyn, *The Peopling of British North America: An Introduction* (New York: Alfred A. Knopf, 1986), 29. For a further discussion, see Bodnar, *The Transplanted*, 3.

8. Thomas Capek, *The Czechs (Bohemians) in America: A Study of Their National, Cultural, Political, Social, Economic, and Religious Life* (1920; repr., New York: Arno Press, 1969), 9. Also see Jan Habenicht, *A History of Czechs in America* (St. Louis: Hlas, 1910), 11. Chroniclers spell the name Herman, Herrman, Harman, Heerman, and Hermans.

9. Habenicht, *History of Czechs in America*, 12–14.

10. Karen Johnson Freeze, "Czechs," in *Harvard Encyclopedia of American Ethnic Groups*, ed. Thernstrom et al., 262.

11. An exception to this would be a small group of Moravian Protestant missionaries who immigrated to Georgia for evangelistic reasons. See Capek, *Czechs in America*, 23.

12. U.S. Immigration Commission, *Reports*, 12:366; Karel Bicha, *The Czechs in Oklahoma* (Norman: University of Oklahoma Press, 1980), 7, 10.

13. A cottager usually owned between five and twenty-five acres and existed primarily as a subsistence farmer. See Lynch, "Czech Farmers in Oklahoma," 89.

14. Bodnar, *The Transplanted*, 55–56; Balch, *Our Slavic Fellow Citizens*, 75. Many of the mid-nineteenth-century Bohemian immigrants came from the areas of Plzen, Budweis, Tabor, Pisek, Kuttenberg, and Caslau.

15. U.S. Immigration Commission, *Reports*, 12:361.

16. Bodnar, *The Transplanted*, 34, 37; Richard A. Easterlin, "Immigration: Economic and Social Characteristics," in *Harvard Encyclopedia of American Ethnic Groups*, ed. Thernstrom et al., 484.

17. Robert Kutak, *The Story of a Bohemian-American Village: A Study of Social Persistence and Change* (1933; repr., New York: Arno Press and the New York Times, 1970), 11. The other reasons given for coming to America were political (3), religious (2), to escape military service (5), and to join relatives or friends already in the United States (15).

18. Freeze, "Czechs," 261.

19. Rose Rosicky, *A History of Czechs (Bohemians) in Nebraska* (Omaha: Czech Historical Society of Nebraska, 1929), 26. Also see Capek, *Czechs in America*, 36–48.

20. Lynch, "Czech Farmers in Oklahoma," 89, 105.

21. Capek, *Czechs in America*, 36–47.

22. Freeze, "Czechs," 262.

23. Henry W. Casper, *History of the Catholic Church in Nebraska* (Milwaukee: Bruce, 1966), vol. 4, *Catholic Chapters in Nebraska Immigration: 1870–1900*, 101. For a further discussion, see Capek, *Czechs in America*, 60.

24. The Moravian immigrants to the Lone Star State embarked from Liverpool and landed in the United States in Galveston rather than in New York. See Habenicht, *History of the Czechs in America*, 63. Also see Capek, *Czechs in America*, 60. Capek gathered his quantitative information from the *Thirteenth Census of the United States, 1910*, Mother Tongue of the Foreign White Stock, table 17, 985–86.

25. Capek, *Czechs in America*, 60–61.

26. U.S. Immigration Commission, *Reports*, 12:385.

27. Stasko, *Slovaks in the United States of America*, 35.

28. See M. Mark Stolarik, "Slovaks," in *Harvard Encyclopedia of American Ethnic Groups*, ed. Thernstrom et al., 928.

29. Alan M. Kraut, *The Huddled Masses: The Immigrant in American Society, 1880–1921* (Arlington Heights, IL: Harlan Davidson, 1986), 106.

30. Capek, *Czechs in America*, 112.

31. Of the 156,891 Czech foreign-born in the 1900 census, 118,883 lived in the north-central region of the United States. See *Census Reports: 1900*, vol. 1, *Population*, table lxxxii, p. clxxiii.

32. Bicha, *Czechs in Oklahoma*, 15–21.

33. Ibid., 18.

34. Ibid., 973.

35. Ibid., 19–20. See William Earl Martin, "The Cultural Assimilation of the Czechoslovak in Oklahoma City: A Study of Culture Contrasts" (MA thesis, University of Oklahoma, 1935), 118. Oklahoma towns containing ethnic Czechs and foreign-born included Yukon, Hennessey, Kingfisher, Perry, and Garber. See Paul M. Nemecek, *Historical and Cultural Essays on Czechs in America* (privately published, 2005), 98. See also *Census of Population: 1920*, 1034.

36. Bicha, *Czechs in Oklahoma*, 20–22. See also Vera Laska, ed., *The Czechs in America: 1633–1977: A Chronology and Fact Book* (Dobbs Ferry, NY: Oceana, 1978), 35.

Chapter 2

1. Lincoln County Historical Society, *Lincoln County*, 1362. See also *Prague Record*, 12 September 1929. The 1929 newspaper account was written as part of an article about Frank Vlasak's death.

2. Lynch, "Czech Farmers in Oklahoma," 14. See also Lincoln County Historical Society, *Lincoln County*, 1362.

3. The Davenport, Oklahoma, newspaper, the *Monthly New Era*, in 2000 published maps of the first people to file for homesteads in 1891 in South Creek Township, Lincoln County. There were twenty-one original filings by Czechs, including the following families: Bontty, Bruza, Vlasak, Barta, Eret, Beranek, Provaznik, Sestak, Suva, Muisack, Hruska, Hrdy, and Bartosh. For a complete listing of homestead filings, see the *Monthly New Era*, April 26 and June 28, 2000. See Tower, "A General History of the Town of Prague," 8. Also see Brown, *Czech-Town*, 25.

4. Lynch, "Czech Farmers in Oklahoma," 15, 89, 91.

5. The Davenport, Oklahoma, newspaper in 2000 reproduced maps from the Federal Tract Books showing the names of the first persons to file for a homestead in North and South Creek Townships. See the *Monthly New Era*, April 26 and June 28, 2000.

6. Lynch, "Czech Farmers in Oklahoma," 15, 91. See also Tower, "A General History of the Town of Prague," 5. After 1900, farmers could file to have their remaining debt forgiven.

7. Brown, *Czech-Town*, 28.

8. Lynch, "Czech Farmers in Oklahoma," 14.

9. Brown, *Czech-Town*, 26. Bohemians harbored a historical animosity toward German-speaking Austria, which dominated them politically.

Nevertheless, Czechs frequently lived near German immigrants in America. See Capek, *The Czechs in America,* 19.

10. Brown, *Czech-Town,* 16, 23. The three doctors (Frank Isles, F. N. Norwood, and S. A. Buercklin) moved to Prague soon after it was organized.

11. Ibid., 17, 19–20, 30–31. Also see Tower, "A General History of the Town of Prague," 6. Dent lay one mile southeast of Prague.

12. Bicha, *Czechs in Oklahoma,* 21.

13. The county officially received its name after the November 8, 1892, election. The three choices were Lincoln, Sac and Fox, and Springer.

14. Oklahoma Geological Survey, *Bulletin No. 19: Petroleum and Natural Gas in Oklahoma, Part II: A Discussion of the Oil and Gas Fields, and Undeveloped Areas of the State by Counties* (Norman: Oklahoma Geological Survey, 1917), 297.

15. Lynch, "Czech Farmers in Oklahoma," 63–65, 89, 105.

16. Ibid., 91.

17. Rosicky, *A History of Czechs (Bohemians) in Nebraska,* 54–58.

18. Lynch, "Czech Farmers in Oklahoma," 93.

19. Kutak, *The Story of a Bohemian-American Village,* 10.

20. Western Czech Brotherhood Association (Zapadni Ceske Bratrska Jednota), Bohemian Hall membership rolls, Lodge 46, Prague (hereafter Bohemian Hall).

   See also Brown, *Czech-Town,* 134–35. According to Brown, the five original members were Frank R. Vlasak, V. Ladra, Jiri Walla, John Sefcik, and Jan Vobornik. However, the membership rolls list Vobornik as joining the society in 1900. There are thirteen others listed as becoming members in 1897. The rolls do not list the month in which they joined, so it is impossible to discern who was the final charter member. The other 1897 members were Josef Bruza, Vaclav Bruza, Anton Cerny, Josef Cerny, Maximilian Hruska, Jan Kaiser, Josef Leder, Frantisek Sekavec, Antonin Smika, Frank Stasta, Frantisek Terfler, Vaclav Ulrich, and Hynes Vojtech.

21. Manuscript Census, 1900, South Creek Township, Lincoln County, OK; Bohemian Hall membership rolls, 1897–1904. By the 1920s the membership of the Bohemian Hall exceeded two hundred.

22. Bohemian Hall membership rolls, 1911–13.

23. Lynch, "Czech Farmers in Oklahoma," 96; Brown, *Czech-Town,* 118–19. The Barta and Simek families are buried in the Catholic cemetery.

24. Manuscript Census, 1900, South Creek Township. Of the 341 families, 269 were U.S.-born white, 42 were Czech, 13 were African American,

and 17 claimed foreign birth from someplace other than Bohemia or Moravia. One of the Austrian-born immigrants, Joseph Custas, may in fact have been Czech. However, Joseph Custas is listed nowhere in any Czech organization, and he fails to appear in the 1910 census. Thus it is impossible to ascertain whether he was Czech or German.

25. Manuscript Census, 1900, South Creek Township.
26. Manuscript Census, 1910, South Creek Township.
27. Manuscript Census, 1920, South Creek Township.
28. Bicha, *Czechs in Oklahoma*, 21.
29. Manuscript Census, 1910, 1920, 1930, Yukon Township, Canadian County, OK.
30. Manuscript Census, 1910, South Creek Township.
31. The bulk of the German community lived in North Creek Township. According to the 1920 census, there were twenty-two families headed by a German immigrant or second-generation ethnic.
32. Manuscript Census, 1900, South Creek Township.
33. Manuscript Census, 1910, South Creek Township.
34. Manuscript Census, 1900, South Creek Township.
35. Ibid. For a good analysis of tracking the movement of families, see Richard C. Rohrs, "Settlement and Migration Patterns of Immigrants and Their Children: A Research Note," *Immigration History Newsletter* 19 (November 1987): 6–8.
36. Manuscript Census, 1900, South Creek Township.
37. Manuscript Census, 1910, South Creek Township.
38. Urban areas seldom contained many blocks inhabited exclusively by a single ethnic group. Usually only limited sections held a 50 percent or higher concentration of a single group. See Humbert S. Nelli, *Italians in Chicago, 1800–1930: A Study in Ethnic Mobility* (New York: Oxford University Press, 1970), 25, 90. See also Herbert J. Gans, *The Urban Villagers: Group and Class in the Life of Italian-Americans* (New York: Free Press, 1962), 11.
39. Kutak, *The Story of a Bohemian-American Village*, 85

Chapter 3

1. This vignette was paraphrased from the depiction given in Brown, *Czech-Town*, 119–20.
2. For examples of arrival experiences and the obstacles confronting newcomers from southern and eastern Europe, see Oscar Handlin, *The Uprooted: The Epic Story of the Great Migrations That Made the American People* (Boston: Little, Brown, 1951), 135–39. See also Kraut, *The Huddled*

Masses, 67–73, 109, and Thomas J. Archdeacon, *Becoming American: An Ethnic History* (New York: Free Press, 1983), 72–73.

3. Jay P. Dolan, *In Search of an American Catholicism: A History of Religion and Culture in Tension* (London: Oxford University Press, 2002), 63.

4. Harold J. Abramson, "Religion," in *Harvard Encyclopedia of Ethnic Groups*, ed. Thernstrom et al., 873.

5. Bodnar, *The Transplanted*, 144, 146; Abramson, "Religion," 872, 875.

6. Dolan, *American Catholicism*, 92–93.

7. Bodnar, *The Transplanted*, 167–68.

8. Peter D. Salins, *Assimilation, American Style* (New York: Basic Books, 1997), 36–37.

9. Maldwyn Allen Jones, *American Immigration* (Chicago: University of Chicago Press, 1960), 317–18.

10. Bodnar, *The Transplanted*, 167; Bruce Garver, "Czech-American Freethinkers on the Great Plains, 1871–1914," in *Ethnicity on the Great Plains*, ed. Frederick C. Luebke (Lincoln: University of Nebraska Press, 1980), 148.

11. Gordon Stein, ed., *The Encyclopedia of Unbelief* (Buffalo, NY: Prometheus Books, 1985), 247, 531; Susan Jacoby, *Freethinkers: A History of American Secularism* (New York: Metropolitan Books, 2004), 4–5, 151.

12. Balch, *Our Slavic Fellow Citizens*, 390–91; Garver, "Czech-American Freethinkers," 149, 164; Rosicky, *A History of the Czechs (Bohemians) in Nebraska*, 286.

13. Bicha, *Czechs in Oklahoma*, 34.

14. Rosicky, *A History of Czechs (Bohemians) in Nebraska*, 286. Hlas translates as "the voice."

15. Joseph Chada, *The Czechs in the United States* (Chicago: Czechoslovak Society of Art and Sciences, 1981), 92–93.

16. Garver, "Czech-American Freethinkers," 148; Chada, *Czechs in the United States*, 17.

17. Garver, "Czech-American Freethinkers," 150, 156; Clinton Machann, "Religious Attitudes in Early Immigrant Autobiographies Written by Czechs in Texas," *MELUS* 22 (Winter 1997): 168–69.

18. Rosicky, *A History of Czechs (Bohemians) in Nebraska*, 279; Garver, "Czech-American Freethinkers," 155.

19. Progressivism, especially regarding religion, is characterized by a willingness to question tradition and the literal interpretation of scripture.

20. Balch, *Our Slavic Fellow Citizens*, 69; Garver, "Czech-American Freethinkers," 151; Ernest J. Zizka, *Czech Cultural Contributions* (Chicago: Benedictine Abbey Press, 1942), 70.

21. Casper, *History of the Catholic Church in Nebraska,* 4:103; Machann, "Religious Attitudes," 164.

22. Rosicky, *A History of Czechs (Bohemians) in Nebraska,* 285.

23. Ibid., 80.

24. Garver, "Czech-American Freethinkers," 163.

25. Ibid., 158; Bicha, *Czechs in Oklahoma,* 37; Rosicky, *A History of Czechs (Bohemians) in Nebraska,* 287.

26. Casper, *History of the Catholic Church in Nebraska,* 4:103.

27. Garver, "Czech-American Freethinkers," 148.

28. Machann, "Religious Attitudes," 168.

29. Lynch, "Czech Farmers in Oklahoma," 97, 137.

30. Garver, "Czech-American Freethinkers," 149.

31. Bicha, *Czechs in Oklahoma,* 28–29.

32. For a few examples, see *Prague Record,* 12 May 1926, 27 April 1927, 6 March 1929.

33. Kutak, *The Story of a Bohemian-American Village,* 92.

34. Clinton Machann and James W. Mendl Jr., trans. and eds., *Czech Voices: Stories from Texas in the Amerikán Národní Kalendář* (College Station: Texas A&M University Press, 1991), xxvi; Clinton Machann and James W. Mendl Jr., *Krasna Amerika: A Study of the Texas Czechs, 1851–1939* (Austin, TX: Eakin Press, 1983), 129; Sean N. Gallup, *Journeys into Czech-Moravian Texas* (College Station: Texas A&M University Press, 1998), 102; Robert L. Skrabanak, *We're Czechs* (College Station: Texas A&M University Press, 1988), 193; Estelle Hudson and Henry R. Maresh, *Czech Pioneers of the Southwest* (Dallas: Southwest Press, 1934), 347–48.

35. Bicha, *Czechs in Oklahoma,* 42.

36. Ibid., 30.

37. Brown, *Czech-Town,* 115.

38. The first church building in Prague was the Methodist Episcopal Church, South. Tower, "A General History of the Town of Prague, Oklahoma," 42.

39. Lynch, "Czech Farmers in Oklahoma," 96; Brown, *Czech-Town,* 118–19.

40. Lynch, "Czech Farmers in Oklahoma," 94; Bicha, *Czechs in Oklahoma,* 31. St. Wenceslaus Catholic Church issued a memorial pamphlet in 1949, the golden anniversary of the first permanent structure. The volume listed 186 members, of which 133 sported Czech surnames.

41. Rosicky, *A History of Czechs (Bohemians) in Nebraska,* 293.

42. Bicha, *Czechs in Oklahoma,* 31. The parish, formed in 1891, retained a Bohemian priest until 1927.

43. Dolan, *American Catholicism*, 72.

44. Abramson, "Religion," 874.

45. Bicha, *Czechs in Oklahoma*, 43.

46. Lynch, "Czech Farmers in Oklahoma," 97; Kutak, *The Story of a Bohemian-American Village*, 44–45.

47. Martin, "The Cultural Assimilation of the Czechoslovak," 143; Zizka, *Czech Cultural Contributions*, 48.

48. C. Merton Babcock, "Czech Songs in Nebraska," *Western Folklore* 8 (October 1949): 321.

49. Rosicky, *A History of Czechs (Bohemians) in Nebraska*, 337.

50. Chada, *Czechs in the United States*, 120–21.

51. Tower, "A General History of the Town of Prague," 42. There were twenty-five charter members, according to the 1903 membership rolls of the First United Methodist Church of Prague. None had Czech surnames.

52. Ibid., 44.

53. *Prague Record*, 1 March 1917, 16 July 1915.

54. First United Methodist Church of Prague church records. The *Prague Record*, 11 January 1928, also listed the election of new Methodist officials.

55. Spevacek Family History, three-ring binder, Prague Historical Museum. Stoklasa was listed as a member of Sokol Hall in the pamphlet *Prague, Oklahoma: City of Opportunities*, 37–39. He is buried in the Czech National Cemetery.

56. *Prague Record*, 7 July 1927.

57. *Prague Record*, 8 February 1927.

58. Tower, "A General History of the Town of Prague," 32.

59. *Prague Record*, 23 June 1916.

60. *Prague Record*, 8 February 1928.

61. Until 1929 and the formation of a Nazarene congregation, the Catholic, Methodist, Baptist, and Christian churches were the primary churches in Prague.

62. Prague Baptist Church changed its name to First Baptist Church in 1957.

63. *Prague Record*, 14 September 1927, 10 March 1921.

64. Mildred D. Bouda Young, "The Trials and Tribulations of the Boudas," 1991, three-ring binder in the Prague Historical Museum.

Chapter 4

1. Upon returning to Prague, Blumel wrote a detailed article about the European trip for the *Prague Record,* 16 September 1920.
2. For details concerning Blumel's family, occupation, and homeownership, see Census, 1920, South Creek Township. Blumel was also a member of the Western Czech Brotherhood Association. See Bohemian Hall membership rolls.
3. *Prague Record,* 16 September 1920.
4. *Prague News,* 27 July 1915.
5. Capek, *The Czechs in America,* 258.
6. Lynch, "Czech Farmers in Oklahoma," 95; Brown, *Czech-Town,* 134–35.
7. Rose Rosicky lists the death benefit as $250. See Rosicky, *A History of Czechs (Bohemians) in Nebraska,* 356–57.
8. Garver, "Czech-American Freethinkers," 160.
9. Bohemian Hall membership rolls.
10. Rosicky, *A History of Czechs (Bohemians) in Nebraska,* 357.
11. Lynch, "Czech Farmers in Oklahoma," 94. See also Bohemian Hall membership rolls.
12. John Barta is found nowhere on the membership lists of Lodge 46. In addition, he is buried not in the Czech National Cemetery but in the city cemetery.
13. The *Prague Patriot, Prague News,* and later the *Prague Record* seldom published an issue without a short article or advertisement on the next event to be held at the ZCBJ Lodge (Bohemian Hall). Lynch and Brown both discuss the importance of the Bohemian Hall to the Czech community. See Lynch, "Czech Farmers in Oklahoma," 96; Brown, *Czech-Town,* 135–36.
14. *ZCBJ Handbook,* 1939, quoted in Lynch, "Czech Farmers in Oklahoma," 95.
15. Martin, "The Cultural Assimilation of the Czechoslovak," 137. See also Lynch, "Czech Farmers in Oklahoma," 97.
16. *Sokol* means falcon in Czech.
17. Chicago formed the second Sokol in 1866, and New York City residents created their own club the following year. Laska, *Czechs in America,* 86.
18. The Czech National Alliance in Great Britain, *Austrian Terrorism in Bohemia* (London: Czech National Alliance in Great Britain, n.d.), 28–29.
19. *Prague News,* 5 April 1906. See also Lynch, "Czech Farmers in Oklahoma," 96, and Bicha, *Czechs in Oklahoma,* 44.
20. Chada, *Czechs in the United States,* 145.

21. Zizka, *Czech Cultural Contributions*, 72.

22. Chada, *Czechs in the United States*, 88–89.

23. Joseph Roucek, "The Passing of American Czechoslovaks," *American Journal of Sociology* 39, no. 5 (March 1934): 623.

24. The Prague Historical Museum contains photographs of early-twentieth-century Sokol uniforms, and Mary Anne Pritchett, daughter of Sokol member Frank Sefcik, still has her father's uniform.

25. *Prague Record*, 12 September 1929.

26. The Catholic Bible of Frank Vlasak's mother is on display at the Prague Historical Museum.

27. *Prague News*, 5 and 12 April 1906.

28. *Prague Record*, 16 September 1920. The group visited Paris, Vienna, Prague, and several towns in Germany. The Prague Sokol visited Oklahoma City and Ft. Worth in 1926. See *Prague Record*, 23 June 1926, 1 September 1926.

29. *Prague Record*, 6 March 1929.

30. Lynch, "Czech Farmers in Oklahoma," 99.

31. *Prague News*, 4 July 1907.

32. Bicha, *Czechs in Oklahoma*, 39–40.

33. Martin, "The Cultural Assimilation of the Czechoslovak," 137.

34. Ibid.

35. Rosicky, *A History of Czechs (Bohemians) in Nebraska*, 357.

36. Ibid., 286.

37. Zizka, *Czech Cultural Contributions*, 48.

38. H. Louis Rees, "The Czechs during World War I (Especially 1917–1918): Economic and Political Developments Leading toward Independence" (PhD diss., Ohio State University, 1990), 20–21.

39. Joseph Jahelka, "The Role of Chicago Czechs in the Struggle for Czechoslovak Independence," *Journal of the Illinois State Historical Society* 31, no. 4 (December 1938): 381, 383.

40. Lewis B. Namier, *The Case of Bohemia* (London: Czech National Alliance, 1917), 5–7, 9–10.

41. Czech National Alliance in Great Britain, *Austrian Terrorism in Bohemia*, 23.

42. Chada, *Czechs in the United States*, 49.

43. Charles Pergler, *Bohemia's Claim to Independence: An Address Delivered by Charles Pergler, LL.B., before the Committee on Foreign Affairs of the House of Representatives of the United States on February 25, 1916* (Chicago: Bohemian National Alliance, 1916), 8.

44. Charles Pergler, *The Bohemians (Czechs) in the Present Crisis: An Address Delivered by Charles Pergler LL.B. on the 28th Day of May, 1916, in Chicago, at a Meeting Held to Commemorate the Deeds of Bohemian Volunteers in the Great War* (Chicago: Bohemian National Alliance, 1916), 8.

45. Vojta Benes, *Economic Strength of the Bohemian (Czechoslovak) Lands* (Chicago: Bohemian [Czech] National Alliance, 1918), 2.

46. Thomas G. Masaryk, *Declaration of the Bohemian (Czech) Foreign Committee: Comments of London Papers* (Chicago: Bohemian National Alliance of America, n.d.), 6.

47. *Prague Record*, 3 and 10 May 1917.

48. Bohemian National Alliance, *The Position of the Bohemians (Czechs) in the European War* (Chicago: Bohemian National Alliance in America, n.d.), 17.

49. Czechoslovak Arts Club, *The Czech Declaration of January 6, 1918* (New York: Czechoslovak Arts Club, 1918), 2.

50. Czechoslovak Arts Club, *The Independence of the Czechoslovak Nation: Quotations from Wilson, Viviani, Balfour, Palacky, Masaryk, Seton-Watson, & Others* (New York: Czechoslovak Arts Club, 1918), 6.

51. Jahelka, "The Role of Chicago Czechs," 392–93.

52. *Prague Record*, 11 January 1917.

53. *Prague Record*, 10 May 1917.

54. Manuscript Census, 1910, South Creek Township.

55. Tower, "A General History of the Town of Prague, Oklahoma," 55.

56. Manuscript Census, 1910, South Creek Township. Both Ray Tower and Melva Losch Brown recorded that O. R. Blumel, owner of Prague's harness shop, had arrived in Oklahoma in 1905 directly from Austria, where his parents and extended family still lived. They reported that his sympathies were with Austria and the Central Powers during the Great War. See Tower, "A General History of the Town of Prague," 56; Brown, *Czech-Town*, 111–12. However, according to the Manuscript Census Schedules of 1910, Blumel listed his arrival in the United States as being in 1894. Furthermore, his first two children were born in Texas. Finally, if this is the same O. R. Blumel who accompanied Prague's Sokol club to Czechoslovakia in 1920—and it definitely appears to be so—then despite being born in Austria, he most likely was of Czech ancestry.

57. Tower, "A General History of the Town of Prague," 56–58; Richard C. Rohrs, *The Germans in Oklahoma* (Norman: University of Oklahoma Press, 1980), 42, 44–45.

58. *Prague News*, 27 May 1915.

59. *Prague News*, 9 July 1915. Sarah Hrbek's name is sometimes printed as Hrbkova, which is the feminine form of Hrbek.
60. *Prague Record*, 21 June 1917.
61. Paul Robert Magocsi, "Loyalties: Dual and Divided," in *Harvard Encyclopedia of American Ethnic Groups*, ed. Thernstrom et al., 680; Laska, *Czechs in America*, 45.
62. Brown, *Czech-Town*, 111.
63. The statue commemorating Walla still stands in the Prague National Cemetery, and Prague's American Legion Post also retains Walla's name.
64. Magocsi, "Loyalties," 683.
65. The Bohemian Hall records continued to be written in Czech until late in 1938.
66. Bohemian Hall records show that the lodge purchased cigars (*doutniky*) almost monthly. It is assumed the members smoked them at meetings or unofficial gatherings.

Chapter 5

1. *Prague News*, 15 September 1904. See also Brown, *Czech-Town*, 53.
2. Lincoln County Historical Society, *Lincoln County: Oklahoma History*, 198–99. Keokuk Falls no longer exists. After weeks of heavy rains in the spring of 1923, a flood covered the entire area with silt and mud destroying the once beautiful natural falls, which had been a favorite recreational area for early settlers.
3. *Prague News*, 28 August 1902.
4. *Prague Record*, 5 October 1916. See also *Prague News*, 28 August 1902; Tower, "A General History of the Town of Prague," 13; Brown, *Czech-Town*, 52.
5. Bicha, *Czechs in Oklahoma*, 61.
6. Balch, *Our Slavic Fellow Citizens*, 308; Roucek, "The Passing of American Czechoslovaks," 616.
7. *Prague News*, 15 September 1904. See also Tower, "A General History of the Town of Prague," 23–25.
8. *Prague News*, 1 December 1904.
9. *Prague News*, 9 May 1907.
10. The *Prague News*, 28 September 1905, listed the Ragsdale & Perkins Saloon as Prague's first saloon. Other saloons mentioned in the newspapers during the prestatehood period include the Ramsdal Saloon, Hardy Saloon, First Chance Saloon, Phil's Place, Dorcey and Roberts Saloon,

Watts Saloon, and Hendrix Saloon. See the *Prague Patriot,* 25 May 1905, and the *Prague News,* 5 and 19 January 1905, 31 May 1906, 1 and 29 November 1906, and 4 July 1907.

11. Lincoln County Historical Society, *Lincoln County,* 198.

12. *Prague Record,* 6 June 1916. For another account of the illegal liquor trade after statehood, see *Prague Record,* 14 September 1916.

13. James Edward Klein, *Grappling with Demon Rum: The Cultural Struggle over Liquor in Early Oklahoma* (Norman: University of Oklahoma Press, 2008), 136. Klein goes into greater detail in his PhD dissertation, "A Social History of Prohibition in Oklahoma, 1900–1920," Oklahoma State University, 2003, 257.

14. *Prague News,* 5 December 1907.

15. Bicha, *Czechs in Oklahoma,* 53, 56; Lynch, "Czech Farmers in Oklahoma," 99–100.

16. Handlin, *The Uprooted,* 95.

17. Ibid., 94.

18. Lynch, "Czech Farmers in Oklahoma," 13.

19. Emily Balch also wrote about how Czech farmers helped each other more than their American counterparts. See Balch, *Our Slavic Fellow Citizens,* 319–20.

20. *Prague News,* 28 August 1902. The first issue of the weekly *Prague News* appeared 24 July 1902. The paper was eight pages in length. Newhouse was not Czech. Soon there was a rival newspaper, the *Prague Patriot.*

21. Brown, *Czech-Town,* 34.

22. *Prague News,* 24 July 1902. As mentioned earlier, Frank Barta also built a hotel in the fall of 1902 that operated until 1961. Regarding the Dobry Lumber Company, the Czech word *dobry* means good.

23. *Prague News,* 2 July 1915. Frank Vlasak called his business Vlasak's Cash Store.

24. Tower, "A General History of the Town of Prague," 21–22. I could find no issues of the *Prague News, Prague Patriot,* or *Prague Record* that did not include an advertisement by a Czech business from 1902 to 1930.

25. *Prague Record,* 1 June 1916.

26. *Prague Record,* 7 September 1916.

27. Brown, *Czech-Town,* 73. George Sadlo later moved to Cleveland, Oklahoma, accepting the position of high school band director. In 1928, the Cleveland High School band, under Sadlo's direction, won Oklahoma's Class B State Championship. See *Prague Record,* 23 May 1928.

28. *Prague Record*, 29 June 1916, 1. See also Lincoln County Historical Society, *Lincoln County*, 404–5.

29. Tower, "A General History of the Town of Prague," 21–22. Lincoln County Bank was later renamed Prague National Bank.

30. *Prague News*, 24 July 1902.

31. *Prague Record*, 7 September 1916.

32. *Prague Record*, 1 June 1916. The listed newspaper issue is an example of White's and Kolodny's advertisements. Both ran ads on a weekly basis. All three Jewish merchants claimed to be Russian Jews. In 1920, Sol White was the oldest at fifty-three with Blumenthal next at forty-eight and Kolodny being the youngest at thirty-five. See Census, 1920, South Creek Township. For Kolodny's relocation to Wetumka, see *Prague Record*, 10 February 1926.

33. For an example of O'Kane's advertisements, see *Prague News*, 17 September 1915.

34. *Prague Record*, 16 November 1916. Jacob Mertes, owner of Mertes Hardware, died in November 1916. The newspaper listed his place of birth as Obermehlen, Germany. He is also listed as born in Germany on the census records. See Census, 1910, South Creek Township.

35. *Prague Record*, 9 June 1916. The proprietors of the Rexall Drugstore were listed in the newspaper as "Brannigan and McDowell." The 1910 census lists Clayton Brannigan as a druggist. However, he was not listed on the 1920 census. There is no listing for anyone named McDowell on either the 1910 or 1920 census. It is very plausible that McDowell arrived in Prague after the 1910 census and departed before the 1920 census. Furthermore, there are no advertisements in the newspaper for Rexall after 1919, as the store apparently had gone out of business. See Census, 1920, South Creek Township.

36. *Prague News*, 10 November 1904.

37. *Prague News*, 24 August 1905. Dr. Mraz moved his practice to an office in the Prague National Bank building sometime in 1905.

38. *Prague Record*, 7 October 1920. For information on Frank Klabzuba's dental office, see *Prague Record*, 31 August 1927.

39. Brown, *Czech-Town*, 60. The *Prague Record* ran a short article about the beloved "Uncle" William: "William Woods, one of our respected colored citizens, who has been quite sick, was able to be out again Monday." See *Prague Record*, 22 June 1916.

40. See Manuscript Census, 1900, 1910, 1920, South Creek Township.

41. For a provocative examination of why blacks fared worse than white immigrants, see Stanley Lieberson's *A Piece of the Pie: Blacks and White Immigrants since 1880* (Berkeley: University of California Press, 1980). In the work, Lieberson agrees that blacks migrating north suffered more discrimination than the previous immigrants from central, eastern, and southern Europe. However, he maintains that race was not the ultimate cause of why they economically did worse than white immigrants.

42. Manuscript Census, 1900, South Creek Township.

43. Manuscript Census, 1910, South Creek Township.

44. Manuscript Census, 1920, South Creek Township.

45. Bicha, *Czechs in Oklahoma*, 51.

46. *Prague Record*, 7 October 1920.

47. The *Prague Record* wrote that "J. F. Walenta sold a load of corn to B. F. Whitmore at 75 cents a bushel." The paper also reported that another Czech, Joe Piter, "sold a load of hay to B. F. Whitmore." See *Prague Record*, 10 August and 7 September 1916. Whitmore's birthplace was Missouri. In addition, his parents were born in the United States. Whitmore's wife, Elizabeth, was born in Illinois. However, her father was a German immigrant. See Census, 1910, South Creek Township.

48. *Prague Record*, 23 September 1920.

49. *Prague News*, 9 February and 13 April 1905.

50. *Prague News*, 24 November 1904.

51. *Prague News*, 21 November 1907.

52. E. E. Long ran a candy store inside the Klabzuba building; Frank Tugwell worked at Hatcher & Co.'s drugstore in the Cerveny building on Broadway Avenue; Henry Cheek operated a restaurant in the Vlasak building on the corner of Main and Broadway. See *Prague News*, 26 December 1907, 2 January 1908, 29 August 1908.

53. *Prague News*, 30 July 1915.

54. *Prague News*, 2 July 1915.

55. *Prague Record*, 20 July 1916.

56. For an example of the auctioneers' advertisement, see *Prague Record*, 29 June 1916.

57. For example, see *Prague Record*, 6 January 1926. See also *Prague Record*, 13 January 1926. The advertisements do not mention Barrett's first name. There is a Barrett listed in the census with the first name of David. However, in 1920 his age was listed as seventy-five, and he does not show up in the 1930 census. David Barrett may well have been Wes Klabzuba's auctioneering partner. But it is impossible to state this

conclusively, because by 1926 David Barrett would have been around eighty-one.

58. *Prague Record,* 27 July 1917.

59. Tower, "A General History of the Town of Prague," 28.

60. *Prague News,* 13 August 1915.

61. Land Records, Lincoln County: Township 12, Range 6, Sections 20–29, Lincoln County Courthouse, Chandler, Oklahoma. Oil exploration was rampant during the second and third decades of the twentieth century. Other oil companies leasing land in the Prague area included Quaker Oil and Gas Company, Transcontinental Oil Company, Keystone Oil and Gas Company, Atlantic Oil Production Company, Mountain State Oil Company, and Mid-Kansas Oil and Gas Company.

62. For examples of the call for better roads, see *Prague News,* 15 July and 6 August 1915.

63. *Prague Record,* 27 July 1916.

64. *Prague Record,* 31 August 1916.

65. Ibid.

66. Tower, "A General History of the Town of Prague," 51. See also Brown, *Czech-Town,* 45.

67. *Prague News,* 16 July 1915. See also *Prague News,* 6 August 1915.

68. *Prague Record,* 8 June 1916.

69. *Prague Record,* 20 July 1927. See also *Prague Record,* 17 August 1927.

70. Brown, *Czech-Town,* 94; Lynch, "Czech Farmers in Oklahoma," 7.

71. *Prague News,* 6 October 1904.

72. For information on the hailstorm, see *Prague Record,* 22 June 1916. War profits article appeared in *Prague Record,* 11 January 1917.

73. *Prague Record,* 7 December 1916. Vlasak sold his farm holdings to C. A. Gripe and A. C. Sahm; neither were Czech.

74. Tower, "A General History of the Town of Prague," 18.

75. Lynch, "Czech Farmers in Oklahoma, 98. See also Brown, *Czech-Town,* 100.

76. *Prague Record,* 1 June 1916.

77. Due to financial difficulties during the Great Depression, the Ft. Smith and Western Railroad Company abandoned their Prague coaling station on 7 August 1939. See Lynch, "Czech Farmers in Oklahoma," 98.

78. *Prague Record,* 12 September 1929.

79. *Prague Record,* 1 June 1916; Lincoln County Historical Society, *Lincoln County,* 404–5. Although Zabloudil left Prague for Abilene, Texas, he kept abreast of his adopted town via the newspapers. In 1926, the *Prague*

Record listed its subscribers, which included Abilene's Jake Zabloudil. See *Prague Record*, 14 April 1926.

80. Bicha, *Czechs in Oklahoma*, 60.
81. Bodnar, *The Transplanted*, 133, 183.
82. Nemecek, *Historical and Cultural Essays on Czechs in America*, 38–42. Most Czechs lived in the southwestern part of Chicago.
83. Kutak, *The Story of a Bohemian-American Village*, 18; Rosicky, *A History of Czechs (Bohemians) in Nebraska*, 54, 60, 84, 89, 119, 121.
84. Hudson and Maresh, *Czech Pioneers of the Southwest*, 167–68; Gallup, *Journeys into Czech-Moravian Texas*, 72.
85. Chada, *Czechs in the United States*, 37.
86. Roucek, "The Passing of American Czechoslovaks," 617.
87. Dostalick, scrapbook.
88. Bohemian Hall membership rolls.

Chapter 6

1. This won/lost record of the baseball team is from the articles in the Prague newspapers during 1916. This is assuming that the *Prague Record* covered all baseball games, which they probably did, due to the intense interest.
2. *Prague Record*, 24 August 1916. For a list of Prague's Czechs in World War I, see Prague Historical Museum, American Legion Honor Roll of Prague Czechs serving in World War I.
3. For examples, see *Prague Record*, 25 January 1917 and 9 November 1919.
4. *Prague Record*, 2 November 1919.
5. For examples, see *Prague Record*, 24 March 1926 (Babe Ruth) and *Prague Record*, 7 April 1926 (Ty Cobb). There were many other baseball stories concerning various big league players throughout the 1920s.
6. *Prague News*, 16 July 1915; *Prague Record*, 24 August 1916.
7. *Prague Record*, 23 September 1920.
8. *Prague Record*, 6 July 1916. See also Lynch, "Czech Farmers in Oklahoma," 97.
9. Census, 1920, South Creek Township.
10. *Prague Record*, 25 August 1916. During the period covered, 1916 appears to be Prague's best baseball season.
11. *Prague Record*, 12 April 1917.
12. Although George Sadlo's father, Cyril, arrived in the United States in 1889, his mother, Emma, was born in Missouri. However, both of Emma's parents were born in Bohemia. Wesley Pastusek's parents

emigrated from the Austro-Hungarian Empire in 1873 and lived in Texas prior to migrating to Oklahoma. See Census, 1920, South Creek Township. Apparently Pastusek left Prague sometime between 1917 and 1920. According to the *Prague Record*, 4 November 1920, Wesley Pastusek lived in Texas in the fall of 1920.

13. Marcus Lee Hansen, "The Problem of the Third Generation Immigrant," in *Theories of Ethnicity: A Classical Reader*, ed. Werner Sollors (New York: New York University Press, 1996), 204.

14. Bicha, *Czechs in Oklahoma*, 33, 60.

15. Kutak, *The Story of a Bohemian-American Village*, 144.

16. Roucek, "The Passing of American Czechoslovaks," 625.

17. Kutak, *The Story of a Bohemian-American Village*, 63–65, 70.

18. Josef Barton, "Land, Labor, and Community in Nueces: Czech Farmers and Mexican Laborers in South Texas, 1880–1930," in *European Immigrants in the American West: Community Histories*, ed. Frederick C. Luebke (Albuquerque: University of New Mexico Press, 1998), 152.

19. Bicha, *Czechs in Oklahoma*, 58.

20. Vivian Rakoff, "Children of Immigrants," in *Strangers in the World*, ed. Leo Eitinger and David Schwarz (Bern: Hans Huber, 1981), 133, 144–45.

21. Leo Eitinger, "Feeling at Home: Immigrants' Psychological Problems," in *Strangers in the World*, ed. Leo Eitinger and David Schwarz (Bern: Hans Huber, 1981), 95.

22. Bodnar, *The Transplanted*, 213; Weiss, *American Education*, xxi.

23. Tamara K. Hareven and John Modell, "Family Patterns," in *Harvard Encyclopedia of American Ethnic Groups*, ed. Thernstrom et al., 345; Kathleen Neils Conzen, "Historical Approaches to the Study of Rural Ethnic Communities," in *Ethnicity on the Great Plains*, ed. Frederick C. Luebke (Lincoln: University of Nebraska Press, 1980), 4.

24. Bodnar, *The Transplanted*, 75; Elovitz, "Patterns and Costs of Immigration," 65.

25. Bicha, *Czechs in Oklahoma*, 60.

26. The only nonimmigrant household head was Joseph Klabzuba, a twenty-one-year-old bachelor and second-generation Czech, born in Kansas. Joseph lived with his nineteen-year-old brother, Frank, and another second-generation Czech, Eddie Kryche. There were two households headed by single men and two others headed by widowers. However, in all four of these situations the single head's birthplace was Bohemia. See Census, 1900, South Creek Township. There were also several Czech families residing in North Creek Township.

27. Four male immigrants married second-generation wives, and one immigrant female married a second-generation husband.

28. Nebraska as the couple's place of marriage was deduced using the 1900 census records. The census shows that George and Mary had been married thirteen years. Furthermore, they had a twelve-year-old daughter, Edna, born in Nebraska only a year after their wedding. Finally, George's place of birth was also Nebraska. Thus it appears likely that Mary migrated to Nebraska (home of a substantial Czech colony), met George, and married him sometime in 1887. Furthermore, Laura, the couple's second daughter, was also born in Nebraska in 1891. Therefore, the Banghains did not come to Oklahoma until sometime in 1891 after the birth of their second daughter. I could find no cemetery records recording the entombment of anyone named Banghain. So it was impossible to determine Mary's maiden name.

29. Manuscript Census, 1900, South Creek Township.

30. Bodnar, *The Transplanted,* 75.

31. Manuscript Census, 1900, South Creek Township.

32. See Manuscript Census, 1920, South Creek Township; St. Wenceslaus Cemetery, Prague; Prague City Cemetery; Czech National Cemetery, Prague; *Prague Record; Prague News.*

33. For a few examples, see *Prague Record,* 23 November 1916, 17 February 1926, 14 September 1927, and 8 February 1928. Many other exogamous marriages can be deduced by comparing cemetery records that included the maiden name of the wife with the census manuscripts to ascertain probable ethnicity and the generation of the Czech spouse.

34. See Prague City Cemetery and Czech National Cemetery. William Vlasak along with his wife and daughters, Marie Crute and Gladys Vanhooser, are buried in the city cemetery. Frank Vlasak Jr.'s family including Ednamae Kilgo are buried in the Czech National Cemetery. The cemetery records contain a paragraph on Ednamae's life including her stint as a schoolteacher in Asher and her marriage in 1929 to Herbert Kilgo.

35. Bicha, *Czechs in Oklahoma,* 60.

36. Manuscript Census, 1920, South Creek Township.

37. Agnes Sucha lived in North Creek Township, directly north of Prague. Her father, Stanley Sucha, immigrated in 1890 and owned a farm. See Manuscript Census, 1920, North Creek Township.

38. The three male immigrants marrying non-Czechs were George Sala (Julia Miller), Julius Bontty (Bertha Hall), and John Simek (Lillian

Turner). See Manuscript Census, 1920, South Creek Township. See also Prague City Cemetery.

39. The fourteen women buried alone in the Czech National Cemetery were Ednamae Kilgo (Vlasak), Frances Pruett (Stasta), Libby Spurgeon (Vobornik), Anna Farr (Provaznik), Madeline Choate (Salda), Marie Supler (Svoboda), Ella Simmons (Cerny), Helen Brown (Bruza), Ellen Shivers (Bruza), Minnie Emery (Sekera), Violet English (Cerny), Lottie Switzer (Caha), Rosie Hurley (Kolar), and Mary Frances Darrow (Zbavitel). Third-generation Czechs were Ednamae Kilgo (Vlasak), Libby Spurgeon (Vobornik), Ella Simmons (Cerny), Violet English (Cerny), and Mary Frances Darrow (Zbavitel). In addition, Minnie Emery (Sekera), born in 1915, may have been a third-generation Czech. I could not locate her name in census manuscripts for verification. See Manuscript Census, 1900, 1920, 1930, South Creek Township.

40. There are actually more than five non-Czech graves. However, for this study's purpose, only the tombs of those born before 1930 were considered.

41. The five couples were Joe and Helen Tompkins (Leder), Louis and Anna Holman (Smicka), Joe and Julia Nance (Pantlik), George and Effie Williams (Stastny), and Fred and Emma Pierce (Barta). The *Prague Record* announced the Holman and Smicka wedding. See *Prague Record*, 23 November 1916.

42. Richard D. Alba, "The Twilight of Ethnicity among Americans of European Ancestry: The Case of Italians," in *Ethnicity and Race in the U.S.A.: Toward the Twenty-First Century*, ed. Richard D. Alba (Boston: Routledge & Kegan Paul, 1985), 153.

43. Lynch, "Czech Farmers in Oklahoma," 97, 102.

44. U.S. Immigration Commission, *Reports*, 20:42.

45. *Oklahomske Noviny* published the itinerary of a speaking tour by a Professor Isky of the University of Nebraska. Isky visited and spoke in Prague on 1 November 1905. See *Oklahomske Noviny*, 5 October 1905.

46. Martin, "The Cultural Assimilation of the Czechoslovak," 114.

47. Brown, *Czech-Town*, 42. See also Tower, "A General History of the Town of Prague, Oklahoma," 46–47. Mullen gave the *Patriot* to his son-in-law, W. S. Overstreet, in 1905, and Overstreet then sold the operation to B. S. Edwards. It was Edwards who sold to Nipper.

48. Franklin Newhouse remained in Prague. His wife, Lillian, became the postmaster in Prague, and Franklin assisted her. See Census, 1920, South Creek Township. See also *Prague Record*, 26 April 1917. This issue of the

Record details Nipper's buying of the *Prague News* and his plans to stop publishing it.

49. Tower, "A General History of the Town of Prague," 46–47.
50. *Prague Record*, 1 June 1916, 20 and 27 July 1916, and 3 August 1916.
51. *Prague News*, 12 January 1905.
52. *Prague Record*, 25 January 1917.
53. Although the *Prague Patriot* carried few articles on travel, practically every issue of the *Prague News* and *Prague Record* contained a short note on residents traveling. For a few examples of visits both within Oklahoma and to other states, see *Prague News*, 16 and 27 July 1915. See also *Prague Record*, 25 May 1911, 8 June 1916, 15 June 1916, 29 June 1916, 6 July 1916, 27 July 1916, 17 May 1917, 28 October 1920, 6 January 1926, 13 January 1926, 17 March 1926, and 21 September 1927.
54. *Prague News*, 3 February 1915.
55. *Prague Record*, 22 June 1916, 27 June 1916, and 3 August 1916.
56. *Prague Record*, 6 July 1916.
57. Manuscript Census, 1920, South Creek Township. Joe and Camellia Bartosh are buried in the Czech National Cemetery.
58. *Prague Record*, 22 June 1916.
59. *Prague Record*, 3 February 1926.
60. *Prague Record*, 20 July 1916.
61. Bohemian Hall financial accounts books, 1915–16.
62. *Prague Record*, 27 July 1916.
63. *Prague Record*, 10 August 1916, 17 August 1916, and 24 August 1916.
64. For information on the racetrack, see *Prague Patriot*, 17 November, 1904; for the Dorsey Shooting Gallery, see *Prague Patriot*, 20 October 1904, and *Prague News*, 7 September 1905; and for the bowling alley, see *Prague Patriot*, 17 November 1904.
65. For information on the roller skating rink, see *Prague News*, 30 August 1906. Prague boasted at least five pool halls (billiard halls) over the years. See *Prague News*, 17 and 24 January 1907 for information on the Adams & Sangster Pool Hall. Hooter's Billiard Hall opened in the Watts Saloon shortly after statehood. See *Prague News*, 21 November 1907. John Urban opened a pool hall in 1916. See *Prague Record*, 1 June 1916. Another pool hall operating in 1916 was the Lone Star Pool Parlor. See *Prague Record*, 21 December 1916. The Metropolitan Pool Hall was first mentioned in 1917. See *Prague Record*, 24 November 1917.
66. *Prague News*, 30 July 1915. The 1920 census lists A. P. Slover's age as thirty-eight, so in 1915 Slover would have been at least thirty-two years old. See Census, 1920, South Creek Township.

67. *Prague Record*, 22 March 1917.

68. For example, see *Prague Record*, 27 July 1916 and 30 September 1920.

69. *Prague News*, 22 March 1906.

70. The first instance of a price increase appeared in *Prague Record*, 30 September 1920.

71. *Prague Record*, 18 January 1917.

72. *Prague Record*, 5 October 1916 and 20 March 1920.

73. *Prague Record*, 23 November 1916.

74. *Prague Record*, 17 March 1921.

75. *Prague Record*, 31 March 1921. The Western Czech Brotherhood also held a benefit dance to help a Czech invalid's family and enable him to buy a wheelchair. See *Prague Record*, 20 January 1926.

76. *Prague Record*, 4 April 1928. The translation of the Czech word *osel* is jackass or donkey. However, as in English, the word in many cases refers to a fool or someone easily deceived.

77. *Prague Record*, 3 February 1921.

78. *Prague Record*, 9 May 1917.

79. For the Wild West show, see *Prague News*, 23 July 1915. For information on the circus, see *Prague News*, 17 September 1915.

80. *Prague News*, 9 July 1915.

81. *Prague Record*, 28 September 1916.

82. *Prague Record*, 10 August 1916. The three plays performed by the Franklin Show were *The Sultan's Daughter*, *St. Elmo*, and *Why Lindy Ran Away*.

83. *Prague Record*, 1 June 1922.

84. See any Prague newspaper issued in October after the fair for winners. For a good example, see *Prague Record*, 12 October 1916.

85. *Prague News*, 2 July 1915. This issue of the *News* published the entire program for the upcoming Independence Day celebration. Other years mentioned food and entertainment but did not list specific events. The band performing at Prague's Independence Day celebration in 1916 was Bontty's Coronet Band. See *Prague Record*, 15 June 1916.

Chapter 7

1. Details of the football game between Prague and Seminole and a roster of players are found in the *Prague Record*, 23 September 1920.

2. A booklet published in the late 1920s featured photos of Prague's finest homes and included the Joseph J. Klabzuba residence. Prague Chamber of Commerce, *City of Opportunities*, 9.

3. Manuscript Census, 1920, South Creek Township.

3. Manuscript Census, 1920, South Creek Township.

4. Kraut, *The Huddled Masses,* 134–37; Salins, *Assimilation, American Style,* 7.

5. Lincoln County Historical Society, *Lincoln County,* 186.

6. Brown, *Czech-Town,* 68.

7. Tower, "A General History of the Town of Prague," 36–37; Brown, *Czech-Town,* 67–69.

8. *Prague Times-Herald,* 6 August 1987. The members of the first graduating class of Prague High School were Nora Jenkins, Walter Schoggen, Gertrude Jukes, Mabel Jukes, Mattie Roberts, Alda Heatley, Beatrice Mansur, Lora Jenkins, and George Sadlo.

9. Prague Historical Society, *Prague, the First 100 Years: Prague, Oklahoma, 1902–2002* (Rich Hill, MO: Bell Books, 2001), 53. Black children attended a separate school. Like most American towns during this period, Prague practiced segregation of the races. *Prague News,* 7 September 1905.

10. Michael R. Olneck and Marvin Lazerson, "Education," in *Harvard Encyclopedia of American Ethnic Groups,* ed. Thernstrom et al., 307; Weiss, *American Education,* xiii.

11. Salins, *Assimilation, American Style,* 7.

12. Milton M. Gordon, *Assimilation in American Life: The Role of Race, Religion, and National Origins* (New York: Oxford University Press, 1964), 35.

13. Will Herberg, *Protestant, Catholic, Jew: An Essay in American Religious Sociology,* rev. ed. (Garden City, NY: Anchor Books, 1960), 16.

14. Matthew Spinka, *John Hus: A Biography* (Princeton: Princeton University Press, 1968), 130–64; W. N. Schwarze, *John Hus, the Martyr of Bohemia* (New York: Fleming H. Revell, 1915), 68–70, 134–35.

15. Elizabeth Wiskemann, *Czechs and Germans: A Study of the Struggle in the Historic Provinces of Bohemia and Moravia* (London: Oxford University Press, 1938), 6–7; Howard Kaminsky, *A History of the Hussite Revolution* (Berkeley: University of California Press, 1967), 58–59, 140–41, 369; Rosicky, *A History of Czechs (Bohemians) in Nebraska,* 284.

16. R. W. Seton-Watson, *A History of the Czechs and Slovaks* (1943; repr., Hamden, CT: Archon Books, 1965), 113; Wiskemann, *Czechs and Germans,* 9–10.

17. Zizka, *Czech Cultural Contributions,* 70; Bicha, *Czechs in Oklahoma,* 26.

18. Zizka, *Czech Cultural Contributions,* 48.

19. Garver, "Czech-American Freethinkers," 156.

20. Martin, "The Cultural Assimilation of the Czechoslovak," 137.

21. Unfortunately, only ten of the twenty-two students recorded could be

found in cemetery records. Some, no doubt, moved away from Prague before their death. Female students were particularly difficult to locate in cemetery records unless the tombstone recorded their maiden name.

22. The original photograph of the Czech school is in the Prague Historical Museum.

23. No instructional material remains, so the language of instruction cannot be ascertained with complete certainty. However, since this early school was a definite attempt on the part of the immigrant community to maintain their heritage, including their language, there is a high probability that classes were taught in Czech.

24. Interest in Sokol Hall waned during the 1930s Depression. After World War II, activity resumed, but by the early 1970s the organization attracted few members. The town tore down the Sokol Hall building in 1976 and deeded the land to the American Legion. On paper the lodge existed until 1992 and then was officially disbanded after almost ninety years of existence. The last three directors were Jim Pospisil, Frank Sefcik, and Leonard Walenta. Prague Historical Society, *Prague, the First 100 Years*, 69.

25. Joshua A. Fishman, "Language Maintenance," in *Harvard Encyclopedia of American Ethnic Groups*, ed. Thernstrom et al., 630; Martin, "The Cultural Assimilation of the Czechoslovak," 145–47.

26. Brown, *Czech-Town*, 66.

27. Frank Vlasak appears to be an exception. Vlasak, although owning farmland, operated a general store in Dent soon after the 1891 land run. He continued his business proclivities after the opening of Prague by opening a store in the new town.

28. U.S. Immigration Commission, *Reports*, 12:87. See chapter 2 for specifics of the commission's findings.

29. Manuscript Census, 1900, South Creek Township. Illiterate is normally defined as someone who can neither read nor write. Thus if one can read but not write, a better term for that person might be *uneducated* rather than the offensive term *illiterate*. Only two adult Czechs in 1900 fell under the category "illiterate."

30. Although it is unclear exactly when the family left Texas for Oklahoma Territory, the Pechaceks lived in Oklahoma Territory in 1898. Josef Pechacek joined the Bohemian Hall in 1898, at that time located in Dent, Oklahoma; Matilda joined in 1899. See Bohemian Hall membership rolls, 1898–1904.

31. Manuscript Census, 1900, South Creek Township.

32. The Pechacek family is not found on the 1910 census. Bohemian Hall updated their membership records in 1912 and showed the name Matilda Pechacek. There is an annotation beside her name, "gone." Josef Pechacek is not mentioned on the 1912 membership rolls. See Bohemian Hall membership rolls, 1912.

33. Manuscript Census, 1900, South Creek Township.

34. The three non-English speakers were Vaclav and Mary Baestam and Elizabeth Petecka. Manuscript Census, 1920, South Creek Township.

35. Ibid.

36. Manuscript Census, 1910, 1920, South Creek Township.

37. Agnes Martinek's mother was fifty-seven. She married Vincent Martinek at age thirty-four. The couple had two children, Agnes and Esther. All three women claimed on the census that they could speak English. Manuscript Census, 1910, South Creek Township.

38. Manuscript Census, 1920, South Creek Township.

39. Ellen Whitmore, Ensley Barbour, Leoti Overstreet, Cora Casey, Alma Thomas, and Dora Newhouse constituted Prague's first eighth-grade graduating class in 1904.

40. There are no existing records of the tuition amount of the Czech school. As a private institution it needed operational funds to buy books and materials and to pay the teacher. Where the money came from, if not from parents, is uncertain. Author found nothing in the records of the ZCBJ Lodge to suggest the Bohemian Hall financed the school.

41. Of the three families, the Sestaks and Leders were prominent in the Czech community, but the Martineks, who were Catholic, appear more sectarian and less involved.

42. Bicha, *Czechs in Oklahoma*, 39.

43. *Prague Record*, 3 February 1926.

44. Paul White, a non-Czech, attended Creighton with the Klabzubas. The *Prague Record* reported the three traveled home together for a visit in 1926. *Prague Record*, 6 January 1926.

45. *Prague Record*, 6 January and 31 March 1926.

46. *Prague Record*, 23 May 1928; Brown, *Czech-Town*, 73.

47. *Prague Record*, 23 May 1927, 4 June 1928.

48. *Prague Record*, 27 August 1915; Tower, "A General History of the Town of Prague," 38.

49. *Prague Record*, 14 April 1929.

50. *Prague Times-Herald*, 6 August 1987.

51. George Sadlo graduated high school in 1913, two years before Prague

fielded a football squad. Otherwise, he probably would have excelled in this sport also.

52. Prague Historical Society, *Prague, the First 100 Years,* 47. Other farming families mentioned as supplying living quarters for young teachers were the Eddy Hillmans, Jerry Nelsons, and Blant Southerns.

53. Ibid., 47–53. Czech farmers living in Arlington area were found in the Manuscript Census, 1900, North Creek Township.

54. Olneck and Lazerson, "Education," 307. Victor Greene also writes about how Czechs valued public schools and in some instances actually used state universities to help preserve their culture. Greene, "Ethnic Confrontations with State Universities," 199.

55. Kutak, *The Story of a Bohemian-American Village,* 63.

56. Brown, *Czech-Town,* 73.

57. Prague Historical Society, *Prague, the First 100 Years,* 45. Czech students identified as members of the *beseda* dance team were Eddie, Ernest, and Helen Sestak, Rose and Raymond Svoboda, Emily Bruza, John Sefcik, Marie Pospisil, Emil Kucera, Helen Soukup, Rose Vobornik, Elba Cerney, and Henry Womastek.

Chapter 8

1. The *Prague News,* 7 June 1906, listed the location of the Mertes and Heatley Store as being on the west side of Broadway Avenue. In November 1906, the *Prague News* placed the Vobornik and Kinsey Meat Market at the corner of Broadway and Main.

2. Paraphrased from stories found in *Prague News,* 9 May 1907; Lynch, "Czech Farmers in Oklahoma," 103; and Brown, *Czech-Town,* 137–38.

3. Manuscript Census, 1900, South Creek Township.

4. Brown, *Czech-Town,* 138.

5. Kutak, *The Story of a Bohemian-American Village,* 31–32, 35.

6. Rosicky, *A History of Czechs (Bohemians) in Nebraska,* 444.

7. Balch, *Our Slavic Fellow Citizens,* 394.

8. Chada, *Czechs in the United States,* 33–34.

9. Balch, *Our Slavic Fellow Citizens,* 392–93. Garver "Czech-American Freethinkers," 148, puts the number of Czech freethinkers at about one in six. Laska's *Czechs in America,* 53, names Cleveland as the hotbed of Czech socialism.

10. Lincoln County Historical Society, *Lincoln County,* 404–5; *Prague Record,* 6 July 1916.

11. *Prague News,* 1 September 1904.

12. *Prague News*, 4 May 1905. The *Prague News* reported on 10 May 1906 that James Harris had defeated A. F. Wood for police judge by six votes. Neither was Czech.

13. Zizka, *Czech Cultural Contributions*, 100.

14. *Prague News*, 10 May 1906. The Bohemian Political Association remained active until after World War II. Prague's Czechs became especially incensed after the Munich Conference in 1938 and Hitler's takeover of Czechoslovakia. The *Tulsa Tribune*, 20 March 1939, reported that both of Prague's fraternal organizations, the ZCBJ and Sokol, sent letters of protest to Great Britain.

15. Lynch, "Czech Farmers in Oklahoma," 103.

16. *Prague Record*, 5 April 1917.

17. *Prague Record*, 7 April 1926.

18. The *Prague News*, 27 July 1915, included a directory of the local lodges.

19. A few examples can be seen in *Prague Record*, 27 July 1915, 1 June 1916, 6 July 1916, 23 November 1916, 23 September 1920, and 13 January 1926. Czechs prided themselves on their lodge associations and in some cases etched their memberships on their tombstones. This is especially true of those belonging to the Masonic order.

20. *Prague Record*, 27 April 1927, 31 August 1927. W. H. Hartman was the Chamber's first president, and George Jepsen, a cotton buyer and part-owner of the Union Cotton Oil Company and Jepsen Gin Company, was the first vice president.

21. *Prague Record*, 25 May 1927.

22. Prague Chamber of Commerce, *Prague, Oklahoma: City of Opportunities*, 32–34, 37–39.

23. *Prague Record*, 15 June 1922.

24. *Prague Record*, 7 September 1922. See James Lowell Showalter, "Payne County and the Hooded Klan, 1921–1924" (PhD diss., Oklahoma State University, 2000).

25. Most revival announcements and short articles appeared in Prague's newspapers during the summer months of the second and third decades of the town. For examples, see *Prague Record*, 1 June 1916, 1 July 1927. In 1927 Prague's churches held a "Union Revival" throughout the summer. Today this event probably would be called a nondenominational or interdenominational meeting. It should be noted that, although filled with emotion, these revivals were not Pentecostal in the modern-day sense of the word; they were led by Methodists, Baptists, and Presbyterians. The charismatic or tongue's movement did not start

until 1906 in California. It only slowly made its way eastward. Prague's first Pentecostal Holiness Church did not open its doors until 1945. The first Assembly of God building was erected in 1947. Brown, *Czech-town*, 124–25.

26. *Prague Record*, 6 July 1916.

27. Martin, "The Cultural Assimilation of the Czechoslovak," 167.

28. A Czech did not always lead the band. Ludie Johnston directed Prague's twenty-four-member town band in 1926, which included the following Czechs: Eddie Bartosh, Joe Lanik, Elmer Sojka, Lada Kucera, Billie Kanak, Alfred Spaniel, and Julius Bontty. *Prague Record*, 22 September 1926.

29. Prague Chamber of Commerce, *City of Opportunities*, 23. Other Czechs on the 1929 Municipal Band included Charles Suva, Jake Simek, Frank Navrah, Charles Jezek, and Frank Sleva.

30. Ibid. The other Czech member of the fire department was August Bartosh. Both Bartosh and Babek belonged to the Catholic Church.

31. *Prague Record*, 8 February 1917; *Prague News*, 15 March 1906. The newspaper listed the partners of the cigar factory as J. Hajek, A. J. Balaun, Wes Wostichil, and Mr. Halousek.

32. Tower, "A General History of the Town of Prague," 50.

33. Prague Chamber of Commerce, *Prague, Oklahoma: City of Opportunities*, 30–40. The ten Czechs featured in the booklet were Charles Klabzuba, Frank Svoboda, Frank Zajic, C. M. Sadlo, Steve Kanak, Julius Bonty, Charles Babek, Joe Stoklasa, Charles Jezek, and Frank Jezek.

34. Kraut, *The Huddled Masses*, 117.

35. Handlin, *The Uprooted*, 94.

36. Kutak, *Story of a Bohemian-American Village*, x–xii, 49.

37. Ibid., 63, 65.

38. Ibid., 69.

39. Ibid., 90–91. Many Czechs loved to drink beer. However, this was the time of Prohibition.

40. Ibid., 67.

41. Ibid., 2, 4.

42. Skrabanak, *We're Czechs*, xii.

43. Ibid., 3, 228.

44. *Greenhorn* was the common term for a newly arrived immigrant, someone who understood little about the culture of America.

45. Lincoln County Historical Society, *Lincoln County*, 1362.

46. *Prague News*, 20 September 1906; *Prague Record*, 30 January 1928.

47. *Prague Record,* 12 September 1929.

48. Bicha, *Czechs in Oklahoma,* 48.

Epilogue

1. Prague did not hold a Kolache Festival between 1955 and 1965. It has been continuous since 1966.

2. Diana Kinzey, interview by Philip D. Smith, telephone, Prague, Oklahoma, 10 January 2016.

3. Valdean Sestak, interview by Philip D. Smith, telephone, Prague, Oklahoma, 16 February 2016. The Bohemian Hall officers for 2016 were Ross Sestak, president, Marjorie Jezek VanDyke, vice president; Cindy Fredrich, secretary; and Valdean Kozel Sestak, treasurer.

4. Thomas and Holman family tree, 21 July 2016, http://ancestry.com, search Vaclav Ladra. See also http://pladra.com.

5. Weir, Bell, and Allied families tree, 20 July 2016, http://ancestry.com, search Jan Sefcif.

6. U.S. Find a Grave Index, 1600s—Current, Provo, Utah (for Jack Barta's obituary), http://ancestry.com, 23 July 2016, search Josephine Barta.

7. Robinc Family Tree, 18 July 2016, http://ancestry.com, search Olinka Hrdy.

8. Search C. M. Sadlo and George Sadlo on http://ancestry.com. Obituary for Kathryn Sadlo Wilson from Dundee *Daily Herald,* 28 November 2008. Search Kathryn Sadlo Wilson, http://ancestry.com.

9. When I interviewed Bohemian Hall treasurer Valdean Sestak, I asked if the ethnic organization still proclaimed freethought as one of their tenets. Ms. Sestak replied that she knew nothing about freethought. Valdean Sestak, interview by Philip D. Smith, telephone, Prague, Oklahoma, 16 February 2016.

Bibliography

Primary Sources

Benes, Vojta. *Economic Strength of the Bohemian (Czechoslovak) Lands.* Chicago: Bohemian (Czech) National Alliance, 1918.

Bohemian National Alliance. *The Position of the Bohemians (Czechs) in the European War.* Chicago: Bohemian National Alliance in America, n.d.

Czech National Alliance in Great Britain. *Austrian Terrorism in Bohemia.* London: Czech National Alliance in Great Britain, n.d.

Czech National Cemetery, Prague, OK.

Czechoslovak Arts Club. *The Czech Declaration of January 6, 1918.* New York: Czechoslovak Arts Club, 1918.

———. *The Independence of the Czechoslovak Nation: Quotations from Wilson, Viviani, Balfour, Palacky, Masaryk, Seton-Watson, & Others.* New York: Czechoslovak Arts Club, 1918.

Dillingham, William P. Dillingham Family Papers. Woodson Research Center, Rice University, Houston.

———. Miscellaneous papers and printed materials. Assorted collections. Waterbury Historical Society, Waterbury, VT.

Dostalik, Carmen. "Carmen Dostalik's Scrapbook: Interesting Clippings of Prague Residents and Personal Writings of Family Histories." Three-ring binder. Prague Historical Museum, n.d.

First Baptist Church. Church records. Prague, OK.

First Methodist Church. Membership rolls. Prague, OK.

Land Records. Lincoln County. Township 12, Range 6, Sections 20–29. Lincoln County Courthouse, Chandler, OK.

Masaryk, Thomas G. *Declaration of the Bohemian (Czech) Foreign Committee: Comments of London Papers.* Chicago: Bohemian National Alliance of America, n.d.

Namier, Lewis B. *The Case of Bohemia.* London: Czech National Alliance, 1917.

Oklahoma Geological Survey. *Bulletin No. 19: Petroleum and Natural Gas in Oklahoma, Part II: A Discussion of the Oil and Gas Fields, and Undeveloped Areas of the State by Counties.* Norman: Oklahoma Geological Survey, 1917.

Pergler, Charles. *The Bohemians (Czechs) in the Present Crisis: An Address Delivered by Charles Pergler, LL.B., on the 28th Day of May, 1916, in Chicago,* at a Meeting Held to Commemorate the Deeds of Bohemian Volunteers in the Great War. Chicago: Bohemian National Alliance, 1916.

———. Bohemia's Claim to Independence: An Address Delivered by Charles Pergler, LL.B., before the Committee on Foreign Affairs of the House of Representatives of the United States on February 25, 1916. Chicago: Bohemian National Alliance, 1916.

Prague Chamber of Commerce. Prague, Oklahoma: City of Opportunities. Brochure.

Prague City Cemetery. Prague, OK.

Prague Historical Museum. Archives and Photo Collection. Prague, OK.

Rolvaag, Edvart. Giants in the Earth: A Saga of the Prairie. New York: Harper & Brothers, 1927; reprint, New York: First Perennial Classics, 1999.

St. Wenceslaus Catholic Cemetery. Prague, OK.

U.S. Bureau of the Census. Fourteenth Census of the United States, 1920. Washington, DC: National Archives and Records Administration, 1920.

———. Thirteenth Census of the United States, 1910. Washington, DC: National Archives and Records Administration, 1910; Washington, DC: Government Printing Office, 1913.

———. Twelfth Census of the United States, 1900. Washington, DC: National Archives and Records Administration, 1900.

———. Manuscript Census Schedules for South Creek Township and North Creek Township, Lincoln County, OK, 1900, 1910, 1920, and 1930.

———. Manuscript Census Schedules for Yukon Township, Canadian County, OK, 1900, 1910, and 1920.

U.S. Department of Commerce Immigration Commission. Reports of the Immigration Commission. 42 vols. Washington, DC: Government Printing Office, 1911.

Western Czech Brotherhood Association (Zapadni Ceske Bratrska Jednota). Bohemian Hall financial account books, Lodge 46, Prague, OK.

———. Bohemian Hall meeting minutes, Lodge 46, Prague, OK.

———. Bohemian Hall membership rolls, Lodge 46, Prague, OK.

Periodicals

Monthly New Era (Davenport, OK, 2000)

New York Times (1919)

Oklahomske Noviny (Chicago) (1905–6)

Prague News (1902–17)

Prague News-Record (1920–30)

Prague Patriot (1903–9)
Prague Record (1909–20)
Prague Times-Herald (1987)
Tulsa Tribune (1945)

Secondary Sources

Books

Alexander, Charles C. *The Ku Klux Klan in the Southwest*. Lexington: University of Kentucky Press, 1965.

Anderson, Benedict. *Imagined Communities: Reflections on the Origin and Spread of Nationalism*. Rev. ed. London: Verso, 1991.

Archdeacon, Thomas J. *Becoming American: An Ethnic History*. New York: Free Press, 1983.

Avrich, Paul. *The Haymarket Tragedy*. Princeton: Princeton University Press, 1984.

Baca, Leo. *Czech Immigration Passenger Lists*. 3 vols. Halletsville, TX: Old Homestead; Richardson, TX: Copies from L. Baca, 1983–89.

Bailyn, Bernard. *The Peopling of British North America: An Introduction*. New York: Alfred A. Knopf, 1986.

Balch, Emily Greene. *Our Slavic Fellow Citizens*. New York: Charities Publication Committee, 1910; repr., New York: Arno Press, 1969.

Barkan, Elliott R. *And Still They Come: Immigrants and American Society, 1920 to the 1990s*. Wheeling, IL: Harlan Davidson, 1996.

Bernard, Richard. *The Poles in Oklahoma*. Norman: University of Oklahoma Press, 1980.

Bicha, Karel D. *The Czechs in Oklahoma*. Norman: University of Oklahoma Press, 1980.

Blanshard, Paul. *American Freedom and Catholic Power*. Boston: Beacon Press, 1958.

Blessing, Patrick. *The British and Irish in Oklahoma*. Norman: University of Oklahoma Press, 1980.

Bodnar, John. *The Transplanted: A History of Immigrants in Urban America*. Bloomington: Indiana University Press, 1985.

Brown, Kenny L. *The Italians in Oklahoma*. Norman: University of Oklahoma Press, 1980.

Brown, Melva Losch. *Czech-Town U.S.A., Prague (Kolache-Ville), Oklahoma*. Norman: Hooper Printing, 1978.

Buenker, John. *Urban Liberalism and Progressive Reform*. New York: Charles Scribner's Sons, 1973.

Capek, Thomas. *American Czechs in Public Office*. Omaha: Czech Historical Society of Nebraska, 1940.

———. *The Czechs (Bohemians) in America: A Study of Their National, Cultural, Political, Social, Economic, and Religious Life*, 1920; repr., New York: Arno Press, 1969.

Carter, Stephen L. *The Culture of Disbelief*. New York: Basic Books, 1993.

Casper, Henry W. *History of the Catholic Church in Nebraska*. 4 vols. Milwaukee: Bruce, 1966.

Chada, Joseph. *Czech-American Catholics, 1850–1920*. Chicago: Benedictine Abbey Press, 1964.

———. *The Czechs in the United States*. Chicago: Czechoslovak Society of Art and Sciences, 1981.

Child, Irvin. *Italian or American? Second Generation in Conflict*. New Haven: Yale University Press, 1943.

Crispino, James. *The Assimilation of Ethnic Groups: The Italian Case*. Staten Island: Center for Migration Studies, 1980.

Diner, Steven J. *A Very Different Age: Americans of the Progressive Era*. New York: Hill & Wang, 1998.

Dobra, Daniel, ed. *Czech and Slovak Leaders in Metropolitan Chicago*. Chicago: Slavonic Club, University of Chicago, 1934.

Dolan, Jay P. *In Search of an American Catholicism: A History of Religion and Culture in Tension*. New York: Oxford University Press, 2002.

Dvornik, Francis. *Czech Contributions to the Growth of the United States*. Chicago: Benedictine Abbey Press, 1962.

Erickson, Charlotte, ed. *Emigration from Europe, 1815–1914: Select Documents*. London: Adam and Charles Black, 1976.

Fishman, Joshua A. *Language Loyalty in the United States: The Maintenance and Perpetuation of Non-English Mother Tongues by American Ethnic and Religious Groups*. London: Mouton, 1966.

Franklin, Jimmie Lewis. *The Blacks in Oklahoma*. Norman: University of Oklahoma Press, 1980.

Gallup, Sean N. *Journeys into Czech-Moravian Texas*. College Station: Texas A&M University Press, 1998.

Gambino, Richard. *Blood of My Blood*. Garden City, NY: Anchor Books, 1975.

Gans, Herbert J. *The Urban Villagers: Group and Class in the Life of Italian-Americans*. New York: Free Press, 1962.

Garis, Roy L. *Immigration Restriction: A Study of Opposition to and Regulation of Immigration into the United States*. New York: Macmillan, 1927.

Glazer, Nathan, and Daniel Patrick Moynihan. *Beyond the Melting Pot.* Cambridge: MIT Press, 1963.

Gordon, Milton M. *Assimilation in American Life: The Role of Race, Religion, and National Origins.* New York: Oxford University Press, 1964.

Gottfried, Alex. *Boss Cermak of Chicago: A Study of Political Leadership.* Seattle: University of Washington Press, 1962.

Graham, Otis L. *Unguarded Gates: A History of America's Crisis.* Lanham, MD: Rowman & Littlefield, 2004.

Greeley, Andrew. *Ethnicity in the United States: A Preliminary Reconnaissance.* New York: Wiley, 1974.

———. *Why Can't They Be Like Us? America's White Ethnic Groups.* New York: E. P. Dutton, 1971.

Gregory, Robert. *Oil in Oklahoma.* Muskogee, OK: Leake Industries, 1976.

Habenicht, Jan. *A History of Czechs in America.* St. Louis: Hlas, 1910.

Haldeman-Julius, Emanuel. *The Germans from Russia in Oklahoma.* Norman: University of Oklahoma Press, 1980.

———. *The Militant Agnostic.* Amherst, NY: Prometheus Books, 1995.

Handlin, Oscar. *Boston's Immigrants, 1790–1880: A Study in Acculturation.* Cambridge, MA: Harvard University Press, 1941.

———. *The Uprooted: The Epic Story of the Great Migrations That Made the American People.* Boston: Little, Brown, 1951.

Hansen, Marcus Lee. *The Atlantic Migration, 1607–1860.* Cambridge, MA: Harvard University Press, 1940.

Hareven, Tamara K. *Families, History, and Social Change: Life-Course and Cross-Cultural Perspectives.* Boulder, CO: Westview Press, 2000.

Harlow, Victor E. *Oklahoma: Its Origins and Development.* Oklahoma City: Harlow, 1935.

Herberg, Will. *Protestant, Catholic, Jew: An Essay in American Religious Sociology.* Rev. ed. Garden City, NY: Anchor Books, 1960.

Higham, John. *Send These to Me: Immigrants in Urban America.* Rev. ed. Baltimore: Johns Hopkins University Press, 1984.

———. *Strangers in the Land: Patterns of American Nativism, 1860–1925.* 2nd ed. New Brunswick, NJ: Rutgers University Press, 1988.

Hudson, Estelle, and Henry R. Maresh. *Czech Pioneers of the Southwest.* Dallas: Southwest Press, 1934.

Jacoby, Susan. *Freethinkers: A History of American Secularism.* New York: Metropolitan Books, 2004.

Jerabek, Esther. *Czechs and Slovaks in North America: A Bibliography.* New York: Czechoslovak Society of Arts and Sciences in America, 1976.

Jones, Maldwyn Allen. *American Immigration*. Chicago: University of Chicago Press, 1960.

Kallen, Horace. *Cultural Pluralism and the American Idea: An Essay in Social Philosophy*. Philadelphia: University of Pennsylvania Press, 1956.

———. *Culture and Democracy in the United States: Studies in the Group Psychology of the American People*. Salem, NH: Ayer, 1924.

Kaminsky, Howard. *A History of the Hussite Revolution*. Berkeley: University of California Press, 1967.

Kann, Robert A. *A History of the Habsburg Empire, 1526–1918*. Berkeley: University of California Press, 1974.

Kerner, Robert J., ed. *Czechoslovakia*. Berkeley: University of California Press, 1945.

Kimmel, Michael. *Manhood in America: A Cultural History*. New York: Free Press, 1996.

King, Desmond. *The Liberty of Strangers: Making the American Nation*. New York: Oxford University Press, 2005.

Klein, James Edward. *Grappling with Demon Rum: The Cultural Struggle over Liquor in Early Oklahoma*. Norman: University of Oklahoma Press, 2008.

Kraut, Alan M. *The Huddled Masses: The Immigrant in American Society, 1880–1921*. Arlington Heights, IL: Harlan Davidson, 1986.

Kutak, Robert. *The Story of a Bohemian-American Village: A Study of Social Persistence and Change*. 1933. Reprint, New York: Arno Press and the New York Times, 1970.

Larson, Orvin. *American Infidel: Robert G. Ingersoll*. New York: Citadel Press, 1962.

Laska, Vera, ed. *The Czechs in America, 1633–1977: A Chronology and Fact Book*. Dobbs Ferry, NY: Oceana, 1978.

Ledbetter, Eleanor E. *The Czechs of Cleveland*. Cleveland: Mayor's Advisory War Committee, 1919.

Lieberson, Stanley. *Ethnic Patterns in American Cities*. New York: Free Press, 1963.

———. *A Piece of the Pie: Blacks and White Immigrants since 1880*. Berkeley: University of California Press, 1980.

Lincoln County Historical Society. *Lincoln County: Oklahoma History*. Saline, MI: McNaughton & Gunn, 1988.

Luebke, Frederick C., ed. *Ethnicity on the Great Plains*. Lincoln: University of Nebraska Press, 1980.

Macdonald, George E. *Fifty Years of Freethought*. 2 vols. New York: Truth Seeker, 1929.

Machann, Clinton, and James W. Mendl Jr., trans. and eds. *Czech Voices: Stories from Texas in the Amerikán Národní Kalendář.* College Station: Texas A&M University Press, 1991.

———. *Krasna Amerika: A Study of the Texas Czechs, 1851–1939.* Austin, TX: Eakin Press, 1983.

Mangione, Jerre. *Mount Allegro: A Memoir of Italian American Life.* New York: Columbia University Press, 1981.

McReynolds, Edwin C. *Oklahoma: A History of the Sooner State.* Norman: University of Oklahoma Press, 1954.

Miller, Kenneth D. *The Czecho-Slovaks in America.* New York: George H. Doran, 1922.

Miller, Randall, and Thomas Marzik, ed. *Immigrants and Religion in Urban America.* Philadelphia: Temple University Press, 1977.

Monahan, David, ed. *One Family, One Century: A Photographic History of the Catholic Church in Oklahoma, 1875–1975.* Oklahoma City: Archdiocese of Oklahoma City, 1977.

Nelli, Humbert S. *Italians in Chicago, 1800–1930: A Study in Ethnic Mobility.* New York: Oxford University Press, 1970.

Nemecek, Paul M. *Historical and Cultural Essays on Czechs in America.* Privately published, 2005.

Novak, Michael. *The Rise of the Unmeltable Ethnics.* New York: Macmillan, 1971.

O'Neill, William L. *The Progressive Years: America Comes of Age.* New York: Dodd, Mead, 1975.

Petrin, Ronald A. *French Canadians in Massachusetts Politics, 1815–1915: Ethnicity and Political Pragmatism.* Philadelphia: Balch Institute Press, 1990.

Polenberg, Richard. *One Nation Divisible: Class, Race, and Ethnicity in the United States.* New York: Viking Press, 1980.

Prague Historical Society. *Prague, the First 100 Years: Prague, Oklahoma, 1902–2002.* Rich Hill, MO: Bell Books, 2001.

Reese, Linda Williams. *Women of Oklahoma, 1890–1920.* Norman: University of Oklahoma Press, 1997.

Reichman, John J. *Czechoslovaks of Chicago.* Chicago: Czechoslovak Historical Society of Chicago, 1937.

Rogers, Daniel T. *Atlantic Crossings: Social Politics in a Progressive Era.* Cambridge, MA: Harvard University Press, 1998.

Rohrs, Richard C. *Crossroads Oklahoma: The German-American Experience in Oklahoma.* Stillwater: Oklahoma State University, 1981.

————. *The Germans in Oklahoma*. Norman: University of Oklahoma Press, 1980.

Rosicky, Rose. *A History of Czechs (Bohemians) in Nebraska*. Omaha: Czech Historical Society of Nebraska, 1929.

Roucek, Joseph Slabey, and Bernard Eisenberg, eds. *America's Ethnic Politics*. Westport, CT: Greenwood Press, 1982.

Ryan, Joseph A. *White Ethnics: Life in Working-Class America*. Englewood Cliffs, NJ: Prentice-Hall, 1973.

Salins, Peter D. *Assimilation, American Style*. New York: Basic Books, 1997.

Schrag, Peter. *The Decline of the WASP*. New York: Simon and Schuster, 1971.

Schwarze, W. N. *John Hus, the Martyr of Bohemia: A Study of the Dawn of Protestantism*. New York: Fleming H. Revell, 1915.

Seton-Watson, R. W. *A History of the Czechs and Slovaks*. 1943. Hamden, CT: Archon Books, 1965.

Skrabanek, Robert L. *We're Czechs*. College Station: Texas A&M University Press, 1988.

Smith, Michael M. *The Mexicans in Oklahoma*. Norman: University of Oklahoma Press, 1980.

Solomon, Barbara Miller. *Ancestors and Immigrants: A Changing New England Tradition*. Cambridge, MA: Harvard University Press, 1956.

Spinka, Matthew. *John Hus: A Biography*. Princeton: Princeton University Press, 1968.

Stasko, Joseph. *Slovaks in the United States of America: Brief Sketches of Their History, National Heritage, and Activities*. Cambridge, ON: Dobrá Kniha, 1974.

Stein, Gordon, ed. *The Encyclopedia of Unbelief*. Buffalo, NY: Prometheus Books, 1985.

Steinberg, Stephen. *The Ethnic Myth: Race, Ethnicity, and Class in America*. New York: Atheneum, 1981.

Strickland, Rennard. *The Indians in Oklahoma*. Norman: University of Oklahoma Press, 1980.

Thomson, S. Harrison. *Czechoslovakia in European History*. Princeton: Princeton University Press, 1953.

Tobias, Henry J. *The Jews in Oklahoma*. Norman: University of Oklahoma Press, 1980.

Tucker, Richard. *The Dragon and the Cross: The Rise and Fall of the Ku Klux Klan in Middle America*. Hamden, CT: Archon Books, 1991.

Turner, James. *Without God, without Creed: The Origins of Unbelief in America*. Baltimore: Johns Hopkins University Press, 1985.

Ward, David. *Cities and Immigrants*. New York: Oxford University Press, 1971.

Warren, Sidney. *American Freethought, 1860–1914*. New York: Columbia University Press, 1996.

Weisberger, Bernard A. *Many People, One Nation*. Boston: Houghton Mifflin, 1987.

Weiss, Bernard J., ed. *American Education and the European Immigrant, 1840–1940*. Urbana: University of Illinois Press, 1982.

Wepman, Dennis. *Immigration: From the Founding of Virginia to the Closing of Ellis Island*. New York: Facts on File, 2002.

Whitehead, Fred, and Verle Muhrer. *Free-Thought on the American Frontier*. Buffalo: Prometheus Books, 1992.

Wickett, Murray R. *Contested Territory: Whites, Native Americans, and African Americans in Oklahoma, 1865–1907*. Baton Rouge: Louisiana State University Press, 2000.

Wiskemann, Elizabeth. *Czechs and Germans: A Study of the Struggle in the Historic Provinces of Bohemia and Moravia*. London: Oxford University Press, 1938.

Zeidel, Robert. *Immigrants, Progressives, and Exclusion Politics: The Dillingham Commission, 1900–1927*. DeKalb: Northern Illinois University Press, 2004.

Zizka, Ernest J. *Czech Cultural Contributions*. Chicago: Benedictine Abbey Press, 1942.

Articles and Book Chapters

Abramson, Harold J. "Religion." In *Harvard Encyclopedia of Ethnic Groups*, ed. Stephan Thernstrom, Ann Orlov, and Oscar Handlin, 150–60. Cambridge, MA: Belknap Press of Harvard University Press, 1980.

Alba, Richard D. "Social Assimilation among American Catholic National-Origin Groups." *American Sociological Review* 41 (March 1981): 1030–46.

———. "The Twilight of Ethnicity among Americans of European Ancestry: The Case of Italians." In *Ethnicity and Race in the U.S.A.: Toward the Twenty-First Century*, ed. Richard D. Alba, 134–58. Boston: Routledge & Kegan Paul, 1985.

Alba, Richard, and Mitchell Chamlin. "A Preliminary Examination of Ethnic Identification among Whites." *American Sociological Review* 48 (April 1983): 240–47.

Babcock, C. Merton. "Czech Songs in Nebraska." *Western Folklore* 8 (October 1949): 320–27.

Barton, Josef. "Land, Labor, and Community in Nueces: Czech Farmers and Mexican Laborers in South Texas, 1880–1930." In *European Immigrants in the American West: Community Histories,* ed. Frederick C. Luebke, 147–60. Albuquerque: University of New Mexico Press, 1998.

———. "Religion and Cultural Change in Czech Immigrant Communities, 1850–1920." In *Immigrants and Religion in Urban America,* ed. Randall M. Miller and Thomas D. Marzik, 3–24. Philadelphia: Temple University Press, 1977.

Bicha, Karel D. "Czech-American Historiography: 1964–1987." *Czechoslovak and Central European Journal* 9 (Summer–Winter 1990): 144–50.

———. "Settling Accounts with an Old Adversary: The Decatholization of Czech Immigrants in America." *Social History* 4 (November 1972): 45–60.

———. "The Survival of the Village in Urban America: A Note on Czech Immigrants in Chicago to 1914." *International Migration Review* 5 (Spring 1971): 72–74.

Blochowiak, Mary Ann. "'Woman with a Hatchet': Carry Nation Comes to Oklahoma Territory." *Chronicles of Oklahoma* 59, no. 2 (Summer 1981): 132–51.

Bodnar, John. "Schooling and the Slavic American Family." In *American Education and the European Immigrant: 1840–1940,* ed. Bernard J. Weiss, 78–95. Urbana: University of Illinois Press, 1982.

Brimelow, Peter. "Looking Back at America's History of Immigration: United States Ethnic Foundation Was White, Anglo-Saxon, and Protestant." In *Opposing Viewpoints in World History: Immigration,* ed. Tamara L. Roleff, 193–202. Farmington Hills, MI: Greenhaven Press, 2004.

Capek, Thomas. "Sociological Factors in Czech Immigration." *Slavonic and East European Review* 22 (December 1944): 93–98.

Chadima, Helen. "The Beseda: The Czech National Dance in Cedar Rapids, Iowa." *Dance Research Journal* 22, no. 2 (Autumn 1990): 23–28.

Chandler, William E. "Shall Immigration Be Suspended?" *North American Review* 156 (January 1893): 1–8.

Conzen, Kathleen Neils. "Historical Approaches to the Study of Rural Ethnic Communities." In *Ethnicity on the Great Plains,* ed. Frederick C. Luebke, 1–18. Lincoln: University of Nebraska Press, 1980.

Covello, Leonard. "Accommodation and the Elementary School Experience." In *White Ethnics: Life in Working-Class America,* ed. Joseph A. Ryan, 100–112. Englewood Cliffs, NJ: Prentice-Hall, 1973.

Dubovicky, Ivan. "Czech-Americans: An Ethnic Dilemma." *Nebraska History* 74 (Fall–Winter 1993): 195–208.

Dudek, J. B. "The Bohemian Language in America." *American Speech* 2 (April 1927): 299–311.

Easterlin, Richard A. "Immigration: Economic and Social Characteristics." In *Harvard Encyclopedia of American Ethnic Groups*, ed. Stephan Thernstrom, Ann Orlov, and Oscar Handlin, 476–86. Cambridge, MA: Belknap Press of Harvard University Press, 1980.

Eitinger, Leo. "Feeling at Home: Immigrants' Psychological Problems." In *Strangers in the World*, ed. Leo Eitinger and David Schwarz, 84–106. Bern, Switzerland: Hans Huber, 1981.

Elovitz, Paul H. "Patterns and Costs of Immigration." In *Immigrant Experiences: Personal Narrative and Psychological Analysis*, ed. Paul H. Elovitz and Charlotte Kahn, 60–73. Madison, NJ: Fairleigh Dickinson University Press, 1997.

Fischer, LeRoy H. "Oklahoma Territory, 1890–1907." *Chronicles of Oklahoma* 53 (Spring 1975): 3–8.

Fishman, Joshua A. "Language Maintenance." In *Harvard Encyclopedia of American Ethnic Groups*, ed. Stephan Thernstrom, Ann Orlov, and Oscar Handlin, 629–38. Cambridge, MA: Belknap Press of Harvard University Press, 1980.

Fowler, James H. "Creating an Atmosphere of Suppression, 1914–1917." *Chronicles of Oklahoma* 59 (Summer 1981): 202–23.

———. "Tar and Feather Patriotism: The Suppression of Dissent in Oklahoma during World War One." *Chronicles of Oklahoma* 56 (Winter 1978–79): 409–30.

Freeze, Karen Johnson. "Czechs." In *The Harvard Encyclopedia of American Ethnic Groups*, ed. Stephan Thernstrom, Ann Orlov, and Oscar Handlin, 261–72. Cambridge, MA: Belknap Press of Harvard University, 1980.

Gans, Herbert. "Symbolic Ethnicity: The Future of Ethnic Groups and Cultures in America." *Ethnic and Racial Studies* 2, no. 1 (January 1979).

Garver, Bruce. "Czech-American Freethinkers on the Great Plains, 1871–1914." In *Ethnicity on the Great Plains*, ed. Frederick C. Luebke, 147–69. Lincoln: University of Nebraska Press, 1980.

———. "Czech-American Protestants: A Minority within a Minority." *Nebraska History* 74 (Fall–Winter 1993): 150–67.

Greene, Victor R. "Ethnic Confrontations with State Universities, 1860–1920." In *American Education and the European Immigrant, 1840–1940*, ed. Bernard J. Weiss, 189–207. Urbana: University of Illinois Press, 1982.

Gumprecht, Blake. "A Saloon on Every Corner: Whiskey Towns of Oklahoma Territory, 1889–1907." *Chronicles of Oklahoma* 74 (Summer 1996): 146–73.

Hale, Douglas. "European Immigrants in Oklahoma: A Survey." *Chronicles of Oklahoma* 53 (Summer 1975): 179–203.

Hansen, Marcus Lee. "The Problem of the Third Generation Immigrant." In *Theories of Ethnicity: A Classical Reader,* ed. Werner Sollors, 202–16. New York: New York University Press, 1996.

———. "The Study of Man: The Third Generation in America." *Commentary* 14 (November 1952): 492–500.

Hareven, Tamara K., and John Modell. "Family Patterns." In *Harvard Encyclopedia of American Ethnic Groups,* ed. Stephan Thernstrom, Ann Orlov, and Oscar Handlin, 345–54. Cambridge, MA: Belknap Press of Harvard University Press, 1980.

Jahelka, Joseph. "The Role of Chicago Czechs in the Struggle for Czechoslovak Independence." *Journal of the Illinois State Historical Society* 31, no. 4 (December 1938): 381–410.

Johnson, W. H. "The Saloon in Indian Territory." *North American Review* 146 (March 1888): 340–41.

Kennedy, Ruby Jo Reeves. "Single or Triple Melting-Pot? Intermarriage Trends in New Haven, 1870–1940." *American Journal of Sociology* 49 (January 1944): 331–39.

Lowenbach, Jan. "Czech Composers and Musicians in America." *Musical Quarterly* 29 (1943): 313–28.

Luebke, Frederick C. "Czech-American Immigration: Some Historiographical Observations." *Nebraska History* 74 (Fall–Winter 1993): 218–22.

Lynch, Russell Willford. "Czech Farmers in Oklahoma: A Comparative Study of the Stability of a Czech Farm Group in Lincoln County, Oklahoma, and the Factors Relating to Its Stability." *Bulletin of Oklahoma Agriculture and Mechanical College* 39, no. 13 (June 1942).

Machann, Clinton. "Religious Attitudes in Early Immigrant Autobiographies Written by Czechs in Texas." *MELUS* 22 (Winter 1997): 168–69.

Magocsi, Paul Robert. "Loyalties: Dual and Divided." In *Harvard Encyclopedia of American Ethnic Groups,* ed. Stephan Thernstrom, Ann Orlov, and Oscar Handlin, 676–89. Cambridge, MA: Belknap Press of Harvard University Press, 1980.

Meaders, Nobuko Yoshizawa. "The Transcultural Self." In *Immigrant Experiences: Personal Narrative and Psychological Analysis,* ed. Paul H. Elovitz and Charlotte Kahn, 47–59. Madison, NJ: Fairleigh Dickinson University Press, 1997.

Morawska, Ewa. "In Defense of the Assimilation Model." *Journal of American Ethnic History* 13, no. 2 (Winter 1994): 76–87.

Naramore, Ronald. "Ethnicity on the American Frontier: A Study of Czechs in Oklahoma." *Papers in Anthropology* 14 (Spring 1973): 104–14.

Nelson, Candace, and Marta Tienda. "The Structuring of Hispanic Ethnicity: Historical and Contemporary Perspectives." In *Ethnicity and Race in the U.S.A.: Toward the Twenty-First Century,* ed. Richard D. Alba, 49–74. Boston: Routledge & Kegan Paul, 1985.

Nolte, Claire E. "Our Brothers across the Ocean: The Czech Sokol in America to 1914." *Czechoslovak and Central European Journal* 11 (Winter 1993): 15–37.

Olneck, Michael R., and Marvin Lazerson. "Education." In *Harvard Encyclopedia of American Ethnic Groups,* ed. Stephan Thernstrom, Ann Orlov, and Oscar Handlin, 303–19. Cambridge, MA: Belknap Press of Harvard University Press, 1980.

Opatrny, Josef. "Problems in the History of Czech Immigration to America in the Second Half of the Nineteenth Century." *Nebraska History* 74 (Fall–Winter 1993): 120–29.

Park, Robert. "Racial Assimilation in Secondary Groups with Particular Reference to the Negro." *American Journal of Sociology* 19 (March 1914): 606–23.

Rakoff, Vivian. "Children of Immigrants." In *Strangers in the World,* ed. Leo Eitinger and David Schwarz, 133–46. Bern: Hans Huber, 1981.

Richards, Eugene S. "Trends of Negro Life in Oklahoma as Reflected by Census Reports." *Journal of Negro History* 33 (January 1948): 38–52.

Rohrs, Richard. "Settlement and Migration Patterns of Immigrants and Their Children: A Research Note." *Immigration History Newsletter* 19 (November 1987): 6–8.

Roucek, Joseph. "The Passing of American Czechoslovaks." *American Journal of Sociology* 39, no. 5 (March 1934): 611–25.

———. "Problems of Assimilation: A Study of Czechoslovaks in the United States." *Sociology and Social Research* 17 (September–October 1931): 62–71.

Smith, Timothy L. "Religion and Ethnicity in America." *American Historical Review* 83 (December 1978): 1155–81.

Stolarik, M. Mark. "Slovaks." In *The Harvard Encyclopedia of American Ethnic Groups,* ed. Stephan Thernstrom, Ann Orlov, and Oscar Handlin, 926–34. Cambridge, MA: Belknap Press of Harvard University Press, 1980.

Svoboda, Joseph G. "Czech-Americans: The Love of Liberty." *Nebraska History* 74, nos. 3–4 (Fall–Winter 1993): 109–19.

Theses and Dissertations

Klein, James Edward. "A Social History of Prohibition in Oklahoma, 1900–1920." PhD diss., Oklahoma State University, 2003.

Martin, William Earl. "The Cultural Assimilation of the Czechoslovak in Oklahoma City: A Study of Culture Contrasts." MA thesis, University of Oklahoma, 1935.

Rees, H. Louis. "The Czechs during World War I (Especially 1917–1918): Economic and Political Developments Leading toward Independence." PhD diss., Ohio State University, 1990.

Showalter, James Lowell. "Payne County and the Hooded Klan, 1921–1924." PhD diss., Oklahoma State University, 2000.

Smith, Philip D. "The Decline of Czechoslovak America: An Examination of Czechoslovak Immigration and Adjustment to the United States since 1960." MA thesis, University of Tulsa, 1992.

Tower, William Ray. "A General History of the Town of Prague, Oklahoma, 1902–1948." MA thesis, Oklahoma Agricultural and Mechanical College, 1948.

Interviews

Kinzey, Diana. Telephone interview by author, 10 January 2016.

Sestak, Valdean. Telephone interview by author, 16 February 2016.

Index

Hruska, Maximilian, 144n3, 145n20
Hudspeth, Kate, 60
Hull House, 32
Hungarians: dominating the Slovaks, 14; among "new immigrants," 14
Hus, Jan: commemoration of, 35, 61; honored by Milligan Czechs 132; medieval martyr, 35, 108; New York Presbyterian Church, 40–41; and World War I, 56

Illinois, 13–16, 26–27, 60, 100, 139, 156n47
immigration, 7, 9, 10–11, 14–15, 39–40, 47, 73, 97, 142n3, 142n6, 142n12, 143nn15–16, 143n23, 146n35, 147n9, 159n24. *See also* U.S. Immigration Commission
Independent Order of Odd Fellows, 46, 124
Indian Territory: alcohol smuggled into, 66–67; as "dry" territory, 65; and Fort Smith and Western Railroad, 3; Harris family in, 26–27; and Keokuk Falls, 65
Ingersoll, Robert, 33
Iowa, 13–15, 18–19, 24, 92–93, 98; Cedar Rapids, 98; Waterloo, 18
Ireland, 25
Irvine, F. S., 78
Italians: and Catholicism, 31; overall numbers in United States, 16; urban problems, 74, 129

Jepsen, George, 128, 168n20
Jezek, Charles, 169n29, 169n33
Jezek, Frank, 169n33
Jezek VanDyke, Marjorie, 170n3
Jim Crow laws, 126

Jim Thorpe Boulevard, 135
Johnson, Fr. George V., 135
Jones, Junia Heath, 99

Kahanek, Wesley, 118
Kaiser, Anna (wife of Jan), 113
Kaiser, Annie (daughter of Jan and Anna), 113
Kaiser, Jan (husband of Anna), 113, 145n20
Kanak, Billie, 169n28
Kanak, Steve, 125, 169n33
Kentucky Liquor House, 66
Keokuk Falls, Okla., 20, 65–66, 153n2
Keystone Oil and Gas Company, 157n61
Kilgo, Ednamae (wife of Herbert), 160n34, 161n39. *See also* Vlasak, Ednamae (wife of Herbert Kilgo)
Kilgo, Herbert (husband of Ednamae), 94–95, 160n34
Kingfisher, Okla.: Czech influence in, 16; and settlement of Czechs, 17, 144n35
Kinsey, C. E., 76, 167n1
Klabzuba, Charles "Charlie" (son of Joseph), 78, 105, 118, 124, 169n33
Klabzuba, Eddie, 102, 117
Klabzuba, Frank, 72, 155n38
Klabzuba, Joseph (Josef): member of ZCBJ, 64; owner of Kentucky Liquor House, 66–67; and second generation, 159n26
Klabzuba, Rose (wife of Harmon Veatch), 42
Klabzuba, Wes, 73, 76, 156n57
knedliky (dumplings), 135

McAdams, Ollie (husband of Rose Bouda), 42

McElvany, Rev. William, 125

McKim, Vern: livery business, 72; takes job at Vlasak's garage, 76

Medford, Okla., 17

Mertes, Jacob, 121, 155n34

Mertes, John, 60

Mertes, Nola, 72

Methodist Church, First United, 149n51, 149n54

Methodist-Episcopal Church, 41, 102, 148n38

Metropolitan Pool Hall, 162n65

Mid-Kansas Oil and Gas Company, 157n61

Miles, Fred, 101

Miller, Julia (wife of George Sala), 160n38

Milligan, Nebr., 13, 27, 38, 80, 88, 129–32; politics, 122, 128, 130; public school, 119. *See also* Nebraska

Minnesota, 13–15, 19, 24

Mishak, Okla., 16

Mitacek, Mike, 59, 70

M. L. Clark and Sons Circus, 103, 163n79

Modern Woodmen of America, 46

Moravia, Moravians, 4, 20–22, 98, 111, 133, 136, 142n11, 146n24, 164n15; animosity toward Austria, 144n5; and Austro-Hungarian Empire, 6–7; called "Czechs," 7; in Central Europe, 6, 12; creation of Sokols, 49–50; emigration from, 13; and freethought, 38–39; migration to Prague, Okla., 16, 20, 24–25; missionaries, 142n11; number

of families in Prague, Okla., 75, 87; participation in World War I, 55–58, 63; reasons for leaving, 11–13; and religion, 39, 44, 74; and Texas, 14, 24–25, 75, 80, 131, 143n24, 148n34, 158n84

Moravian Brethren Church, 38, 40, 80

Mountain State Oil Company, 157n61

Mraz, Gerald: and Musical Art Institute of Oklahoma, 70; relocates to Oklahoma City, 82

Mraz, John Z.: death of wife, 99; as physician, 72, 155n37

Muisack family, 144n3

Mullen, Frank, 98, 161n47

Mustang, Okla., 16

Nation, Carry, 65

nativists, nativism: attacking Catholics, 74; hostility toward immigrants, 97; and native-born people in Prague, Okla., 77; settlement of Prague, Okla., 5

Navrah, Frank, 169n29

Nebraska: Creighton University, 72, 117, 166n44; town of Ord, 82; town of Saline City, 35; town of Wilber, 27, 80, 88. *See also* Milligan, Nebr.; University of Nebraska

New Amsterdam, N.Y., 11

Newhouse, Frank N., 69, 98–99, 154n20, 161n48

New York Bargain Store, 71, 77, 99, 101. *See also* Kolodny, Sam

New York City, 9, 18, 30, 58, 140, 150n17

Nietzsche, Friedrich, 33

Wilson, Woodrow: on self-determination, 58; support for allies, 59; support for creation of Czechoslovakia, 63, 122

Wisconsin, 13–16, 19, 24, 93, 98, 113; Racine, 14

Womastek, Henry, 167n57

Wood, A. F., 123, 168n12

Woodmen of the World, 46, 124

Woods, William, 72, 155n39

World War I: Bohemian Political Association, 168n14; changing political allegiances during, 122; and cotton production in Prague, Okla., 78, 128; and Edward Sefcik, 138; and freethought, 32; and George Sadlo, 139; and Habsburg family, 6; KKK re-emerges after, 125; and Prague, Okla., 76, 98; Prague, Okla., sends 111 men to join AEF, 62, 158n2; religious discord among Czechs during, 34, 38; and Sokols, 50, 165n24; tensions between Czechs and Germans, 60, 83, 95, 97

Wostichil, Wes, 169n31

Wostrcil, Anna, 36

Yukon, Okla.: as "Czech capital" of Oklahoma, 16–17; Czech influence in, 16, 144n35; influx of Moravians, 24

Zabloudil, Jake: born in Ord, Nebr., 82; cashier at First State Bank, 70; honorary tribal member, 82; as politician, 123; subscriber to *Prague Record*, 158n79

Zajic, Frank, 169n33

ZCBJ. *See* Western Czech Brotherhood Association (Zapadni Cesko Bratrska Jednota; ZCBJ)

Zizka, Jan, 109

CPSIA information can be obtained
at www.ICGtesting.com
Printed in the USA
LVHW090045090821
694731LV00016B/1266